300 best
Casserole
recipes

Tiffany Collins

Robert
ROSE

For complete cataloguing information, see page 339.

Disclaimer
The recipes in this book have been carefully tested by our kitchen and our tasters. To the best of our knowledge, they are safe and nutritious for ordinary use and users. For those people with food or other allergies, or who have special food requirements or health issues, please read the suggested contents of each recipe carefully and determine whether or not they may create a problem for you. All recipes are used at the risk of the consumer.

We cannot be responsible for any hazards, loss or damage that may occur as a result of any recipe use.

For those with special needs, allergies, requirements or health problems, in the event of any doubt, please contact your medical adviser prior to the use of any recipe.

Design and Production: Daniella Zanchetta/PageWave Graphics Inc.
Editors: Sue Sumeraj and Jennifer MacKenzie
Proofreader: Sheila Wawanash
Indexer: Gillian Watts
Photography: Colin Erricson
Associate Photographer: Matt Johannsson
Food Styling: Kathryn Robertson
Prop Styling: Charlene Erricson

Cover image: Beef Ziti with Silky Béchamel (page 220)

We acknowledge the financial support of the Government of Canada through the Book Publishing Industry Development Program (BPIDP) for our publishing activities.

Published by Robert Rose Inc.
120 Eglinton Avenue East, Suite 800, Toronto, Ontario, Canada M4P 1E2
Tel: (416) 322-6552 Fax: (416) 322-6936
www.robertrose.ca

Printed and bound in Canada

1 2 3 4 5 6 7 8 9 SP 18 17 16 15 14 13 12 11 10

To my amazing daughter, Kennedy, who
inspires me to be the best mommy ever.
To my daddy, John Tacker, for your never-ending
pride and support, and to my mother, Fay,
for constantly sending culinary wisdom
from the heavens above.

Contents

Acknowledgments 6
Introduction 8
Casserole Basics 10

Breakfast and Brunch Casseroles 15
Appetizers 47
Hearty Vegetable and Pasta Casseroles 67
Fish and Seafood Casseroles 103
Chicken and Turkey Casseroles. 129
Pork Casseroles 167
Beef and Lamb Casseroles 193
Healthy Choices 237
Side Dishes. 261
Kid Stuff 295
Desserts 317

Index 340

Acknowledgments

This book would not have been possible without the support of my family, friends and neighbors, not to mention people whom I have never even met but who contributed their talents from afar to make this book the best it could be. I give endless thanks to my agent, Lisa Ekus-Saffer, who continues to believe in me and discover opportunities. Thank you to Bob Dees, my publisher, for trusting me with another title; to Karen Tripton, my copywriter; to Sue Sumeraj, my editor, for her amazing patience and talent; to Jennifer MacKenzie, my recipe editor, for sharing her extensive food knowledge and cooking expertise; to Daniella Zanchetta of PageWave Graphics for the beautiful design; and to Colin Erricson, Kathryn Robertson and Charlene Erricson for bringing my recipes to life with stunning photographs.

I cannot imagine having been able to complete this book without my dear friend Ellen Harrison. Ellen gave me endless hours over several months, pushing me, reminding me, scolding me, shopping, writing and editing copy, testing recipes and brainstorming casserole ideas. And thanks to Trevor, my friend and Ellen's hubby, for watching Patrick so that Ellen could do *more* casserole work. I love you guys!

My family helped out tremendously by tracking down copies of our treasured family recipes, often found tucked in a random cookbook, Bible or drawer — even written on the inside of cabinet doors. Daddy and Cheryl Younger Tacker, my stepmother, spent countless hours going through my mother's cookbooks, files and notebooks and retyping recipes for my interpretation. Thank you also to my brother, Bud, and sister, Jill, for sharing your memories and your versions of our childhood casseroles.

Thank you to all of my friends who offered recipes, suggestions and opinions: Marcia Smith, Tina Straseske and Melissa Saucedo, my workout partners, for suggesting healthy options; the Johnson family — Roger, TJ, Alissa and Sara — for sharing your mom's prized casserole recipes (thank you, Carol!); Robyn Canard, Stephanie and Bobby Collins, Judy Colognesi, Susan Condon, Lorinda Drake, Nancy Farrington, Dina Foley, Barbara Garrison, Babsie Hambrick, Sandy Hancock, Vicki Hansen, Stacia Hernstrom, Lia Huber with The Nourish Network, Donna Hutchinson, Shari Jones, Jayna and Debra Judd, Sara Juraschek, Pam Lecy, Beth Markin, Betty McCullough, Gloria McDonald, Patty Moncus, Linda Pearl Motley, Michaele Musel, Michele Northrup, David and Lana Oberg, Jen O'Neil, Tom and Lisa Perini, Jean Phillips, Meg Plotsky, Marianne Rohde, Candace Arslanian Rosenberg, Chris Russo, Larry Russo, Patty Russo,

Pat Schermerhorn, Karin Schwob, Nozik Smith, Tim Stamper, Cathy and John Sullivan, Linda Sullivan, Jody Tacker, Becky Terrell, Helen and Td Todd, Jane Tollette, Jeri Tribo, Pamela Weatherford, Debi Williams of Hummingbird Farms, Jack and Nicole Williams and Jennifer Windom. Special thanks to Ruth "Gammy" Collins, Kennedy's grandmother, for finally agreeing to let me use your family favorites.

To Kennedy, my sweet little tester and daughter, thank you for tasting casseroles you were not too fond of and not saying "Mommy, it isn't good" about the ones I know you hated ... I could tell by the look on your face!

Thank you to my friends at the Texas Beef Council, who offered suggestions for beef casseroles and assisted with beef-related questions.

Finally, thank you to Greg Blackmon for getting me through the home stretch! Yeah!

Introduction

Whenever I am asked what my favorite recipes are, my mind always drifts back to my childhood, to beloved family recipes that made frequent appearances at our dinner table: tuna casserole, cornbread dressing, King Ranch casserole, tamale pie — all one-dish meals, or casseroles!

The French word *casserole*, meaning "saucepan," is a diminutive of the Old French *casse*, meaning "pan." Since we adopted the word into the English language, it has come to mean both a baking dish, usually with a cover, and the one-dish meal cooked in it. Many countries have a tradition of one-dish meals, each with its own name, including cassoulet (France), lasagna (Italy), pastitsio (Greece), hot pot (Great Britain), tagine (Morocco) and paella (Spain).

In North America, casseroles became a common family meal in the 1950s and reached their peak of popularity in the 1960s. In the 1970s, in the interest of saving both time and money, many families chose canned ingredients over fresh in their casseroles. As a result, the casserole's image suffered a bit of a blow. But it has fought back and held its ground, and today casseroles are once again embraced by the masses.

Why have casseroles been so popular for so long? It's simple, really: they offer a relatively easy, economical, convenient way to prepare delicious food. And the possible combinations are endless — the 300 offerings in this book, for example, are just the tip of the iceberg when it comes to casserole options. Every family, it seems, has its own treasured recipe, its own version of the best casserole *ever*.

With such a huge variety of possibilities to choose from, there's something for everyone in the casserole world. But casseroles are also easy to adapt to your taste: you can simply leave out ingredients you don't like or add those you do. In a layered casserole, you can even use slightly different ingredients in one half of the dish than in the other, to satisfy the various requirements of picky eaters in the same family.

Sure, casseroles will never qualify as fast food; they all need some quality time in the oven to allow the flavors to blend and intensify. But getting them to the oven is easy. You may need to brown some meat, sauté some vegetables or cook some pasta or rice first, but for the most part, preparing a casserole is a simple matter of mixing or layering ingredients in a dish.

Assembling a casserole is also a great way to get your whole family into the kitchen, learning to appreciate the camaraderie and sense of accomplishment that come from cooking together. Since casseroles often involve many different components, there's a task for everybody. Even little ones can help with the stirring and layering. The preparation is often a multigenerational endeavor: I have fond memories of cooking with my great-grandmother, my grandmothers, my parents and my siblings. It's a great time to share stories about your day while teaching kids about food preparation and nutrition.

Casseroles can be as big or as small as you want them to be, and most reheat well — some are even better the next day! They're a great option for singles and couples who want a good hot meal with leftovers to carry them through another day or two, but they can also serve a crowd and are easy to transport; thus, their ubiquity at potlucks and buffet tables.

Their portability and freezer-friendliness also make them a good choice when you're preparing food to help out a friend, family member or neighbor, and indeed, casseroles have a long tradition as gifts for people moving house, coming home with a new baby or coping with the loss of a loved one — anyone who needs a little help with the everyday chores of life to get through a trying or chaotic time. (Foil pans are perfect for casseroles you plan to give away; make sure to include thawing and baking instructions.)

The bottom line is that casseroles are comfort food at its best. This collection of recipes will reacquaint you with the classics you remember from your childhood, many of them family heirlooms in their own right, and introduce you to new, modern dishes that incorporate flavors from around the world. You're sure to create your own wonderful family memories as you explore the options in this book and discover your favorites!

Casserole Basics

Before you start exploring the recipes in this book, take a few minutes to review the basics: your options when it comes to casserole dishes, important information about the ingredients used in this book, instructions on freezing casseroles and some general tips and advice.

Casserole Dishes and Pans

Casserole dishes and pans come in many sizes, shapes and materials. All of the recipes in this book were tested in glass or ceramic baking dishes. If you use another type, you may need to adjust the cooking time.

- **Ovenproof glass baking dishes** cook evenly, retain heat well and can go from freezer to oven to table to dishwasher. Coating them with nonstick spray makes cleanup easy.

- **Ceramic casserole dishes** are beautiful but chip easily. However, they are relatively inexpensive, hold heat moderately well and are easy to clean.

- **Glazed earthenware baking dishes** come in many colors and shapes, each with its own personality and beauty, so they make attractive serving pieces. They cook evenly and hold heat very well, and therefore are best used for casseroles with long cooking times. Don't subject them to drastic temperature changes, though, or they will crack. Cool them on something other than a granite or tile countertop. They are easy to clean, though they chip easily.

- **Stainless steel baking pans** are very durable but do not retain heat well unless the bottom is reinforced with copper or aluminum — which increases the expense. Stainless steel pans scratch easily, so when it comes to cleaning them, it is best to soak them in hot water for 10 to 15 minutes, then use a nylon scouring pad to remove any remaining food. Most are dishwasher-safe, but they should be hand-dried rather than left to dry in the high heat of the dishwasher.

- **Copper-lined baking pans** provide the most even cooking of all metal pans and retain heat well. However, they do react with acidic foods, resulting in a metallic taste. Use only wood, nylon or silicone utensils with copper pans. They are extremely durable, though they are heavy and can be quite expensive. They make beautiful serving pieces. They should be hand-washed, and cleanup can sometimes be difficult, depending on the ingredients used. Don't let food sit in a copper pan for more than 2 hours (which means you should not store food in it).

- **Anodized aluminum baking pans** are heavy and resist sticking, which makes cleanup easier. They have the added convenience of being able to travel from stovetop to oven, and they absorb heat quickly and distribute it evenly. The drawback is that they can be expensive.

- **Enameled cast-iron casserole dishes** are very heavy, but they're durable, cook evenly, retain heat well and are easy to clean.

Approximate Casserole and Baking Dish Equivalents

If you don't have the specific casserole dish recommended in a recipe, here are alternatives that will work just as well.

4-cup or 1-quart (1 L) casserole dish

8- by 6- by $1\frac{1}{2}$-inch (20 by 15 by 4 cm) baking dish
8-inch (20 cm) round baking dish
9-inch (23 cm) pie plate
6- by 3-inch (15 by 7.5 cm) soufflé dish

6-cup or 1$\frac{1}{2}$-quart (1.5 L) casserole dish

8- by 8- by $1\frac{1}{2}$-inch (20 by 20 by 4 cm) square baking dish
9-inch (23 cm) round baking dish
10-inch (25 cm) pie plate
7- by 3-inch (18 by 7.5 cm) soufflé dish

8-cup or 2-quart (2 L) casserole dish

9- by 9- by $1\frac{1}{2}$-inch (23 by 23 by 4 cm) square baking dish
8- by 8- by 2-inch (20 by 20 by 5 cm) square baking dish
11- by 7- by $1\frac{1}{2}$-inch (28 by 18 by 4 cm) baking dish
8- by 3-inch (20 by 7.5 cm) soufflé dish

10-cup or 2$\frac{1}{2}$-quart (2.5 L) casserole dish

10- by 10- by $1\frac{1}{2}$-inch (25 by 25 by 4 cm) square baking dish
9- by 9- by 2-inch (23 by 23 by 5 cm) square baking dish
9- by 3-inch (23 by 7.5 cm) soufflé dish

12-cup or 3-quart (3 L) casserole dish

13- by 9- by 2-inch (33 by 23 by 5 cm) baking dish
8- by 8- by $3\frac{1}{2}$-inch (20 by 20 by 7.5 cm) square baking dish

Ingredient Essentials

The recipes in this book make some assumptions about what is standard when it comes to basic ingredients.

- All eggs used are large eggs.
- I used 2% milk and yogurt unless otherwise specified.
- Butter is salted unless otherwise specified.
- Fresh vegetables and fruits are medium size unless otherwise indicated. Any inedible peels, skins, seeds and cores are removed unless otherwise indicated.
- "Onions" means regular cooking onions unless otherwise indicated.
- "Mushrooms" means white button mushrooms unless otherwise indicated.
- With canned tomatoes and tomato products, the juice is also used unless the recipe instructs you to drain it.
- I used air-chilled poultry, which has a firmer texture and holds its shape better and is more tender when baked in casseroles.
- When I call for broth (chicken, beef or vegetable), homemade is the ideal, but ready-to-use broth in Tetra Paks come a close second. If you can only find canned broth, make sure to dilute it as directed on the can before use.
- Canned soups are used undiluted unless otherwise specified.
- Canned tuna is water-packed.
- I used dried pasta unless fresh or frozen is indicated.
- Where recipes call for vegetable oil to brown meats and sauté vegetables, I used a combination of olive oil and canola oil.

Healthy Choices

I try to make healthy choices for myself and my family. But we all need to splurge sometimes. Use your best judgment when selecting ingredients and make wise decisions about when to splurge. Here are some tips on how to prepare the healthiest casseroles:

- When grocery shopping, shop the perimeter of the store as much as possible, choosing fresh or frozen ingredients over canned or packaged foods.
- Use fat-free, light or olive oil mayonnaise.
- Choose breast meat over dark meat, and always remove the skin.
- Avoid "seasoned" meats and poultry, which have been treated with additional water and sodium phosphate or other ingredients and tend to make foods watery and salty.
- Trim any fat from meat and poultry.

- Choose lean or even extra-lean ground meats.
- Use fat-free or light broths and soups.
- Whenever you have a reduced-sodium option — for soups, broths, other canned goods, condiments and so on — choose it.
- Add flavor with fresh herbs, ground or toasted spices, flavored vinegars and fresh garlic, shallots or chile peppers. Use table salt with a very light hand.
- Use whole-grain bread and pasta.
- Save casseroles made with cream sauces for special occasions and serve casseroles with broth-based sauces regularly.
- Use nonstick cooking spray, rather than oil or melted butter, to lightly grease casserole dishes.
- Use nonstick skillets and saucepans to reduce the amount of fat required for cooking.

Freezing Casseroles

Most casseroles can be successfully frozen, and it can be a great relief on a busy weeknight to know you have an assembled casserole waiting for you at home, ready to be popped into the oven and heated up. I often spend a weekend day assembling several casseroles to freeze for such occasions.

It's best to freeze a casserole before baking it, to prevent it from drying out (but make sure any meat in the casserole is fully cooked). If you plan to freeze a casserole, line the baking dish with foil, leaving a couple of inches of foil overhanging the dish, and give it a light coating of nonstick cooking spray. After assembling the casserole, let it cool to room temperature if necessary, then cover and freeze until solid. Use the foil handles to lift the casserole from the dish and transfer it to a large freezer-proof plastic bag. Label the bag with the name of the casserole, the date you assembled it and the baking instructions (or the page number the recipe is on). Freeze for up to 3 months — but keep in mind that casseroles lose moisture over time.

You'll need to decide a day or two in advance when you want to serve a casserole, as it is best to thaw it in the refrigerator. Simply remove the casserole from the freezer, peel off the foil and return the casserole to its original dish. Thaw in the refrigerator for at least 1 day; large, dense casseroles may need 2 days or more to thaw completely.

Once the casserole is thawed, you can follow the baking instructions as given in the recipe, though you may need to add 5 or 10 minutes to the cooking time, since you're starting with cold food.

Here are some other tips to keep in mind when freezing casseroles:

- Potatoes do not tend to freeze well. If you plan to freeze a casserole that includes potatoes, it would be best to leave them out of the initial assembly, adding them once the casserole is thawed.

- Casseroles with pasta or rice will benefit from a little extra liquid (which can be water, broth or milk, depending on the recipe), as this type of casserole tends to be a bit dry after freezing. Alternatively, as with potatoes, you can omit the starch in the initial assembly, adding it when the casserole is thawed.

- Leave off toppings such as bread crumbs or crushed crackers or chips. Add them during the last 10 minutes of baking to prevent a soggy topping.

- Foods containing peppers, onions, garlic, cloves or curry powder can experience flavor changes during freezing. Season your casserole lightly before it goes in the freezer and jazz it up right before baking.

- Sauces thickened with flour may separate when thawed. Instead, use cornstarch or instant tapioca to thicken a casserole you plan to freeze.

Final Words of Advice

- Most cookbooks stress the importance of accurate measuring, but it's not all that important when it comes to casseroles. We can be a bit more relaxed about adding a pinch of this and a handful of that. Casseroles, after all, are all about experimentation and trying out fun new combinations of flavors — they don't have to taste exactly the same every time you make them. However, if you have strayed from the exact measurements or ingredients called for in the recipe, be careful when transferring the mixture to the baking dish; if your changes have increased the volume of the mixture, you may have too much for your dish. Even if it still fits, you may need to increase the baking time to account for the extra ingredients.

- If your oven has a convection setting, by all means use it to save time. Follow the oven manufacturer's instruction manual for guidance on converting the baking time.

- If you're not enthusiastic about spending an entire day cooking by yourself, turn casserole-making into a social event. Gather some friends together, have fun and catch up while creating a variety of casseroles, assembly-line fashion, to load up your refrigerators or freezers.

- Plan ahead to make casserole preparation quicker and easier. Cook extra meat, vegetables, pastas and rice when preparing meals, collecting casserole ingredients over a couple of days in your fridge (or storing them for longer periods in your freezer). Then, when it's time to make a casserole, all you have to do is assemble the ingredients and bake! (Keep in mind, though, that foods that have been frozen shouldn't be refrozen in a casserole — it's best to bake those and eat them right away.)

Breakfast and Brunch Casseroles

French Toast Casserole. 16

Apple French Toast Casserole. 17

Orange French Toast Bake 18

Hummingbird Farms Lavender French Toast Bake. 19

Apricot Breakfast Bake 20

Crème Brûlée Bake. 21

Ellen's Mushroom, Spinach and Sausage
 Breakfast Casserole 22

Christmas Omelet Casserole. 23

Deviled Egg Casserole 24

Eggs Benedict Bake 25

Sausage Egg Casserole 26

Santa Fe Breakfast Casserole 27

Country Breakfast Casserole. 28

Brunch Casserole 29

Elegant Brunch Bake 30

Cheesy Grits Casserole with Mushrooms and Prosciutto . . . 31

Cheesy Hash Brown Casserole. 32

Tiffany's Breakfast Torta 33

Cathy's Cheese Strata. 34

Southwest Strata 35

Crab Strata. 36

Garden Vegetable Frittata 37

Spinach and Cheese Pie. 38

Artichoke Quiche 39

Spinach-Mushroom Quiche. 40

Bacon and Leeks in a Quiche 41

Sausage and Cheddar Quiche 42

Crustless Pizza Quiche 43

Taco Quiche 44

Tex-Mex Green Chile Quiche. 45

Noodle Quiche 46

French Toast Casserole

My Alabama friends Helen and Td Todd love, love, love casseroles and were thrilled when they heard about this book. Helen insisted I add her favorite brunch casserole.

Tip

If you like it super-sweet, drizzle maple syrup over each serving.

- 13- by 9-inch (33 by 23 cm) glass baking dish

¾ cup	packed brown sugar	175 mL
½ cup	butter	125 mL
2 tbsp	light or golden corn syrup	30 mL
¾	loaf French bread, torn into bite-size pieces (about 4 cups/1 L)	¾
5	eggs	5
1½ cups	half-and-half (10%) cream	375 mL
1 tsp	vanilla extract	5 mL
¼ cup	granulated sugar	60 mL
2 tbsp	ground cinnamon	30 mL
¼ cup	confectioners' (icing) sugar	60 mL

1. In a microwave-safe bowl, combine brown sugar, butter and corn syrup; microwave on High for 45 to 55 seconds or until butter is melted and sugar is dissolved (or melt in a saucepan over medium-low heat). Stir well and pour into baking dish. Arrange bread pieces evenly over butter mixture.

2. In a large bowl, whisk eggs until blended. Whisk in cream and vanilla. Pour evenly over bread, pressing bread down until moistened.

3. In a small bowl, combine granulated sugar and cinnamon. Sprinkle evenly over casserole. Cover and refrigerate for at least 6 hours or overnight.

4. Preheat oven to 350°F (180°C).

5. Uncover baking dish. Bake for 30 to 40 minutes or until set and golden brown. Sift confectioners' sugar over top. Serve immediately.

Apple French Toast Casserole

The wonderful flavors of baked apples and cinnamon are layered in this easy breakfast casserole, perfect for weekend houseguests or a brunch party.

Tip
Serve with maple syrup or your favorite syrup.

- 9-inch (23 cm) quiche dish or glass pie plate or 11- by 7-inch (28 by 18 cm) glass baking dish, greased

4	large slices sourdough bread, cut into 1-inch (2.5 cm) cubes	4
1	package (8 oz/250 g) cream cheese, cut into cubes	1
1	large baking apple, peeled and chopped	1
6	eggs	6
1 cup	mllk	250 mL
1 tsp	ground cinnamon	5 mL
2 tbsp	confectioners' (icing) sugar	30 mL

1. Place half the bread cubes in prepared baking dish. Top evenly with cream cheese and apple. Arrange the remaining bread cubes on top.

2. In a large bowl, whisk together eggs, milk and cinnamon until well blended. Pour evenly over bread mixture. Cover and refrigerate overnight.

3. Preheat oven to 375°F (190°C).

4. Bake, covered, for 45 minutes or until set. Uncover and bake for 5 minutes. Let cool for 10 minutes. Sift confectioners' sugar over top. Serve immediately.

Orange French Toast Bake

Makes 8 to 10 servings

Our family friend Pam Lecy prepares this fragrant casserole with orange juice, sugar, vanilla and almonds. What a treat!

Tip

For an extra-special presentation, serve with fresh berries.

• 13- by 9-inch (33 by 23 cm) glass baking dish, greased

1	loaf French bread, cut into ½-inch (1 cm) slices	1
4	eggs	4
⅔ cup	orange juice	150 mL
⅓ cup	milk	75 mL
¼ cup	granulated sugar	60 mL
1 tsp	vanilla extract	5 mL
¼ tsp	ground nutmeg	1 mL
¼ cup	butter, melted	60 mL
½ cup	sliced almonds	125 mL

1. Arrange bread slices in prepared baking dish, overlapping as necessary.

2. In a large bowl, whisk eggs until blended. Whisk in orange juice, milk, sugar, vanilla and nutmeg. Pour evenly over bread. Cover and refrigerate for at least 6 hours or overnight.

3. Preheat oven to 375°F (190°C).

4. Uncover baking dish. Drizzle butter over top and sprinkle with almonds. Bake for 45 to 50 minutes or until set.

Hummingbird Farms Lavender French Toast Bake

This recipe, courtesy of Debi Williams of Hummingbird Farms, is elegant enough for Easter, Mother's Day or a bridal brunch. It is easy to prepare the night before and makes a beautiful presentation.

Tips

There are multiple varieties of lavender, and some are too harsh for cooking, so be sure you select culinary-grade lavender.

Lavender has a strong flavor, so keep in mind a little goes a long way. It should be used to enhance other flavors in your recipe, not to dominate. As with vanilla, you should know it is there, but it shouldn't be the main player.

The potency of lavender increases as the flowers dry. If you replace dried lavender with fresh, use three times as much.

• 13- by 9-inch (33 by 23 cm) glass baking dish

1½ cups	half-and-half (10%) cream	375 mL
1 tsp	dried culinary lavender flowers	5 mL
1¼ cups	packed brown sugar	300 mL
½ cup	butter	125 mL
2 tbsp	pure maple syrup	30 mL
1	large loaf soft white Italian or French bread, cut into 1-inch (2.5 cm) slices, crusts removed	1
5	eggs	5
1 tsp	vanilla extract	5 mL
1 tsp	ground cinnamon	5 mL
¼ tsp	ground nutmeg	1 mL
¼ tsp	salt	1 mL
	Confectioners' (icing) sugar	
	Pure maple syrup	

1. In a small saucepan, over medium-low heat, warm cream and lavender for 5 minutes or until steaming. Remove from heat and let cool while you prepare the remaining ingredients.

2. In another small saucepan, over medium heat, combine brown sugar, butter and maple syrup, stirring until smooth and sugar has dissolved. Pour into baking dish. Arrange bread slices in a single layer on top, pushing the slices tightly together.

3. In a large bowl, whisk together eggs, vanilla, cinnamon, nutmeg and salt.

4. Strain cream mixture through a fine sieve into egg mixture, discarding lavender; whisk to combine. Pour evenly over bread. Cover and refrigerate for at least 6 hours or overnight.

5. Preheat oven to 350°F (180°C). Meanwhile, let casserole stand at room temperature for 15 minutes.

6. Uncover and bake for 35 to 40 minutes or until bubbling and golden brown. Serve hot, with a sprinkling of confectioners' sugar and a light drizzle of maple syrup.

Apricot Breakfast Bake

In this breakfast dish, tangy dried apricots are enhanced by a hint of nutmeg and vanilla.

Tips

Liquid egg substitute works very well in this recipe. One cup (250 mL) egg substitute equals 4 whole eggs, so for this recipe, use 1¼ cups (300 mL) egg substitute.

Butter is easiest to cube when it's cold and in stick form.

- 11- by 7-inch (28 by 18 cm) glass baking dish, greased

5	eggs	5
2 cups	milk	500 mL
2 tbsp	granulated sugar	30 mL
⅛ tsp	ground nutmeg	0.5 mL
1 tsp	vanilla extract	5 mL
¼ tsp	salt	1 mL
1	package (16 oz/500 g) frozen ready-to-bake yeast rolls, thawed	1
½ cup	chopped dried apricots	125 mL
2 tbsp	butter, cut into ¼-inch (0.5 cm) cubes	30 mL

1. In a large bowl, whisk together eggs, milk, sugar, nutmeg, vanilla and salt until blended.

2. Break apart rolls and cut into bite-size pieces. Arrange in a single layer in prepared baking dish. Top evenly with apricots. Pour egg mixture evenly over top; dot with butter. Cover and refrigerate for at least 6 hours or overnight.

3. Preheat oven to 325°F (160°C).

4. Uncover baking dish. Bake for 55 to 60 minutes or until set and golden brown. Let cool for 5 minutes before serving.

Crème Brûlée Bake

This luscious dessert casserole is laced with creamy goodness. It's perfect as a selection with savory brunch dishes for a buffet.

Tip

To dress this dish up even more, serve with warm maple syrup, fresh berries and whipped cream.

- 13- by 9-inch (33 by 23 cm) baking dish

1 cup	packed brown sugar	250 mL
1/2 cup	butter	125 mL
2 tbsp	corn syrup	30 mL
8	slices (1 inch/2.5 cm thick) French bread	8
5	eggs	5
1 1/2 cups	half-and-half (10%) cream	375 mL
1 tsp	vanilla extract	5 mL
2 tbsp	Grand Marnier or other orange-flavored liqueur	30 mL
1/4 tsp	salt	1 mL

1. In a microwave-safe bowl, combine brown sugar, butter and corn syrup; microwave on High for 45 to 55 seconds or until butter is melted and sugar is dissolved (or melt in a saucepan over medium-low heat). Stir well and pour into baking dish. Arrange bread slices in a single layer over butter mixture.

2. In a large bowl, whisk eggs until blended. Whisk in cream, vanilla, Grand Marnier and salt. Pour evenly over bread. Cover and refrigerate for at least 6 hours or overnight.

3. Preheat oven to 350°F (180°C).

4. Uncover baking dish. Bake for 50 to 55 minutes or until golden brown.

5. Preheat broiler. Run a knife around edge of casserole and invert a rimmed baking sheet on top of dish. Invert casserole onto baking sheet. Broil for about 3 minutes or until sugar is bubbly. Serve immediately.

Ellen's Mushroom, Spinach and Sausage Breakfast Casserole

Preparing this casserole the night before has two benefits: the flavors marry and intensify as it sits in the fridge overnight, and it's ready to pop in the oven in the morning, allowing you to make breakfast with no fuss.

Variation

Sauté 1 chopped green bell pepper with the mushrooms to add color and texture.

- 13- by 9-inch (33 by 23 cm) glass baking dish, greased

2 cups	seasoned croutons	500 mL
1 lb	spicy pork sausage (bulk or removed from casing)	500 g
1 tbsp	butter	15 mL
10 oz	mushrooms, sliced	300 g
1/2 tsp	salt	2 mL
1/2 tsp	freshly ground black pepper	2 mL
4	eggs	4
2 1/4 cups	milk	550 mL
1	can (10 oz/284 mL) condensed cream of mushroom soup	1
1	package (10 oz/300 g) frozen chopped spinach, thawed and squeezed dry	1
2 cups	shredded Mexican-seasoned Cheddar-Jack cheese	500 mL
1/4 tsp	dry mustard	1 mL
1/4 tsp	hot pepper sauce	1 mL

1. Spread croutons in bottom of prepared baking dish.

2. In a nonstick skillet, over medium-high heat, cook sausage, breaking it up with the back of a spoon, for 8 to 10 minutes or until no longer pink. Drain off fat. Spread sausage over croutons.

3. In the same skillet, melt butter over medium heat. Sauté mushrooms, salt and pepper for about 5 minutes or until tender. Remove from heat and let cool.

4. In a large bowl, whisk together eggs and milk. Stir in soup, spinach, cheese, mustard, hot pepper sauce and mushrooms. Pour evenly over sausage. Cover and refrigerate for at least 6 hours or overnight.

5. Preheat oven to 325°F (160°C).

6. Bake, covered, for 45 minutes. Uncover and bake for about 5 minutes or until browned.

Christmas Omelet Casserole

Vibrant red and green bell peppers make this casserole perfect for Christmas brunch.

Tip

This casserole freezes well for up to 1 month. Let baked casserole cool completely, then wrap well in plastic wrap, then in foil.

- Preheat oven to 325°F (160°C)
- 13- by 9-inch (33 by 23 cm) metal baking pan or glass baking dish, greased

12	eggs	12
3	green onions, chopped	3
1	red bell pepper, diced	1
1	green bell pepper, diced	1
1	can (14 oz/398 mL) diced tomatoes, drained	1
1 lb	pasteurized prepared cheese product, such as Velveeta, diced	500 g
1 cup	sour cream	250 mL
¼ cup	butter, melted	60 mL
1 lb	diced cooked ham (optional)	500 g

1. In a large bowl, whisk eggs until blended. Stir in green onions, red pepper, green pepper, tomatoes, cheese, sour cream, butter and ham (if using). Pour into prepared baking dish.

2. Bake in preheated oven for 1 hour or until a knife inserted in the center comes out clean.

Deviled Egg Casserole

This recipe is perfect for Easter celebrations!

Tip

I love serving this festive casserole on a Sunday brunch buffet with cold fresh fruit and vegetable salads.

- Preheat oven to 400°F (200°C)
- 13- by 9-inch (33 by 23 cm) glass baking dish, greased

12	hard-cooked eggs	12
1 tbsp	table (18%) cream	15 mL
1/2 tsp	Worcestershire sauce	2 mL
1 tsp	grated onion	5 mL
1 1/2 tsp	salt, divided	7 mL
1 tsp	dry mustard, divided	5 mL
1/2 tsp	freshly ground black pepper	2 mL
6 tbsp	butter	90 mL
6 tbsp	all-purpose flour	90 mL
3 cups	milk	750 mL
2 cups	shredded Cheddar cheese	500 mL
1 lb	asparagus, trimmed	500 g
2 cups	cubed cooked ham	500 mL
1 cup	crushed corn flakes cereal	250 mL

1. Cut eggs in half lengthwise and remove yolks. Place yolks in a bowl and mash with a fork. Stir in cream, Worcestershire sauce, onion, 1/2 tsp (2 mL) of the salt, 3/4 tsp (3 mL) of the mustard and pepper until well blended. Spoon yolk mixture into egg white halves; set aside.

2. In a small saucepan, melt butter over medium heat. Whisk in flour, then gradually add milk, whisking. Cook, whisking, for about 5 minutes or until smooth and thickened. Add cheese and the remaining salt and dry mustard; cook, stirring, until cheese is melted.

3. Arrange asparagus in prepared baking dish. Place stuffed eggs on top. Top evenly with ham. Pour cheese sauce evenly over top. Sprinkle with corn flakes.

4. Bake in preheated oven for 25 to 30 minutes or until asparagus is tender.

Eggs Benedict Bake

Our family friend Donna Hutchinson makes this simple version of classic eggs Benedict.

Tips

Steamed or roasted asparagus works beautifully as a side dish with this combo.

Squeeze thawed and drained spinach several times to remove excess moisture.

• 13- by 9-inch (33 by 23 cm) glass baking dish, greased

2	envelopes (each 1 1/4 oz/35 g) Hollandaise sauce mix	2
2 cups	half-and-half (10%) cream	500 mL
1/4 cup	butter, melted	60 mL
12	eggs	12
1 cup	shredded Swiss cheese	250 mL
8 oz	Canadian bacon, chopped	250 g
1	package (10 oz/300 g) frozen chopped spinach, thawed and squeezed dry	1
2 tbsp	freshly squeezed lemon juice	30 mL
1/2 tsp	salt	2 mL
1/2 tsp	freshly ground black pepper	2 mL
6	English muffins, cut into cubes	6

1. In a large bowl, whisk together Hollandaise sauce mix, cream and butter until smooth. Whisk in eggs until smooth. Stir in cheese, bacon, spinach, lemon juice, salt and pepper.

2. Arrange English muffin cubes in bottom of prepared baking dish. Pour egg mixture evenly over top. Cover and refrigerate for at least 6 hours or overnight.

3. Preheat oven to 350°F (180°C).

4. Uncover baking dish. Bake for 45 to 50 minutes or until golden brown.

Sausage Egg Casserole

There are so many versions of breakfast casseroles, and each one has flair. Every family thinks theirs is the best, and I have to agree — all of them are great in their own way. But of course, mine is the best!

Tip

This recipe uses both spicy and mild pork sausage. Feel free to use double the amount of spicy to increase the heat or all mild to omit the heat.

- 13- by 9-inch (33 by 23 cm) metal baking pan or glass baking dish, greased
- Blender

2½ cups	seasoned croutons	625 mL
1 lb	spicy pork sausage (bulk or removed from casings)	500 g
1 lb	mild pork sausage (bulk or removed from casings)	500 g
2 cups	shredded Cheddar cheese	500 mL
4	eggs	4
2½ cups	milk	625 mL
1	can (10 oz/284 mL) condensed cream of mushroom soup	1
½ tsp	dry mustard	2 mL
1	can (4½ oz/127 mL) sliced mushrooms, drained (about ½ cup/125 mL)	1

1. Spread croutons in bottom of prepared baking dish.

2. In a large nonstick skillet, over medium-high heat, cook spicy sausage and mild sausage, breaking it up with the back of a spoon, for 8 to 10 minutes or until no longer pink. Drain off fat. Let cool for 5 minutes.

3. Spread sausage over croutons. Sprinkle with cheese.

4. In blender, combine eggs, milk, soup and mustard; blend until smooth. Pour evenly over cheese mixture. Spread mushrooms on top. Cover and refrigerate overnight.

5. Preheat oven to 350°F (180°C).

6. Uncover baking dish. Bake for about 1 hour or until set and golden brown.

Santa Fe Breakfast Casserole

Sausage, green chiles and Monterey Jack cheese make a tasty combo in this Southwest favorite.

Tips

To save time, I often leave the crust on the bread. It also provides a different texture.

For more heat, try spicy sausage.

- Preheat oven to 350°F (180°C)
- 13- by 9-inch (33 by 23 cm) glass baking dish, greased

8	slices sandwich bread, crusts removed and quartered	8
1 lb	sausage (bulk or removed from casings)	500 g
6	eggs	6
1 cup	sour cream	250 mL
1	can (4½ oz/127 mL) chopped mild green chiles	1
2 cups	shredded Monterey Jack cheese	500 mL

1. Arrange bread in a single layer in prepared baking dish.

2. In a nonstick skillet, over medium-high heat, cook sausage, breaking it up with the back of a spoon, for 8 to 10 minutes or until no longer pink. Drain off fat. Let cool for 5 minutes.

3. In a large bowl, whisk eggs until blended. Whisk in sour cream and chiles. Pour evenly over bread. Top evenly with sausage and sprinkle with cheese.

4. Bake in preheated oven for 45 to 50 minutes or until set and golden brown.

Country Breakfast Casserole

**Makes 10 to
12 servings**

With this recipe, my good friend Karin Schwob shares a family favorite.

Tip

I love to serve fresh fruit salad as a side dish with breakfast casseroles.

- 13- by 9-inch (33 by 23 cm) glass baking dish, greased

1½ lbs	spicy pork sausage (bulk or removed from casings)	750 g
6	eggs, lightly beaten	6
2 lbs	frozen hash brown potatoes	1 kg
1 cup	minced onion	250 mL
2 cups	milk	500 mL
4 cups	shredded Colby-Jack or Cheddar cheese (about 1 lb/500 g), divided	1 L
½ tsp	salt	2 mL
	Salsa	

1. In a large nonstick skillet, over medium-high heat, cook sausage, breaking it up with the back of a spoon, for 8 to 10 minutes or until no longer pink. Drain off fat. Let cool for 5 minutes.

2. In a large bowl, combine sausage, eggs, hash browns, onion, milk, 3 cups (750 mL) of the cheese and salt. Pour into prepared baking dish. Top with the remaining cheese. Cover and refrigerate for at least 6 hours or overnight.

3. Preheat oven to 350°F (180°C).

4. Uncover baking dish. Bake for 50 to 55 minutes or until a knife inserted in the center comes out clean. Cover and let stand for 10 minutes. Cut into squares and serve immediately with salsa.

Brunch Casserole

My friend Carol Johnson created this casserole with Canadian bacon, green onions, mushrooms and tomatoes. So fresh!

Tip

Any type of bread will work, but I especially like French bread in this recipe.

• 13- by 9-inch (33 by 23 cm) glass baking dish, greased

8 cups	cubed day-old French bread	2 L
2 cups	shredded Cheddar cheese	500 mL
10	eggs	10
4 cups	milk	1 L
1 tbsp	Worcestershire sauce	15 mL
1 tsp	dry mustard	5 mL
½ tsp	salt	2 mL
½ tsp	freshly black ground pepper	2 mL
4	green onions, sliced	4
2	tomatoes, chopped	2
8 oz	Canadian bacon, cut into thin strips	250 g
1 cup	sliced mushrooms	250 mL

1. Arrange bread cubes in prepared baking dish. Sprinkle cheese on top.

2. In a large bowl, whisk eggs until blended. Whisk in milk, Worcestershire sauce, mustard, salt and pepper. Pour evenly over bread. Top evenly with green onions, tomatoes, bacon and mushrooms. Cover and refrigerate for at least 6 hours or overnight.

3. Preheat oven to 325°F (160°C).

4. Bake, covered, for 55 minutes or until bubbling. Uncover and bake for 5 minutes.

Elegant Brunch Bake

There are a number of breakfast and brunch casseroles in this book, and I am sure you'll discover your favorite, but I particularly love the slightly different ingredients in this one. The sour cream and Parmesan cheese mixture on top gives it special flair.

Tip

This is great for a breakfast or brunch buffet, accompanied by chilled glasses of Prosecco, an Italian sparkling wine.

• 13- by 9-inch (33 by 23 cm) glass baking dish, greased

1 lb	pork sausage (bulk or removed from casings)	500 g
1/2	loaf French or Italian bread, cubed (about 4 cups/1 L)	1/2
3 tbsp	butter, melted	45 mL
2 cups	shredded Swiss cheese	500 mL
1 cup	shredded Monterey Jack cheese	250 mL
8	eggs	8
2	green onions, chopped	2
1²⁄₃ cups	half-and-half (10%) cream	400 mL
1/4 cup	dry white wine	60 mL
1 tsp	Dijon mustard	5 mL
1/2 tsp	freshly ground black pepper	2 mL
1/4 tsp	cayenne pepper	1 mL
2/3 cup	sour cream	150 mL
1/2 cup	freshly grated Parmesan cheese	125 mL

1. In a large nonstick skillet, over medium-high heat, cook sausage, breaking it up with the back of a spoon, for 8 to 10 minutes or until no longer pink. Drain off fat. Let cool for 5 minutes.

2. Arrange bread cubes in prepared baking dish and drizzle with butter. Sprinkle with Swiss cheese, Monterey Jack and crumbled sausage.

3. In a large bowl, whisk eggs until blended. Whisk in green onions, cream, wine, mustard, black pepper and cayenne. Pour evenly over bread mixture. Cover and refrigerate for at least 6 hours or overnight.

4. Preheat oven to 350°F (180°C).

5. Bake, covered, for 55 minutes or until set. Uncover, spread with sour cream and sprinkle with Parmesan. Bake, uncovered, for 15 minutes.

Cheesy Grits Casserole with Mushrooms and Prosciutto

Grits are the foundation of this casserole, a luscious sauté of portobello and shiitake mushrooms and spectacular prosciutto. I enjoy it with a side of garlicky Caesar salad.

Tips

Leftovers of this casserole are great reheated the next day. Let cool, cover and refrigerate, then bake, covered, in a 350°F (180°C) oven until hot.

You can save money by using cremini mushrooms instead of portobello for this recipe. Portobellos are simply cremini mushrooms grown very large, so their flavor is similar. The large slices do, however, make a dramatic presentation on the plate.

- Preheat oven to 350°F (180°C)
- 11- by 7-inch (28 by 18 cm) glass baking dish, greased

1¼ cups	stone-ground yellow grits	300 mL
¾ cup	shredded Italian cheese blend, divided	175 mL
1 tsp	salt, divided	5 mL
1½ tsp	butter	7 mL
1 cup	chopped onion	250 mL
2	garlic cloves, minced	2
4 cups	thinly sliced portobello mushroom caps	1 L
3 cups	thinly sliced shiitake mushroom caps	750 mL
½ tsp	freshly ground black pepper	2 mL
1 cup	chopped prosciutto (about 3 oz/90 g)	250 mL
⅓ cup	dry white wine	75 mL
3	eggs, lightly beaten	3
2	egg whites, lightly beaten	2
1 tbsp	chopped fresh parsley	15 mL

1. In a large saucepan, bring 5 cups (1.25 L) water to a boil over high heat. Gradually stir in grits. Reduce heat to low and simmer, stirring often, for about 25 minutes or until thick. Remove from heat. Stir in ¼ cup (60 mL) of the cheese and ½ tsp (2 mL) of the salt. Spoon grits mixture into prepared baking dish, smoothing top.

2. In a large nonstick skillet, melt butter over medium-high heat. Sauté onion and garlic for 6 to 8 minutes or until tender. Add the remaining salt, portobello mushrooms, shiitake mushrooms and pepper; sauté for 6 minutes or until mushrooms are tender. Stir in prosciutto and wine; simmer for 5 minutes or until liquid is almost evaporated. Let cool slightly.

3. Add eggs and egg whites to mushroom mixture and stir gently to combine. Spread mushroom mixture over grits mixture and sprinkle with the remaining cheese.

4. Bake in preheated oven for 30 minutes or until cheese is melted and grits are thoroughly heated. Let cool for 5 minutes before serving. Sprinkle with parsley and serve immediately.

Cheesy Hash Brown Casserole

I have seen many variations of this recipe. I add my signature with a bit more onion and extra-sharp Cheddar cheese to boost the flavor, along with more crunch from buttered crushed corn flakes.

Tips

Crush the corn flakes in a food processor or place them in a freezer-proof bag and use a rolling pin to crush them.

I have used cream of celery soup, golden mushroom soup or, in a pinch, whatever cream soup I have in the pantry, with great results.

- Preheat oven to 350°F (180°C)
- 8-cup (2 L) glass baking dish, greased

2 cups	sour cream	500 mL
1	can (10 oz/284 mL) condensed cream of chicken soup	1
¾ cup	butter, melted, divided	175 mL
½ cup	chopped onion	125 mL
2 lbs	frozen hash brown potatoes, thawed	1 kg
2 cups	shredded extra-sharp (extra-old) Cheddar cheese	500 mL
2 cups	coarsely crushed corn flakes cereal	500 mL

1. In a large bowl, whisk together sour cream, soup and ½ cup (125 mL) of the butter. Stir in onion, hash browns and cheese. Spread in prepared baking dish.

2. In a small bowl, combine corn flakes and the remaining butter and sprinkle over hash browns.

3. Bake in preheated oven for 50 minutes or until golden brown and bubbling.

Tiffany's Breakfast Torta

Makes 8 to 10 servings

Several years ago, I developed this recipe for a cooking show in the East Texas area. I had such rave reviews I thought I should definitely include it in this book.

Tips

Control the heat level in this dish with the variety of sausage you use. I use spicy sausage, as my family loves heat.

In Italian, *torta* means pie, tart or cake. In Spanish, *torta* means cake, loaf or sandwich. To me, *torta* means layers of goodness.

- Preheat oven to 350°F (180°C)
- 13- by 9-inch (33 by 23 cm) glass baking dish, greased

1½ lbs	spicy pork sausage (bulk or removed from casings)	750 g
1½ lbs	frozen hash brown potatoes, thawed	750 g
½ cup	chopped green onions	125 mL
½ cup	chopped green bell pepper	125 mL
½ cup	chopped red bell pepper	125 mL
10	eggs	10
½ cup	half-and-half (10%) cream	125 mL
½ tsp	dry mustard	2 mL
½ tsp	dried thyme	2 mL
½ tsp	dried oregano	2 mL
½ tsp	chopped fresh rosemary	2 mL
½ tsp	seasoned salt	2 mL
½ tsp	freshly ground black pepper	2 mL
8	slices sandwich white or whole wheat bread, cubed	8
2½ cups	shredded Cheddar cheese	625 mL

1. In a large nonstick skillet, over medium-high heat, cook sausage, breaking it up with the back of a spoon, for 8 to 10 minutes or until no longer pink. Using a slotted spoon, transfer sausage to a plate and set aside. Drain off all but 2 tbsp (30 mL) of the drippings from the pan.

2. Return skillet to medium-high heat and add hash browns, green onions, green pepper and red pepper; sauté for 8 to 10 minutes or until onions are tender. Let cool for 5 minutes.

3. In a large bowl, whisk eggs until blended. Whisk in cream, mustard, thyme, oregano, rosemary, seasoned salt and pepper.

4. Arrange bread cubes in baking dish. Top evenly with sausage, potato mixture and cheese. Pour egg mixture evenly over top.

5. Bake in preheated oven for 50 to 55 minutes or until set and golden brown.

Cathy's Cheese Strata

This is easily prepared ahead so you can pop it in the oven the next day for easy entertaining — which is especially handy when you have overnight guests.

Tip

For variety, try Cheddar, Monterey Jack, provolone or Swiss cheese in place of the American cheese.

• 13- by 9-inch (33 by 23 cm) glass baking dish

12	slices white sandwich bread, cut into quarters	12
12 oz	American cheese, thinly sliced	375 g
1	package (10 oz/300 g) frozen chopped broccoli, cooked according to package directions and drained	1
2 cups	finely diced cooked ham	500 mL
6	eggs	6
3½ cups	milk	875 mL
1 tbsp	dried minced onion	15 mL
½ tsp	salt	2 mL
½ tsp	freshly ground black pepper	2 mL
¼ tsp	dry mustard	1 mL

1. Arrange half the bread in prepared baking dish, overlapping as necessary. Top with cheese slices, overlapping as necessary. Top evenly with broccoli and ham. Arrange the remaining bread on top.

2. In a large bowl, whisk eggs until blended. Whisk in milk, onion, salt, pepper and mustard. Pour evenly over bread. Cover and refrigerate for at least 6 hours or overnight.

3. Preheat oven to 325°F (160°C).

4. Uncover baking dish. Bake for 55 minutes or until set. Let cool for 10 minutes before serving.

Orange French Toast Bake (page 18)

Southwest Strata (page 35)

Southwest Strata

I make this recipe when I have out-of-town guests. I either assemble it the night before and bake it the next morning or bake it ahead and freeze it for up to a month. Serve with homemade salsa and fresh guacamole.

Tip
Reduce the spice by using regular pork sausage and canned diced tomatoes with mild green chiles or without any chiles.

• 13- by 9-inch (33 by 23 cm) baking dish, greased

1 lb	spicy pork sausage	500 g
1 cup	chopped onion	250 mL
1/2	green bell pepper, chopped	1/2
2	cans (each 10 oz/284 mL) diced tomatoes with green chiles	2
8	10-inch (25 cm) flour tortillas, cut into strips	8
3 cups	shredded Monterey Jack cheese	750 mL
6	eggs	6
2 cups	milk	500 mL
1 tsp	salt	5 mL
1/2 tsp	freshly ground black pepper	2 mL

1. In a large nonstick skillet, over medium-high heat, cook sausage, onion and green pepper, breaking up sausage with the back of a spoon, for 8 to 10 minutes or until sausage is no longer pink and vegetables are tender. Drain off fat and return sausage mixture to skillet.

2. Stir in tomatoes with chiles and bring to a boil. Reduce heat and simmer, stirring occasionally, for 10 minutes. Remove from heat and let cool for 5 minutes.

3. Arrange half the tortilla strips in prepared baking dish. Top with half the sausage mixture and sprinkle with half the cheese. Repeat layers.

4. In a large bowl, whisk eggs until blended. Whisk in milk, salt and pepper; pour evenly over strata. Cover and refrigerate for at least 6 hours or overnight.

5. Preheat oven to 350°F (180°C).

6. Bake, covered, for 55 minutes or until bubbling. Uncover and bake for 10 minutes or until top is golden brown.

Crab Strata

This elegant brunch casserole is just the thing for a special occasion. Serve a mixed green salad on the side.

Tips

For the best texture, use day-old bread with a dense, fine crumb rather than an airy loaf.

I use kitchen shears for rough chopping and to slice fresh herbs, green onions and chives.

- 8-cup (2 L) glass baking dish, greased

4 cups	cubed firm-textured bread	1 L
2	cans (each 6 oz/170 g) crabmeat, drained and flaked	2
2 cups	shredded Swiss cheese	500 mL
1 cup	shredded Cheddar cheese	250 mL
1/4 cup	drained capers	60 mL
3	green onions, chopped	3
6	eggs	6
1 1/3 cups	milk	325 mL
2 tbsp	dry sherry	30 mL
1 tbsp	Dijon mustard	15 mL
1/2 tsp	Worcestershire sauce	2 mL

1. In a large bowl, gently toss bread cubes, crabmeat, Swiss cheese, Cheddar, capers and green onions. Spread in prepared baking dish.

2. In the same bowl, whisk eggs until blended. Whisk in milk, sherry, mustard and Worcestershire sauce. Pour evenly over bread mixture. Cover and refrigerate for at least 6 hours or overnight.

3. Preheat oven to 350°F (180°C).

4. Uncover baking dish. Bake for 45 minutes or until a knife inserted in the center comes out clean. Let cool for 10 minutes before serving.

Garden Vegetable Frittata

This makes a beautiful main course or side dish on a buffet, especially during spring and summer, when vegetables are at their peak of ripeness and flavor.

Tip

Shocking vegetables in ice water stops the cooking process after blanching and sets the color, so you will have brightly colored vegetables even after baking.

- Preheat oven to 350°F (180°C)
- 11- by 7-inch (28 by 18 cm) glass baking dish, greased

1 lb	asparagus, trimmed and cut into 1-inch (2.5 cm) pieces	500 g
	Ice water	
1 tbsp	olive oil	15 mL
4 oz	mushrooms, sliced	125 g
1	clove garlic, minced	1
1	shallot, minced	1
1	small zucchini, cut in half lengthwise and thinly sliced	1
6	eggs	6
1/3 cup	milk	75 mL
1 tbsp	chopped chives	15 mL
1 tsp	salt	5 mL
1/2 tsp	freshly ground black pepper	2 mL
1/8 tsp	ground nutmeg	0.5 mL
2	tomatoes, thinly sliced	2
1/4 cup	freshly grated Parmesan cheese	60 mL

1. In a large pot of boiling water, blanch asparagus for 1 to 2 minutes. Immediately plunge into ice water; let stand until chilled. Drain and place in prepared baking dish.

2. In a skillet, heat oil over medium heat. Sauté mushrooms for about 10 minutes or until tender. Add garlic and shallot; sauté for 2 minutes. Spread over asparagus. Arrange zucchini on top.

3. In a large bowl, whisk eggs until blended. Whisk in milk, chives, salt, pepper and nutmeg. Pour evenly over vegetable mixture. Arrange tomatoes on top. Sprinkle evenly with cheese.

4. Bake in preheated oven for 40 to 45 minutes or until set.

Spinach and Cheese Pie

Makes 6 to 8 servings

I often serve this cheese pie for breakfast or brunch on the weekend, and I love it so much that I usually make two: one to serve right away and one to reheat and serve with fresh fruit or a green salad.

Variation

For a stronger flavor, substitute shredded Gruyère for the Swiss cheese.

• Preheat oven to 425°F (220°C)

1	9-inch (23 cm) unbaked pie shell	1
1	package (10 oz/300 g) frozen chopped spinach, thawed and squeezed dry	1
1 cup	shredded Swiss cheese	250 mL
1/3 cup	sliced green onions	75 mL
4	eggs	4
1/4 cup	freshly grated Parmesan cheese	60 mL
1 1/4 cups	milk	300 mL
1 tbsp	Worcestershire sauce	15 mL
1/2 tsp	salt	2 mL
1/2 tsp	freshly ground black pepper	2 mL

1. Prick pie shell all over with fork. Bake in preheated oven for 5 to 10 minutes or until lightly browned. Let cool slightly. Reduce oven temperature to 325°F (160°C).

2. Layer half each of the spinach, Swiss cheese and green onions in pie crust. Repeat layers.

3. In a large bowl, whisk eggs until blended. Whisk in Parmesan, milk, Worcestershire sauce, salt and pepper. Pour over spinach mixture.

4. Bake for 20 to 25 minutes or until a knife inserted in the center comes out clean. Let cool for 5 to 10 minutes before serving.

Artichoke Quiche

This quiche is particularly delightful for brunch, but let's face it: it's good anytime.

Tips

As the quiche bakes, you may need to cover the edges of the crust with foil to prevent excess browning.

Squeeze thawed and drained spinach several times to remove excess moisture.

• Preheat oven to 425°F (220°C)

1	9-inch (23 cm) unbaked pie shell	1
6	eggs	6
1	package (10 oz/300 g) frozen chopped spinach, thawed and squeezed dry	1
1	can (14 oz/398 mL) artichoke hearts, drained and chopped	1
1	small onion, finely chopped	1
1	clove garlic, minced	1
2 cups	shredded Cheddar cheese	500 mL
½ cup	chopped mushrooms	125 mL
¼ cup	dry bread crumbs	60 mL
½ tsp	salt	2 mL
¼ tsp	freshly ground black pepper	1 mL
¼ tsp	dried oregano	1 mL
¼ tsp	hot pepper sauce	1 mL

1. Prick pie shell all over with a fork. Bake in preheated oven for 5 to 10 minutes or until lightly browned. Let cool slightly. Reduce oven temperature to 350°F (180°C).

2. In a large bowl, whisk eggs until blended. Stir in spinach, artichokes, onion, garlic, cheese, mushrooms, bread crumbs, salt, pepper, oregano and hot pepper sauce. Pour into pie crust.

3. Bake for 55 to 60 minutes or until a knife inserted in the center comes out clean.

Spinach-Mushroom Quiche

This recipe is quick and easy, as it uses a prepared pie crust, which you can find in the refrigerator or freezer section of your supermarket.

Tip

As the quiche bakes, you may need to cover the edges of the crust with foil to prevent excess browning.

• Preheat oven to 425°F (220°C)

1	9-inch (23 cm) unbaked pie shell	1
3	eggs	3
1 cup	milk	250 mL
½ tsp	salt	2 mL
½ tsp	freshly ground black pepper	2 mL
¼ tsp	ground nutmeg	1 mL
2 tbsp	butter	30 mL
2 cups	sliced mushrooms	500 mL
2 cups	shredded Swiss cheese	500 mL
1	package (10 oz/300 g) frozen chopped spinach, thawed and squeezed dry	1

1. Prick pie shell all over with a fork. Bake in preheated oven for 5 to 10 minutes or until lightly browned. Let cool slightly. Reduce oven temperature to 350°F (180°C).

2. In a medium bowl, whisk eggs until blended. Whisk in milk, salt, pepper and nutmeg.

3. In a skillet, melt butter over medium heat. Sauté mushrooms for about 5 minutes or until tender. Let cool slightly.

4. Add mushrooms, cheese and spinach to egg mixture and stir until combined. Pour into pie crust.

5. Bake in preheated oven for 1 hour or until a knife inserted in the center comes out clean.

Bacon and Leeks in a Quiche

I love the name and the flavor of this quiche!

Tip
Keeping the leek roots intact while you wash them holds the leek together, making slicing easier.

Variation
Substitute 1 bunch green onions, sliced, or 2 small sweet onions, thinly sliced, for the leeks.

- Preheat oven to 425°F (220°C)

1	9-inch (23 cm) unbaked pie shell	1
8	slices bacon, cut into 1-inch (2.5 cm) pieces	8
1	bunch leeks (2 or 3 medium)	1
¼ cup	fresh flat-leaf (Italian) parsley leaves, chopped	60 mL
3	eggs	3
1 cup	half-and-half (10%) cream	250 mL
½ tsp	salt	2 mL
¼ tsp	freshly ground black pepper	1 mL
⅛ tsp	ground nutmeg	0.5 mL

1. Prick pie shell all over with a fork. Bake in preheated oven for 5 to 10 minutes or until lightly browned. Let cool slightly. Reduce oven temperature to 350°F (180°C).

2. In a skillet, over medium-high heat, cook bacon until crisp. Using a slotted spoon, transfer to a plate lined with paper towels, reserving drippings in pan. Set both aside.

3. Cut off dark green ends from leeks and discard. Slice leeks in half lengthwise, down to but not through the roots, and rinse under cold running water, removing all sand and dirt. Pat dry and cut crosswise into thin slices.

4. Heat bacon drippings in skillet over medium-high heat. Add leeks and sauté for 6 to 8 minutes or until soft. Spread in pie crust. Sprinkle bacon and parsley over leeks.

5. In a medium bowl, whisk eggs until blended. Whisk in cream, salt, pepper and nutmeg. Pour over leek mixture.

6. Bake for 50 minutes or until a knife inserted in the center comes out clean. Let cool for 10 minutes before serving.

Sausage and Cheddar Quiche

I love quiche any time of day, but it's especially elegant for brunch. Try this simple recipe, made with biscuit mix.

Tip

I enjoy the flavor of extra-sharp (extra-old) Cheddar cheese in this recipe.

* Preheat oven to 350°F (180°C)
* 11- by 7-inch (28 by 18 cm) glass baking dish
* Blender

1 lb	sausage (bulk or removed from casings)	500 g
1	bunch green onions, chopped	1
1 cup	shredded Cheddar cheese	250 mL
1 cup	biscuit mix	250 mL
3	eggs	3
1½ cups	milk	375 mL
¾ cup	sour cream	175 mL
½ tsp	salt	2 mL
½ tsp	freshly ground black pepper	2 mL

1. In a nonstick skillet, over medium-high heat, cook sausage, breaking it up with the back of a spoon, for 8 to 10 minutes or until no longer pink. Drain off fat. Let cool.

2. Spread sausage in baking dish. Sprinkle onions and cheese on top.

3. In blender, combine biscuit mix, eggs, milk, sour cream, salt and pepper; blend until smooth. Pour evenly over sausage mixture.

4. Bake in preheated oven for 40 to 45 minutes or until set. Let cool for 10 minutes before serving.

Crustless Pizza Quiche

Makes 8 to 10 servings

Use chopped pepperoni or salami in this pizza-like quiche, or use a combination of both! Serve with a mixed green salad dressed with Italian vinaigrette.

Tip

Substitute an Italian cheese blend or pizza cheese blend for the mozzarella. These blends are usually a combination of mozzarella, Parmesan, Asiago and/or Romano cheeses.

- Preheat oven to 375°F (190°C)
- 13- by 9-inch (33 by 23 cm) baking pan or dish, greased

2	eggs	2
2 cups	milk	500 mL
1 tsp	salt	5 mL
½ tsp	freshly ground black pepper	2 mL
1½ tsp	dried oregano	7 mL
1½ cups	all-purpose flour	375 mL
2 cups	chopped pepperoni or salami	500 mL
3 cups	shredded mozzarella cheese, divided	750 mL

1. In a large bowl, whisk eggs until blended. Whisk in milk, salt, pepper and oregano. Stir in flour until moistened. Add pepperoni and half the cheese. Pour into prepared baking dish.

2. Bake in preheated oven for 30 minutes or until set. Sprinkle with remaining cheese. Bake for 5 minutes or until cheese is melted.

Taco Quiche

I love ground beef tacos and I love quiche, so why not combine the two, I thought, for a real Tex-Mex twist on breakfast? Both kids and adults will love the result.

Tips

You can leave off the sour cream, lettuce, tomatoes, avocado and olives and this dish would still taste great, but it's so much better with them!

I like using lean ground beef to reduce the fat, especially when a recipe contains a lot of flavor, as this one does.

- Preheat oven to 350°F (180°C)
- 10-inch (25 cm) deep-dish glass pie plate, greased

6	6- to 7-inch (15 to 18 cm) corn tortillas	6
2 lbs	lean ground beef	1 kg
1	small red onion, chopped	1
1	clove garlic, minced	1
1 tsp	chili powder	5 mL
½ tsp	salt	2 mL
¼ tsp	ground cumin	1 mL
¼ tsp	dried thyme	1 mL
¼ tsp	freshly ground black pepper	1 mL
¼ tsp	dried oregano	1 mL
2 cups	shredded Monterey Jack cheese	500 mL
6	eggs	6
2 cups	milk	500 mL
1 cup	sour cream	250 mL
1	small head iceberg lettuce, shredded	1
2	tomatoes, sliced	2
1	large avocado, sliced	1
¼ cup	sliced olives	60 mL

1. Line prepared pie plate with tortillas, tearing them to fit and overlapping as necessary.

2. In a large nonstick skillet, over medium-high heat, brown beef, red onion and garlic, breaking up beef with the back of a spoon, for 8 to 10 minutes or until beef is no longer pink. Stir in chili powder, salt, cumin, thyme, pepper and oregano. Pour over tortillas. Sprinkle with cheese.

3. In a bowl, whisk together eggs and milk. Pour evenly over beef mixture.

4. Bake in preheated oven for 1 hour or until set. Evenly layer sour cream, lettuce, tomatoes, avocado and olives on top. Serve immediately.

Tex-Mex Green Chile Quiche

In this scrumptious quiche, layers of Tex-Mex ingredients are accented with the smoky flavor of crisp bacon.

Tip

Reheat leftover baked quiche for breakfast, lunch or dinner. Simply place it in a microwave-safe dish, cover it loosely with plastic wrap, vent and microwave on High in 30-second intervals until the internal temperature reaches 160°F (71°C).

• Preheat oven to 425°F (220°C)

1	9-inch (23 cm) unbaked pie shell	1
1 cup	shredded Monterey Jack cheese	250 mL
$\frac{1}{4}$ cup	finely chopped onion	60 mL
8	slices bacon, cooked crisp and crumbled	8
1	can ($4\frac{1}{2}$ oz/127 mL) chopped mild green chiles	1
4	eggs	4
$\frac{1}{2}$ cup	half-and-half (10%) cream	125 mL
$\frac{1}{4}$ tsp	salt	1 mL
$\frac{1}{8}$ tsp	freshly ground black pepper	0.5 mL
$1\frac{1}{2}$ tbsp	butter, melted	22 mL

1. Prick pie shell all over with a fork. Bake in preheated oven for 5 to 10 minutes or until lightly browned. Let cool slightly. Reduce oven temperature to 375°F (190°C).

2. Layer cheese, onion, bacon and chiles in pie crust.

3. In a bowl, whisk eggs until blended. Whisk in cream, salt, pepper and butter. Pour evenly over cheese mixture.

4. Bake for 45 minutes or until set. Let cool for 10 minutes before serving.

Noodle Quiche

Makes 6 servings

This dish is so simple and so good! Serve it with a salad to make a complete meal.

Variation

Substituting blue cheese for the Swiss cheese will create a very different dish with a sharper bite of flavor. Use a mild blue cheese, such as Stella.

- Preheat oven to 375°F (190°C)
- 8-cup (2 L) glass baking dish or casserole, greased

8 oz	wide egg noodles, cooked, drained and rinsed	250 g
2 cups	shredded Swiss cheese	500 mL
8	slices bacon	8
1	onion, chopped	1
3	eggs	3
1½ cups	milk	375 mL
1 cup	sour cream	250 mL
½ cup	freshly grated Parmesan cheese	125 mL
½ tsp	salt	2 mL
¼ tsp	ground nutmeg	1 mL
¼ tsp	freshly ground black pepper	1 mL

1. In a large bowl, toss noodles with Swiss cheese. Press evenly onto bottom and sides of prepared baking dish.

2. In a skillet, over medium-high heat, cook bacon until crisp. Using tongs, transfer to a plate lined with paper towels, reserving 2 tbsp (30 mL) of the drippings in the pan. Let bacon cool.

3. Return skillet to medium-high heat and heat drippings. Add onion and sauté for about 5 minutes or until tender. Let cool for 5 minutes.

4. In a large bowl, whisk eggs until blended. Whisk in milk, sour cream, Parmesan, salt, nutmeg and pepper. Stir in bacon and onion. Pour evenly over noodle mixture.

5. Bake in preheated oven for 50 minutes or until set.

Appetizers

Wine-Soaked Bread Bake. 48

Cheddar Cheese Bake 48

Baked Feta with Marinara Sauce. 49

Baked Goat Cheese with Herbed Sun-Dried Tomatoes 49

Tif's Baked Pimento Cheese 50

Bacon Blue Cheese Dip 51

Cheesy Phyllo Appetizers 52

Artichoke Cheddar Squares 53

The Best Artichoke Dip Ever 54

Cheesy Spinach Bacon Dip. 54

Spinach and Artichoke Casserole 55

Creamed Jalapeño Spinach Dip 56

Spinach Quiche Nibbles 57

Onion Frittata with Crème Fraîche Drizzle 58

Zucchini Squares 59

Corn Dip. 60

Creamy Smoked Salmon Dip 60

Crab Bake 61

Creamy Crab and Artichoke Dip 61

Buffalo Chicken Dip 62

Chicken and Cheddar Dip with Four Chiles 63

Sara's Dip. 64

Baked Kielbasa Appetizers 64

Warm Mexican Layered Dip. 65

Layered Italian Antipasto Squares 66

Wine-Soaked Bread Bake

Makes 4 to 6 servings

This recipe is great for a buffet or cocktail party, but you will certainly need to lay out forks and napkins!

- Preheat oven to 400°F (200°C)
- 9-inch (23 cm) square glass baking dish, greased

1/2	baguette, cut into 2-inch (5 cm) slices	1/2
1/2	small onion, thinly sliced	1/2
2 oz	sliced deli ham	60 g
3/4 cup	white wine	175 mL
6 oz	Swiss cheese, shredded	175 g
1/2 tsp	salt	2 mL
1/2 tsp	freshly ground black pepper	2 mL

1. Place baguette slices in prepared baking dish. Layer onion and ham on top. Pour wine over ham and sprinkle with cheese, salt and pepper.

2. Bake in preheated oven for about 20 minutes or until starting to brown at the edges and cheese is melted.

Cheddar Cheese Bake

Makes 8 servings

Serve this cozy appetizer warm, with crackers and a glass of Chardonnay.

Variation

Mix it up by adding in 1/2 cup (125 mL) chopped sun-dried tomatoes or roasted red peppers, or 3 tbsp (45 mL) diced jalapeño pepper.

- Preheat oven to 325°F (160°C)
- 4-cup (1 L) baking dish, greased

1	egg, lightly beaten	1
1 cup	mayonnaise	250 mL
1/4 tsp	garlic salt	1 mL
1/8 tsp	freshly ground black pepper	0.5 mL
3 cups	shredded Cheddar cheese	750 mL
1/2	small onion, minced	1/2

1. In a medium bowl, combine egg, mayonnaise, garlic salt and pepper. Stir in cheese and onion. Spread in prepared baking dish.

2. Bake in preheated oven for 20 to 25 minutes or until bubbling.

Baked Feta with Marinara Sauce

This delectable mélange of melted cheese and marinara sauce is wonderful spread on baguette slices or crackers, or tossed with hot pasta for a seated first course.

Tip

I'm sure you have a favorite marinara sauce (mine is a bottled Cabernet marinara), and you could simply use it plain rather than doctoring it up as I did in this recipe.

- Preheat oven to 350°F (180°C)
- 6- by 3-inch (15 by 7.5 cm) soufflé dish, greased

2	cloves garlic, minced	2
1½ cups	marinara sauce	375 mL
1 tsp	freshly squeezed lemon juice	5 mL
½ tsp	salt	2 mL
¼ tsp	hot pepper flakes	1 mL
4 oz	feta cheese, crumbled	125 g

1. In a bowl, combine garlic, marinara sauce, lemon juice, salt and hot pepper flakes.

2. Sprinkle feta evenly in prepared baking dish and pour marinara mixture evenly over top.

3. Bake in preheated oven for 20 minutes or until bubbling.

Baked Goat Cheese with Herbed Sun-Dried Tomatoes

If, like me, you have friends who turn up their nose at goat cheese, don't tell them what's in this dish until they have a taste. Then you can laugh at their expression when they realize how good goat cheese really is! Serve with crackers or baguette slices, or as a dip with fresh veggies.

Tip

For a more formal bite-size appetizer, spoon into baked mini phyllo cups and bake at 350°F (180°C) until hot.

- Preheat oven to 350°F (180°C)
- 2-cup (500 mL) baking dish, greased

8 oz	soft goat cheese	250 g
2 tbsp	chopped fresh basil	30 mL
¼ tsp	Cajun seasoning	1 mL
⅛ tsp	freshly ground black pepper	0.5 mL
2	cloves garlic, minced	2
¼ cup	drained oil-packed sun-dried tomatoes, chopped	30 mL
1 tsp	chopped fresh rosemary	5 mL

1. In a medium bowl, combine goat cheese, basil, Cajun seasoning and pepper. Spread in prepared baking dish.

2. In a small bowl, combine garlic, sun-dried tomatoes and rosemary. Layer on top of cheese mixture.

3. Bake in preheated oven for 20 minutes or until bubbling.

Tif's Baked Pimento Cheese

Makes 8 servings

My grandmother Effie made a delectable Southern pimento cheese. We would smear it on white bread and have the best tea sandwiches in the world. In my travels, I found a quaint restaurant in Ashville, North Carolina, that *baked* my favorite spread! When I returned home, I *had* to bake my grandmother's recipe. Now I can't decide which way I like it best — baked or unbaked.

Tips

Serve baked pimento cheese with toast points, your favorite crackers or baguette slices.

You can also simply combine the ingredients, without baking, and serve the mixture as a spread with your favorite bread or toast.

- Preheat oven to 350°F (180°C)
- 11- by 7-inch (28 by 18 cm) glass baking dish, greased

1	jar (4½ oz/127 mL) chopped pimentos, drained	1
1½ cups	mayonnaise	375 mL
1 tsp	Worcestershire sauce	5 mL
1 tsp	minced onion	5 mL
¼ tsp	freshly ground black pepper	1 mL
¼ tsp	garlic powder	1 mL
2 cups	shredded extra-sharp (extra-old) Cheddar cheese	500 mL
2 cups	shredded sharp (old) Cheddar cheese	500 mL

1. In a large bowl, combine pimento, mayonnaise, Worcestershire sauce, onion, pepper and garlic powder. Stir in extra-sharp Cheddar and sharp Cheddar. Spoon into prepared baking dish.

2. Bake in preheated oven for 20 minutes or until bubbling.

Baked Goat Cheese with
Herbed Sun-Dried Tomatoes (page 49)

Garden Vegetable Frittata (page 37)

Bacon Blue Cheese Dip

Makes 12 to 15 servings

The bold flavors of bacon and blue cheese in this dip cry out for a bold red wine to be served alongside.

Tips

Gently stir the blue cheese mixture to keep the individual ingredients visually distinct. If you overmix, it will turn a very unappetizing blue color.

Serve this dip with assorted crackers, baguette slices and chopped fruit.

- Preheat oven to 350°F (180°C)
- 6- by 3-inch (15 by 7.5 cm) soufflé dish, greased

8	slices bacon, chopped	8
2	cloves garlic, minced	2
1 lb	cream cheese, softened	500 g
1/3 cup	half-and-half (10%) cream	75 mL
4 oz	blue cheese, crumbled	125 g
2 tbsp	chopped fresh chives	30 mL
3 tbsp	chopped toasted walnuts (see tip, page 74)	45 mL

1. In a large skillet, cook bacon over medium-high heat, stirring, for 10 minutes or until crisp. Using a slotted spoon, transfer bacon to a plate lined with paper towels.

2. Add garlic to skillet and sauté for 1 minute. Remove from heat and let cool slightly.

3. In a bowl, using an electric mixer on medium speed, beat cream cheese until smooth. Add cream and beat until combined. Using a spoon, gently stir in bacon, garlic, blue cheese and chives just until combined. Spoon into prepared baking dish.

4. Bake in preheated oven for 15 minutes or until golden and bubbling. Sprinkle evenly with walnuts.

Cheesy Phyllo Appetizers

The combination of feta, cream cheese and dill layered between tender phyllo sheets makes a great appetizer for a party with a Greek theme.

Tip

Thaw phyllo with a damp towel around it and keep it wrapped as you work, removing one sheet at a time and brushing it with butter as fast as you can to keep it from drying out.

- Preheat oven to 350°F (180°C)
- 13- by 9-inch (33 by 23 cm) glass baking dish, greased

1 lb	feta cheese, crumbled	500 g
12 oz	cream cheese, softened	375 g
5	eggs	5
1 tbsp	chopped fresh dill	15 mL
1/8 tsp	salt	0.5 mL
1/8 tsp	freshly ground black pepper	0.5 mL
12	sheets frozen phyllo pastry, thawed	12
1 cup	butter, melted	250 mL

1. In a large bowl, using an electric mixer on medium speed, beat feta and cream cheese until blended. On low speed, beat in eggs, one at a time, until blended. Beat in dill, salt and pepper.

2. Cut each pastry sheet into a 13- by 9-inch (33 by 23 cm) rectangle, discarding scraps. Brush one sheet lightly with butter and place in prepared baking dish. Working with one sheet at a time, brush 7 more sheets with butter and stack in baking dish. Spread cheese mixture evenly over phyllo. Brush remaining 4 sheets of phyllo and stack on top of cheese mixture.

3. Bake in preheated oven for 45 to 50 minutes or until golden brown. Let cool for 10 minutes before cutting into squares.

Artichoke Cheddar Squares

Here, I've turned popular artichoke dip into a casserole, cut into squares. They're perfect for a buffet or as passed hors d'oeuvres at a party.

Variation

For a different flavor and aroma, substitute smoked mozzarella for the Cheddar.

- Preheat oven to 325°F (160°C)
- 9-inch (23 cm) glass baking dish, greased

1 tbsp	olive oil	15 mL
1	small onion, minced	1
1	clove garlic, minced	1
2	jars (each 6½ oz/184 mL) marinated artichoke hearts, drained and chopped	2
4	eggs	4
¼ cup	dry bread crumbs	60 mL
¼ tsp	salt	1 mL
⅛ tsp	freshly ground black pepper	0.5 mL
⅛ tsp	dried oregano leaves	0.5 mL
⅛ tsp	hot pepper sauce	0.5 mL
2 cups	shredded extra-sharp (extra-old) Cheddar cheese	500 mL
2 tbsp	minced fresh parsley	30 mL

1. In a large nonstick skillet, heat oil over medium heat. Sauté onion and garlic for about 5 minutes or until tender. Stir in artichokes. Let cool slightly.

2. In a large bowl, whisk eggs until blended. Stir in bread crumbs, salt, black pepper, oregano and hot pepper sauce. Gently stir in cheese and parsley. Stir in onion mixture. Pour into prepared baking dish.

3. Bake in preheated oven for 30 minutes or until golden. Let cool slightly, then cut into 1-inch (2.5 cm) squares.

The Best Artichoke Dip Ever

Makes 8 to 10 servings

This dip, created by my friend Cathy Sullivan, wears its title well. Everyone loves it, even folks who don't really care for artichokes. Serve it with melba toast or flatbread crackers.

Tip

For the best consistency, roughly chop the artichokes.

- Preheat oven to 350°F (180°C)
- 9-inch (23 cm) glass pie plate or quiche dish, greased

1	can (14 oz/398 mL) artichoke hearts, drained and chopped	1
1	jar (4½ oz/127 mL) chopped pimentos, drained	1
2 cups	shredded Monterey Jack cheese	500 mL
1 cup	freshly grated Parmesan cheese	250 mL
1 cup	mayonnaise	250 mL
½ cup	packed sliced trimmed fresh spinach	125 mL

1. In a large bowl, combine artichokes, pimentos, Monterey Jack, Parmesan, mayonnaise and spinach. Spread in prepared pie plate.

2. Bake in preheated oven for 25 to 30 minutes or until golden brown and bubbling.

Cheesy Spinach Bacon Dip

Makes 8 to 10 cups (2 to 2.5 L)

My friend Marcia Smith makes this savory dip for our gatherings and serves it with tortilla chips and salsa. Go ahead and splurge!

Tips

This recipe can be cut in half for smaller gatherings and baked in an 8-inch (20 cm) square glass baking dish.

For the best consistency, remove as much moisture as possible from the thawed spinach.

- Preheat oven to 350°F (180°C)
- 13- by 9-inch (33 by 23 cm) glass baking dish, greased

1½ lbs	cream cheese, softened	750 g
1 lb	bacon, cooked crisp and crumbled	500 g
1	package (10 oz/300 g) frozen spinach, thawed and squeezed dry	1
1	onion, chopped	1
2 cups	freshly grated Parmesan cheese	500 mL
1 cup	shredded mozzarella cheese	250 mL
½ cup	mayonnaise	125 mL

1. In a large bowl, thoroughly combine cream cheese, bacon, spinach, onion, Parmesan, mozzarella and mayonnaise. Spread in prepared baking dish.

2. Bake in preheated oven for 30 minutes or until bubbling.

Spinach and Artichoke Casserole

Makes 8 servings

Yummy! Enough said.

Tips

For a chunkier consistency, quarter each artichoke heart rather than chopping them.

Serve with fresh ciabatta.

- Preheat oven to 350°F (180°C)
- 8-inch (20 cm) square glass baking dish, greased

2	packages (each 10 oz/300 g) frozen spinach, thawed and squeezed dry	2
$\frac{1}{2}$ cup	chopped onion	125 mL
$\frac{1}{2}$ cup	melted butter	125 mL
$\frac{1}{2}$ cup	sour cream	125 mL
$\frac{1}{4}$ cup	freshly grated Parmesan cheese, divided	60 mL
$\frac{1}{2}$ tsp	salt	2 mL
$\frac{1}{2}$ tsp	freshly ground black pepper	2 mL
$\frac{1}{4}$ tsp	cayenne pepper	1 mL
2	cans (each 14 oz/398 mL) artichoke hearts, drained and chopped	2

1. In a bowl, combine spinach, onion, butter, sour cream, half the cheese, salt, black pepper and cayenne.

2. Place artichokes in prepared baking dish. Spoon spinach mixture over top and sprinkle with the remaining cheese.

3. Bake in preheated oven for 25 to 30 minutes or until bubbling.

Creamed Jalapeño Spinach Dip

I love this creamy spinach dip served with fiery salsa and tortilla chips.

Tips

Removing the ribs and seeds from fresh chile peppers before mincing them will reduce the amount of heat in your dish.

Squeeze thawed and drained spinach several times to remove excess moisture.

- Preheat oven to 350°F (180°C)
- 11- by 7-inch (28 by 18 cm) glass baking dish, greased

2 tbsp	olive oil	30 mL
2	jalapeño peppers, seeded and minced	2
1	onlon, chopped	1
1	can (4½ oz/127 mL) chopped mild green chiles, with liquid	1
1	can (14 oz/398 mL) diced tomatoes, with juice	1
8 oz	cream cheese, cut into cubes	250 g
1 tbsp	red wine vinegar	15 mL
1	package (10 oz/300 g) frozen spinach, thawed and squeezed dry	1
1 cup	half-and-half (10%) cream	250 mL
3 cups	shredded pepper Jack cheese	750 mL
½ tsp	salt	2 mL

1. In a large skillet, heat oil over medium-high heat until very hot, swirling to coat pan. Sauté jalapeños and onion for about 5 minutes or until tender. Add chiles with liquid and tomatoes with juice; boil for 3 minutes.

2. Stir in cream cheese and vinegar until cheese is melted and thoroughly blended. Stir in spinach, cream, pepper Jack and salt. Pour into prepared baking dish.

3. Bake in preheated oven for 30 minutes or until bubbling.

Spinach Quiche Nibbles

Makes 36 squares

I like to serve these miniature quiches when I host a wine-tasting party. They pair especially well with light red or crisp white wines.

Tip

Baked squares can be stored in an airtight container in the freezer for up to 1 month. Thaw overnight in the refrigerator, then reheat in the microwave until hot.

- Preheat oven to 350°F (180°C)
- 13- by 9-inch (33 by 23 cm) glass baking dish, greased

1	can (8 oz/227 g) refrigerated crescent rolls	1
2 cups	shredded Gruyère cheese	500 mL
½ cup	freshly grated Parmesan cheese	125 mL
3 tbsp	all-purpose flour	45 mL
4	eggs, lightly beaten	4
1¼ cups	milk	300 mL
¼ tsp	salt	1 mL
⅛ tsp	freshly ground black pepper	0.5 mL
⅛ tsp	ground nutmeg	0.5 mL
1	package (10 oz/300 g) frozen chopped spinach, thawed and squeezed dry	1

1. Unroll crescent roll sheet and press into prepared baking dish, pressing ¼ inch (0.5 cm) up the sides to form a crust.

2. In a large bowl, toss together Gruyère, Parmesan and flour. Stir in eggs, milk, salt, pepper and nutmeg until well blended. Stir in spinach. Pour evenly over prepared crust.

3. Bake in preheated oven for 50 minutes or until center is set. Let cool for 5 minutes, then cut into small squares.

Onion Frittata with Crème Fraîche Drizzle

This recipe, served in individual pieces drizzled with silky crème fraîche, makes an elegant brunch menu item.

Tip

Crème fraîche is French-style sour cream, a bit thinner and more delicate-tasting than what we're used to in North America.

- Preheat oven to 350°F (180°C)
- 11- by 7-inch (28 by 18 cm) glass baking dish, greased

1 tsp	butter	5 mL
2 cups	minced onion	500 mL
6	eggs	6
¼ cup	freshly grated Parmesan cheese, divided	50 mL
½ tsp	salt	2 mL
½ tsp	freshly ground black pepper	2 mL
¼ cup	chopped fresh chives	50 mL
¼ cup	crème fraîche	50 mL

1. In a nonstick skillet, melt butter over medium heat. Sauté onion for 5 to 7 minutes or until tender. Spread in prepared baking dish.

2. In a bowl, whisk eggs until blended. Stir in half the Parmesan and season with salt and pepper. Pour evenly over onion. Sprinkle with remaining Parmesan.

3. Bake in preheated oven for 25 to 30 minutes or until set. Sprinkle with chives. Let cool slightly. Cut into 24 pieces and drizzle with crème fraîche.

Zucchini Squares

These squares make great finger food or passed hors d'oeuvres.

Tip

For best results, use a sharp knife or a mandoline to thinly slice zucchini. Be careful when using sharp blades!

- Preheat oven to 450°F (230°C)
- 13- by 9-inch (33 by 23 cm) glass baking dish, greased

2	cloves garlic, minced	2
3 cups	thinly sliced zucchini	750 mL
1/2 cup	minced onion	125 mL
1/2 cup	freshly grated Parmesan cheese	125 mL
2 tbsp	chopped fresh parsley	30 mL
1/2 tsp	dried oregano	2 mL
1/2 tsp	salt	2 mL
1/4 tsp	freshly ground black pepper	1 mL
1 cup	biscuit mix	250 mL
4	eggs, beaten	4
1/2 cup	vegetable oil	125 mL

1. In a large bowl, combine garlic, zucchini, onion, cheese, parsley, oregano, salt and pepper. Spread in prepared baking dish.

2. In a medium bowl, combine biscuit mix, eggs and oil. Pour evenly over zucchini mixture.

3. Bake in preheated oven for about 25 minutes or until golden brown and a tester inserted in the center comes out clean. Cut into 2-inch (5 cm) squares and serve immediately.

Corn Dip

This dip is so yummy you won't be able to stop yourself from indulging! Serve with tortilla chips.

- Preheat oven to 350°F (180°C)
- 11- by 7-inch (28 by 18 cm) glass baking dish, greased

1	can (15 oz/425 mL) whole-kernel corn, drained	1
8 oz	cream cheese, softened	250 g
1 cup	shredded Monterey Jack cheese	250 mL
1/2 cup	freshly grated Parmesan cheese	125 mL
1/2 cup	chopped red bell pepper	125 mL
1	can (4 oz/114 mL) pickled jalapeño peppers, drained and chopped	1
1/4 cup	sliced black olives	60 mL

1. In a bowl, combine corn, cream cheese, Monterey Jack, Parmesan, red pepper and jalapeños. Spread in prepared baking dish.

2. Bake in preheated oven for 30 minutes or until heated through. Sprinkle with olives and serve immediately.

Creamy Smoked Salmon Dip

This creamy dip is delicious served hot or cold, with fresh vegetables, bagel chips or crackers.

- Preheat oven to 350°F (180°C)
- 10-cup (2.5 L) glass baking dish, greased

1 lb	cream cheese, softened	500 g
1 cup	sour cream	250 mL
1/4 cup	milk	50 mL
1/4 tsp	garlic powder	1 mL
1/4 tsp	salt	1 mL
1/4 tsp	freshly ground black pepper	1 mL
4 oz	smoked salmon, chopped	125 g
1/2 cup	chopped red bell pepper, chopped	125 mL
1/4 cup	sliced green onions	60 mL

1. In a large bowl, using an electric mixer on medium speed, beat cream cheese, sour cream, milk, garlic powder, salt and pepper until blended. Using a spoon, gently stir in salmon, red pepper and green onions. Spread in prepared baking dish.

2. Bake in preheated oven for 20 to 25 minutes or until heated through. Serve immediately.

Crab Bake

Makes 2 cups (500 mL)

This creamy appetizer with delicate crabmeat is great served with crusty bread, corn chips or tortilla chips at happy hour.

Tips

If you want to splurge, use 8 oz (250 g) shelled fresh cooked crabmeat instead of the canned.

Minced onion can be substituted for the shallots.

- Preheat oven to 375°F (190°C)
- 8-inch (20 cm) square glass baking dish, greased

8 oz	cream cheese, softened	250 g
1/4 cup	minced shallots	60 mL
1 tbsp	milk	15 mL
1/2 tsp	salt	2 mL
1/4 tsp	freshly ground black pepper	1 mL
1/4 tsp	Worcestershire sauce	1 mL
1	can (6 oz/170 g) crabmeat, drained	1
1/4 cup	sliced green onions	60 mL

1. In a medium bowl, combine cream cheese, shallots, milk, salt, pepper and Worcestershire sauce. Fold in crabmeat. Spread in prepared baking dish and sprinkle with green onions.

2. Bake in preheated oven for 15 to 20 minutes or until bubbling.

Creamy Crab and Artichoke Dip

Makes 8 to 10 servings

This dip is so hearty that it can even leave its appetizer status behind and be smeared on a crusty baguette and served with a green salad for an easy meal.

Tips

Sprinkle hot pepper flakes on top for an extra boost of flavor.

For a dramatic presentation, bake in a hollowed-out sourdough round.

- Preheat oven to 375°F (190°C)
- 9-inch (23 cm) glass pie plate, greased

8 oz	cream cheese, softened	250 g
1 cup	mayonnaise	250 mL
8 oz	cooked crabmeat, flaked	250 g
3 oz	Parmesan cheese, grated	90 g
1	can (14 oz/398 mL) artichoke hearts, drained and chopped	1
1/3 cup	chopped onion	75 mL

1. In a medium bowl, combine cream cheese and mayonnaise until smooth. Stir in crabmeat, cheese, artichokes and onion. Spread in prepared pie plate.

2. Bake in preheated oven for 15 to 20 minutes or until bubbling.

Buffalo Chicken Dip

Makes 8 servings

Buffalo wings and blue cheese dressing are a classic combination — my mouth waters just thinking about it. This appetizer casserole provides the same great flavors, but in a less messy form.

Tip
Serve with celery sticks, tortilla chips and ice-cold beer!

- Preheat oven to 350°F (180°C)
- 13- by 9-inch (33 by 23 cm) glass baking dish, greased

2 lbs	boneless skinless chicken breasts	1 kg
¼ cup	crumbled blue cheese	60 mL
1 cup	hot wings dipping sauce	250 mL
1 lb	cream cheese, cut into cubes	500 g
1	bottle (16 oz/454 mL) blue cheese salad dressing	1
2 cups	shredded extra-sharp (extra-old) Cheddar cheese	500 mL

1. Place chicken breasts in a saucepan and add just enough water to cover. Bring to a simmer over medium heat. Reduce heat and simmer for about 15 minutes or until no longer pink inside. Drain well and let cool. Shred with two forks.

2. Layer shredded chicken in prepared baking dish. Sprinkle evenly with blue cheese. Pour dipping sauce evenly over top.

3. In a large saucepan, combine cream cheese and blue cheese dressing. Heat over medium heat, stirring, until smooth and hot. Pour evenly over chicken mixture.

4. Bake in preheated oven for 30 minutes or until bubbling. Sprinkle Cheddar over top. Bake for 10 minutes or until cheese is melted. Let cool for 10 minutes before serving.

Chicken and Cheddar Dip with Four Chiles

Truly a Texan's dream of Southwest flavors, this dip is great served with tortilla chips and sweet potato chips for dipping or in home-fried small taco shells as part of a Tex-Mex buffet.

Tip

Assemble this casserole a day ahead, cover and refrigerate to allow the flavors to develop, then bake just before serving.

Removing the ribs and seeds from a jalapeño lessens its heat.

- Preheat oven to 350°F (180°C)
- 8-inch (20 cm) square glass baking dish, greased

8 oz	cream cheese, softened	250 g
$\frac{2}{3}$ cup	sour cream	150 mL
$\frac{1}{3}$ cup	mayonnaise	75 mL
1 tsp	chili powder	5 mL
1 tsp	ground cumin	1 mL
3	green onions, minced	3
2	jalapeño peppers, seeded and chopped	2
1	can ($4\frac{1}{2}$ oz/127 mL) chopped mild green chiles	1
2 cups	chopped cooked chicken	500 mL
2 cups	shredded extra-sharp (extra-old) Cheddar cheese	500 mL
$\frac{1}{4}$ cup	chopped fresh cilantro	50 mL
1 tbsp	minced chipotle pepper in adobo sauce	15 mL

1. In a large bowl, using an electric mixer on low speed, beat cream cheese, sour cream, mayonnaise, chili powder and cumin until smooth. With a spoon, gently stir in green onions, jalapeños, green chiles, chicken, Cheddar, cilantro and chipotle pepper. Spread in prepared baking dish.

2. Bake in preheated oven for 25 to 30 minutes or until bubbling.

Sara's Dip

My family would often vacation in Neshkoro, Wisconsin, at a beautiful cottage on the lake. At 4:00 p.m., we'd declare it happy hour, pile into the pontoon boat, grab our beverage of choice and munch on this savory dip, created many years ago by my dear friend Sara Johnson. I can't eat it without thinking of lazy summer afternoons at the cottage.

Tip

Serve with tortilla chips or roll up in a steamed flour or corn tortilla.

- Preheat oven to 350°F (180°C)
- 11- by 7-inch (28 by 18 cm) glass baking dish, greased

8 oz	cream cheese, softened	250 g
1	can (15 oz/426 mL) turkey chili	1
1	jar (8 oz/228 mL) salsa	1
1 cup	shredded Cheddar cheese	250 mL
½ cup	sliced black olives	125 mL

1. Spread cream cheese in bottom of prepared baking dish. Layer chili, salsa, Cheddar and olives on top.

2. Bake in preheated oven for 25 to 30 minutes or until bubbling.

Baked Kielbasa Appetizers

Applesauce is a sweet complement to kielbasa sausage. I offer these appetizers on game day, on a platter with toothpicks.

Tip

For a game-day buffet table, keep the sausages warm in a slow cooker, with crackers or chips handy nearby.

- Preheat oven to 350°F (180°C)
- 13- by 9-inch (33 by 23 cm) glass baking dish, greased

2	jars (each 20 oz/567 mL) unsweetened applesauce	2
½ cup	packed brown sugar	125 mL
2 lbs	cooked kielbasa or Polish sausages, cut into ½-inch (1 cm) pieces	1 kg
1	onion, chopped	1

1. In a large bowl, combine applesauce and brown sugar. Stir in sausages and onion until thoroughly combined. Spread in prepared baking dish.

2. Bake in preheated oven for 45 to 50 minutes or until bubbling.

Warm Mexican Layered Dip

Makes 6 to 8 servings

This layered dip is easy to assemble and is always popular with a crowd. It makes a hearty buffet dish served with tortilla chips or small steamed tortillas.

Tips

I like to use a nonstick skillet when browning ground turkey, chicken or beef, as it eliminates the need for oil or butter.

If you prefer to use pre-shredded cheese or don't have a kitchen scale, you'll need 1 cup (250 mL) each Cheddar and Monterey Jack.

- Preheat oven to 400°F (200°C)
- 9-inch (23 cm) square glass or ceramic baking dish, greased

1 lb	ground turkey or beef	500 g
1	jar (15 oz/426 mL) salsa	1
1	envelope (1¼ oz/37 g) taco seasoning mix	1
1	can (16 oz/454 mL) refried beans	1
1 cup	sour cream	250 mL
4 oz	Cheddar cheese, shredded	125 g
4 oz	Monterey Jack cheese, shredded	125 g

1. Heat a large nonstick skillet over medium-high heat. Cook turkey, breaking it up with the back of a spoon and stirring occasionally, for 8 to 10 minutes or until no longer pink. Stir in salsa and taco seasoning.

2. Spread turkey mixture in prepared baking dish. Layer refried beans, sour cream, Cheddar and Monterey Jack on top.

3. Bake in preheated oven for 25 to 30 minutes or until bubbling.

Layered Italian Antipasto Squares

This layered dish has the components of an antipasto tray, served in bite-size squares. It's absolutely perfect for entertaining!

Tips

You can use leftover meats such as roast beef or turkey in place of the salami, pepperoni or ham.

When pressing out the dough, make sure to seal the perforations between the rolls.

Brushing the crust with egg yolk gives it a beautiful golden gloss.

- Preheat oven to 350°F (180°C)
- 13- by 9-inch (33 by 23 cm) glass baking dish

2	cans (each 8 oz/227 g) refrigerated crescent rolls	2
4 oz	salami, thinly sliced	125 g
4 oz	Swiss cheese, thinly sliced	125 g
4 oz	pepperoni, thinly sliced	125 g
4 oz	fontina cheese, thinly sliced	125 g
4 oz	cooked ham, thinly sliced	125 g
4 oz	provolone cheese, thinly sliced	125 g
2	eggs	2
½ tsp	garlic powder	2 mL
½ tsp	salt	2 mL
½ tsp	freshly ground black pepper	2 mL
1	jar (12 oz/341 mL) roasted red bell peppers, drained	1
½ cup	sliced kalamata olives	125 mL
1	egg yolk, beaten	1

1. Unroll one crescent roll sheet and press into prepared baking dish, pressing ¾ inch (2 cm) up the sides to form a crust. Layer salami, Swiss cheese, pepperoni, fontina, ham and provolone on top.

2. In a small bowl, whisk together eggs, garlic powder, salt and pepper. Pour evenly over meat and cheese layers. Layer roasted peppers and olives on top.

3. Unroll second crescent roll sheet, press into a 13- by 9-inch (33 by 23 cm) rectangle and place on top of dish, pressing to seal edges. Cut a few slits in the top to vent steam. Brush dough with egg yolk. Cover with foil.

4. Bake in preheated oven for 30 minutes. Remove foil and bake for 15 to 20 minutes or until crust is golden brown. Let cool for 10 minutes, then cut into squares. Serve warm.

Hearty Vegetable and Pasta Casseroles

Cheesy Macaroni and Cheese. 68

Smoked Gouda Mac and Cheese 69

Jill's Broccoli Cheese Casserole 70

No-Crust Green Chile Pie 71

Chile Cheese Casserole 72

Summer Harvest Corn Casserole 72

Eggplant Gratin. 73

Eggplant Walnut Bake. 74

Herb-Stuffed Eggplant with Roma Tomato. 75

Eggplant, Pepper, Onion and Tomato Bake 76

Eggplant Parmesan Bake 77

Cremini Mushroom Potato Dish. 78

Caramelized Onion, Mushroom and Barley Casserole 79

Layered Sweet Onions, Potatoes and Tomatoes
    with Romano Cheese. 80

Potato and Leek Swiss Bake. 81

Spinach- and Ricotta-Stuffed Shells 82

Spinach, Zucchini and Sweet Onion Casserole 83

Two-Squash Skillet Bake. 84

Creamy Vegetable Bake with Swiss Cheese 85

Harvest Gratin. 86

Cheesy Baked Vegetables. 87

Harvest Lasagna with Infused Sage White Sauce 88

Layered Vegetable and Ziti Casserole 90

Baked Rigatoni. 92

Ravioli Casserole. 93

Vegetarian Casserole with Indian Spices 94

Vegetable Tamale Pie 96

Ratatouille Casserole. 98

Black Bean Enchilada Casserole 99

Easy Vegan Enchiladas 100

Kidney Bean and Rice Casserole. 101

Couscous Bake 102

Cheesy Macaroni and Cheese

Makes 4 to 6 servings

If you like mac and cheese, you will fall head over heels for this creamy, cheesy dish!

Variation

You can substitute 8 oz (250 g) corkscrews, wheels or mini shells for the traditional elbow macaroni.

- Preheat oven to 350°F (180°C)
- 8-cup (2 L) casserole dish, greased

2 cups	elbow macaroni	500 mL
1 tbsp	butter	15 mL
¼ cup	thinly sliced green onions	60 mL
2 tbsp	all-purpose flour	30 mL
Pinch	freshly ground black pepper	Pinch
2 cups	milk	500 mL
1½ cups	shredded sharp (old) Cheddar cheese	375 mL
3 oz	cream cheese, cubed, softened	90 g
⅓ cup	freshly grated Parmesan cheese	75 mL

1. In a large pot of boiling water, cook macaroni according to package directions until just tender. Drain and set aside.

2. Meanwhile, in a large skillet, melt butter over medium heat. Sauté green onions for about 2 minutes or until tender. Whisk in flour and pepper; sauté for 2 minutes.

3. Gradually whisk in milk; reduce heat and simmer, whisking constantly, for 3 to 5 minutes or until thickened. Remove from heat and stir in Cheddar and cream cheese until melted. Stir in macaroni. Spoon into prepared casserole dish and sprinkle with Parmesan.

4. Bake in preheated oven for 20 to 25 minutes or until bubbling.

Smoked Gouda Mac and Cheese

You'll love this twist on an all-American classic: mac and cheese made with smoked Gouda. It's great as a side dish with barbecued meats.

Tip

Freshly grated or shaved Parmesan cheese is always best right off the wedge, but prepackaged containers can be found in the refrigerated specialty cheese section of your local supermarket.

- Preheat oven to 350°F (180°C)
- 8-cup (2 L) casserole dish, greased

2 cups	elbow macaroni	500 mL
1 tbsp	butter	15 mL
2	cloves garlic, minced	2
1/4 cup	thinly sliced green onions	60 mL
2 tbsp	all-purpose flour	30 mL
2 cups	milk	500 mL
1/2 tsp	salt	2 mL
1/4 tsp	freshly ground black pepper	1 mL
1/2 cup	shredded smoked Gouda cheese	125 mL
6 tbsp	freshly grated Parmesan cheese	90 mL
1/2 cup	dry bread crumbs	125 mL

1. In a large pot of boiling water, cook macaroni according to package directions. Drain and set aside.

2. Meanwhile, in a large saucepan, melt butter over medium heat. Sauté garlic and green onions for about 2 minutes or until tender. Whisk in flour and sauté for 1 minute.

3. Gradually whisk in milk, salt and pepper; reduce heat and simmer, whisking constantly, for 3 to 5 minutes or until thickened. Remove from heat and stir in Gouda and Parmesan until melted. Stir in macaroni. Spoon into prepared casserole dish and sprinkle with bread crumbs.

4. Bake in preheated oven for 20 minutes or until bubbling.

Jill's Broccoli Cheese Casserole

Makes 8 to 10 servings

My sister, Jill, makes this fabulous casserole. I asked her where it came from, as I couldn't recall our mom making it for us. She reminded me that it was my old boyfriend's mom's recipe. We have made a few modifications and call it our own. Enjoy!

Tip

Spice lovers can use jalapeño-flavored processed cheese spread.

- Preheat oven to 350°F (180°C)
- 13- by 9-inch (33 by 23 cm) glass baking dish, greased

1 tbsp	butter	15 mL
1	large onion, chopped	1
2	packages (each 10 oz/300 g) frozen chopped broccoli, thawed	2
2 cups	hot cooked long-grain white rice	500 mL
2	cans (each 10 oz/284 mL) condensed cream of mushroom soup	2
1	jar (15 oz/426 mL) processed cheese spread	1
1 cup	milk	250 mL
½ tsp	salt	2 mL
½ tsp	freshly ground black pepper	2 mL

1. In a large skillet, melt butter over medium-high heat. Sauté onion and broccoli for 5 to 7 minutes or until onion is tender. Stir in rice. Transfer to prepared baking dish.

2. In a medium saucepan, over medium heat, combine soup, cheese spread, milk, salt and pepper. Cook, stirring, until cheese is melted. Pour over onion mixture.

3. Bake in preheated oven for 45 minutes or until bubbling.

No-Crust Green Chile Pie

Makes 6 to 8 servings

Cut into small squares, this recipe is perfect on a buffet, served with a beautiful red Sangría, which pairs well with the green chiles. It's great hot or at room temperature.

Tip

At the end of the cooking time, the center of the custard may still jiggle, but it will continue to cook after you remove it from the oven. Be careful not to overcook.

- Preheat oven to 425°F (220°C)
- 9-inch (23 cm) glass pie plate, greased

6	canned roasted whole green chiles, split in half	6
1¼ cups	shredded fontina cheese	300 mL
4	eggs	4
2 cups	milk	500 mL
½ tsp	salt	2 mL
¼ tsp	freshly ground black pepper	1 mL
2 tbsp	chopped fresh cilantro	30 mL

1. Line prepared pie plate with chiles so they cover the bottom and sides. Sprinkle evenly with cheese.

2. In a medium bowl, whisk together eggs, milk, salt and pepper. Pour over cheese.

3. Bake in preheated oven for 15 minutes. Reduce the heat to 325°F (160°C) and bake for 20 to 30 minutes or until a knife inserted into the custard halfway between the edge and the center comes out clean. Let stand for 5 minutes before serving.

Chile Cheese Casserole

Cottage cheese lends a creamy consistency to this casserole.

Tip

Make the prep for this casserole a breeze by purchasing bags of shredded cheese. Colby-Jack or Cheddar cheese will work as a substitute for the Monterey Jack.

- Preheat oven to 350°F (180°C)
- 9-inch (23 cm) square glass baking dish, greased

6	eggs	6
1 lb	shredded Monterey Jack cheese	500 g
2	cans (each 4½ oz/127 mL) chopped mild green chiles	2
8 oz	cottage cheese	250 g
3 oz	cream cheese, cut into 4 cubes, softened	90 g
½ cup	cornmeal	125 mL
1½ tsp	baking powder	7 mL
1 tsp	salt	5 mL
½ tsp	freshly ground black pepper	2 mL
1 cup	milk	250 mL
2 tbsp	butter, melted	30 mL

1. In a large bowl, whisk together eggs, Monterey Jack, chiles, cottage cheese, cream cheese, cornmeal, baking powder, salt, pepper, milk and butter until well blended. Pour into prepared baking dish.

2. Bake in preheated oven for 40 to 45 minutes or until set.

Summer Harvest Corn Casserole

This casserole is unbelievably good when the corn is freshly picked. Removing the kernels from the cob and chopping them releases their sweet milk, giving you a sweeter, fresher-tasting dish.

Tip

If corn is out of season, you can use frozen or canned corn kernels and still have great results.

- Preheat oven to 350°F (180°C)
- 6-cup (1.5 L) casserole dish, greased

¼ cup	cornstarch	60 mL
4	eggs	4
2 cups	fresh corn kernels, chopped	500 mL
2 cups	milk	500 mL
2 tbsp	butter, melted	30 mL
1 tsp	granulated sugar	5 mL
½ tsp	salt	2 mL
¼ tsp	freshly ground black pepper	1 mL

1. In a large bowl, whisk together cornstarch, eggs, corn, milk, butter, sugar, salt and pepper. Pour into prepared casserole dish.

2. Bake in preheated oven for about 45 minutes or until set. Let stand for 5 minutes before serving.

Eggplant Gratin

Makes 4 to 6 servings

Eggplant lovers will adore this elegant entrée or side dish, which pairs eggplant with flavorful tomatoes, garlic, green onions and mushrooms. Herbes de Provence contribute a fabulous aroma.

Tip

Herbes de Provence is a traditional blend of dried herbs from the south of France. It typically includes thyme, savory, rosemary, sage, marjoram and lavender, among others. If you can't find it, just use a combination of any of these herbs, keeping the total to 1 tsp (5 mL).

- Preheat oven to 350°F (180°C)
- 8-cup (2 L) casserole dish

1	large eggplant (about 1 lb/500 g)	1
1 tsp	salt, divided	5 mL
1/4 cup	all-purpose flour	60 mL
	Olive oil	
4	tomatoes, chopped	4
2	cloves garlic, minced	2
1	bunch green onions (5 or 6), trimmed and sliced	1
1 lb	mushrooms, trimmed and sliced	500 g
1/4 cup	drained capers	60 mL
1 cup	tomato sauce	250 mL
1/2 cup	dry white wine	125 mL
1 tsp	herbes de Provence	5 mL
1/2 tsp	freshly ground black pepper	2 mL
8 oz	mozzarella cheese, sliced and cut diagonally into triangles	250 g

1. Trim ends from eggplant and cut eggplant into 1/2-inch (1 cm) thick slices. Sprinkle with 1/2 tsp (2 mL) of the salt and coat in flour.

2. In a large skillet, heat 1/2 inch (1 cm) of oil over high heat. Fry eggplant for about 4 minutes per side or until browned on both sides. Transfer eggplant to a plate lined with paper towels to drain.

3. Drain all but 2 tbsp (30 mL) oil from skillet. Add tomatoes, garlic, green onions, mushrooms and capers; sauté for 5 minutes or until tomatoes and mushrooms start to release their juices. Reduce heat to low and simmer, stirring occasionally, for 5 to 10 minutes or until slightly thickened.

4. Line bottom and sides of casserole dish with eggplant slices. Pour in tomato mixture.

5. In a small bowl, combine tomato sauce, wine, herbes de Provence, the remaining salt and pepper. Pour evenly over vegetables. Top with cheese triangles.

6. Bake in preheated oven for 25 to 30 minutes or until golden brown.

Eggplant Walnut Bake

With eggplant, walnuts and a hint of nutmeg, this dish makes a nice change from the usual holiday fare and will delight any vegetarians at your table.

Tip

Chopped nuts can be toasted stovetop in a dry skillet over medium heat, stirring often, until brown and fragrant. To toast in the oven, spread walnut halves on a baking sheet and bake in a 350°F (180°C) oven, stirring often, for 10 to 15 minutes or until brown and fragrant. To toast in the microwave, place walnut halves on a microwave-safe plate. Microwave on High for 3 to 4 minutes or until brown and fragrant (turn halfway through cooking time if you do not have a turntable).

- Preheat oven to 325°F (160°C)
- 13- by 9-inch (33 by 23 cm) glass baking dish

1/4 cup	butter	60 mL
1	large eggplant (about 1 lb/500 g), cut crosswise into 12 slices	1
1/2 cup	chopped toasted walnuts	125 mL
3/4 cup	heavy or whipping (35%) cream	175 mL
1/2 tsp	salt	2 mL
1/4 tsp	freshly ground black pepper	1 mL
1/4 tsp	ground nutmeg	1 mL
3/4 cup	dry bread crumbs	175 mL
2 tbsp	butter, melted	30 mL

1. In a large skillet, melt 1/4 cup (60 mL) butter over medium-high heat. In batches, if necessary, fry eggplant for about 4 minutes per side or until browned on both sides. Transfer to a baking sheet lined with paper towels to drain.

2. Arrange half the browned eggplant in bottom of baking dish. Top with half the walnuts. Repeat the layers with the remaining eggplant and walnuts.

3. In a medium bowl, combine cream, salt, pepper and nutmeg. Pour over walnuts.

4. In a small bowl, combine bread crumbs and 2 tbsp (30 mL) melted butter. Sprinkle over cream mixture.

5. Bake in preheated oven for 20 to 25 minutes or until bubbling.

Herb-Stuffed Eggplant with Roma Tomato

Makes 4 servings

Stuffing eggplant with savory Italian ingredients makes for an elegant, delectable main dish everyone will love.

Tips

For the best texture and flavor, choose eggplants that feel heavy for their size and have tight, shiny skins and fresh green stems.

For a sharper taste, replace half the Parmesan cheese with Romano cheese.

- Preheat oven to 350°F (180°C)
- 13- by 9-inch (33 by 23 cm) glass baking dish

2	large eggplants (each about 1 lb/500 g)	2
2 tbsp	olive oil, divided	30 mL
2	cloves garlic, minced	2
1	onion, chopped	1
2 tsp	chopped fresh thyme	10 mL
1 cup	dry bread crumbs	250 mL
1/2 cup	shredded mozzarella cheese	125 mL
1 tbsp	chopped fresh basil	15 mL
1 tbsp	drained capers	15 mL
1/4 tsp	hot pepper flakes	1 mL
1 tsp	salt	5 mL
1 tsp	freshly ground black pepper	5 mL
2 tbsp	freshly squeezed lemon juice	30 mL
12	slices plum (Roma) tomato	12
1/4 cup	freshly grated Parmesan cheese	60 mL

1. Cut eggplants in half and scoop out the flesh, leaving a 1/2-inch (1 cm) shell. Chop the flesh. Set shells aside.

2. In a medium skillet, heat half the oil over medium-high heat. Sauté chopped eggplant for 2 minutes. Add garlic, onion and thyme; sauté for 5 to 7 minutes or until onion is tender.

3. Transfer eggplant mixture to a large bowl and stir in bread crumbs, mozzarella, basil, capers, hot pepper flakes, salt, black pepper and lemon juice. Spoon evenly into eggplant shells.

4. Place stuffed eggplants in baking dish and top with overlapping slices of tomato. Sprinkle with Parmesan and drizzle with the remaining oil.

5. Bake in preheated oven for 30 minutes or until bubbling and cheese is melted.

Eggplant, Pepper, Onion and Tomato Bake

I love making this dish during peak tomato season, when I can pick the fruit right out of my own garden. So fresh and tasty!

Variation

For a little bit of added heat, you can substitute a mild green chile, such as Anaheim, for the bell pepper.

- Preheat oven to 350°F (180°C)
- 8-cup (2 L) casserole dish, greased

1	large eggplant (about 1 lb/500 g)	1
½ cup	all-purpose flour	125 mL
¼ cup	olive oil (approx.)	60 mL
2	green bell peppers, cut into strips	2
2	onions, finely chopped	2
1 cup	seasoned dry bread crumbs, divided	250 mL
2	ripe tomatoes, thickly sliced	2
8 oz	mozzarella cheese, diced	250 g
3	eggs	3
¾ cup	milk	175 mL
¼ tsp	salt	1 mL
¼ tsp	freshly ground black pepper	1 mL
¼ tsp	ground allspice	1 mL
¼ tsp	dried thyme	1 mL
¼ tsp	dried parsley	1 mL

1. Cut eggplant crosswise into slices slightly less than ½ inch (1 cm) thick and coat in flour.

2. In a large skillet, heat oil over medium-high heat. In batches, if necessary, fry eggplant for about 4 minutes per side or until browned on both sides. Transfer to a baking sheet lined with paper towels to drain.

3. Reduce heat to medium and add green peppers and onions to skillet; sauté for 5 to 7 minutes or until tender.

4. Sprinkle prepared casserole dish with 2 tbsp (30 mL) of the seasoned bread crumbs. Evenly layer with half each of the eggplant, tomatoes and pepper mixture. Sprinkle with half the remaining bread crumbs and all of the mozzarella. Top with layers of the remaining eggplant, tomatoes and pepper mixture. Sprinkle with the remaining bread crumbs.

5. In a medium bowl, whisk together eggs, milk, salt, pepper, allspice, thyme and parsley. Pour over eggplant mixture.

6. Bake in preheated oven for 45 to 50 minutes or until golden brown and bubbling. Let cool for 10 minutes before serving.

Eggplant Parmesan Bake

Makes 6 servings

You'll love classic eggplant Parmesan in casserole form. Serve with hot buttered linguini, angel hair pasta or fettuccini.

Tip

Choose ripe tomatoes that yield gently when squeezed and smell fragrant. If they aren't quite ripe, let them ripen at room temperature, away from direct sunlight, for a few days before use. Never refrigerate your tomatoes — it destroys the flavor.

- Preheat oven to 325°F (160°C)
- 11- by 7-inch (28 by 18 cm) glass baking dish

½ cup	all-purpose flour	125 mL
½ tsp	salt, divided	2 mL
½ tsp	freshly ground black pepper, divided	2 mL
2 lbs	eggplant, sliced crosswise into ½-inch (1 cm) slices	1 kg
½ cup	olive oil	125 mL
3 cups	chopped tomatoes, with juice, divided	750 mL
1 tbsp	chopped fresh Italian (flat-leaf) parsley	15 mL
2 tsp	finely chopped fresh oregano (or 1 tsp/5 mL dried, crumbled)	10 mL
1½ cups	shredded mozzarella cheese	375 mL
¾ cup	freshly grated Parmesan cheese	175 mL

1. In a shallow dish, combine flour and half each of the salt and pepper. Add eggplant and turn to lightly coat.

2. In a large skillet, heat oil over medium-high heat. Fry eggplant for about 4 minutes per side or until browned on both sides. Transfer eggplant to a plate lined with paper towels to drain.

3. Spread half the tomatoes with juice over bottom of baking dish. Sprinkle with the remaining salt and pepper. Arrange eggplant over tomatoes, overlapping as necessary. Sprinkle with parsley and oregano. Spread the remaining tomatoes with juice over the top. Sprinkle with mozzarella and Parmesan.

4. Cover and bake in preheated oven for 20 minutes. Uncover and bake for 10 to 15 minutes or until golden brown.

Cremini Mushroom Potato Dish

Savory cremini mushrooms, Yukon gold potatoes and cheeses make this dish spectacular!

Tip

You can substitute button, shiitake or baby bella mushrooms for the cremini.

- Preheat oven to 350°F (180°C)
- 13- by 9-inch (33 by 23 cm) glass baking dish, greased

2	cloves garlic, minced	2
2 cups	shredded Monterey Jack cheese, divided	500 mL
1 cup	ricotta cheese	250 mL
¼ cup	finely chopped fresh parsley	60 mL
1 tsp	dried thyme	5 mL
1 lb	potatoes (peeled or unpeeled), sliced	500 g
1 tsp	salt, divided	5 mL
1 tsp	freshly ground black pepper, divided	5 mL
1 lb	cremini mushrooms, sliced	500 g
2 cups	sliced onions	500 mL

1. In a large bowl, combine garlic, half the Monterey Jack, the ricotta, parsley and thyme. Set aside.

2. Arrange potatoes in a single layer in bottom of prepared baking dish, overlapping as necessary. Sprinkle with half each of the salt and pepper. Spread the cheese mixture over the potato layer.

3. In the same large bowl, combine mushrooms and onions. Layer on top of cheese mixture. Sprinkle with the remaining salt and pepper. Top with the remaining Monterey Jack.

4. Bake in preheated oven for 40 to 45 minutes or until potatoes are tender when pierced with a fork and top is lightly browned.

Caramelized Onion, Mushroom and Barley Casserole

Makes 6 servings

I adore the sweet flavor of caramelized onion paired with umami-rich mushrooms in this recipe.

Tip

The Japanese term "umami" refers to a savory, meaty or brothy flavor. Mushrooms are high in umami, as are fermented products such as soy sauce or oyster sauce.

- Preheat oven to 350°F (180°C)
- 11- by 7-inch (28 by 18 cm) glass baking dish, greased

2 tbsp	butter	30 mL
3	onions, chopped	3
1 tsp	granulated sugar	5 mL
3 cups	sliced cremini mushrooms (about 8 oz/250 g)	750 mL
3 cups	sliced stemmed shiitake mushrooms (about 8 oz/250 g)	750 mL
1½ cups	pearl barley	375 mL
1 tbsp	soy sauce	15 mL
½ tsp	salt	2 mL
½ tsp	freshly ground black pepper	2 mL
¼ tsp	dried thyme	1 mL
4 cups	vegetable broth, heated to boiling and kept hot	1 L

1. In a Dutch oven, melt butter over low heat. Sauté onions and sugar for 20 to 25 minutes or until golden brown. Add cremini and shiitake mushrooms; sauté for 8 to 10 minutes or until tender. Add barley and sauté for 2 minutes. Remove from heat and stir in soy sauce, salt, pepper and thyme. Spoon into prepared baking dish and pour broth over top.

2. Cover and bake in preheated oven for 1 hour or until barley is tender. Let cool for 10 minutes before serving.

Layered Sweet Onions, Potatoes and Tomatoes with Romano Cheese

My dear friend Larry Russo is quite the foodie and often gives me a run for my money in the culinary world. He has bragged about this vegetable dish for years, and for good reason: it is very, very good and so easy.

Tips

Parmesan cheese is a good substitute for the Romano cheese in this recipe.

You can use red onions in place of the sweet onions.

- Preheat oven to 350°F (180°C)
- 13- by 9-inch (33 by 23 cm) glass baking dish, greased

2	large sweet onions (such as Vidalia), thinly sliced	2
2 lbs	potatoes, peeled and thinly sliced	1 kg
1 lb	tomatoes, sliced	500 g
6 tbsp	olive oil	90 mL
1 cup	grated Romano cheese	250 mL
1 tsp	salt	5 mL
1 tsp	freshly ground black pepper	5 mL
1/4 cup	basil leaves, thinly sliced	60 mL

1. On bottom of prepared baking dish, evenly layer half each of the onions, potatoes and tomatoes. Drizzle with 2 tbsp (30 mL) oil. Sprinkle with half each of the salt and pepper and 1/3 cup (75 mL) of the cheese. Repeat layers. Sprinkle with basil, drizzle with the remaining oil and top with the remaining cheese. Gently pour 1/4 cup (60 mL) water over top.

2. Bake in preheated oven for 1 hour or until potatoes are tender when pierced with a fork.

Potato and Leek Swiss Bake

Makes 8 servings

This elegant pie uses refrigerated bread dough to make life simpler, but it also works well in a baked pastry shell. Serve with a salad of bitter greens and a bottle of Riesling.

Tip

Leeks often harbor grit between the layers. Cut off the root end and green part, reserving the green part for another use, then cut the white part in half lengthwise. Rinse well under running water, pulling the layers apart. Drain well, then thinly slice.

- Preheat oven to 375°F (190°C)
- 9-inch (23 cm) glass pie plate, greased
- Blender

1	can (11 oz/312 g) refrigerated breadstick dough	1
1 tsp	olive oil	5 mL
1	baking potato, peeled, halved lengthwise and cut crosswise into 1/8-inch (3 mm) thick slices	1
1 cup	thinly sliced leeks (white part only)	250 mL
1/2 tsp	salt	2 mL
1/4 tsp	freshly ground black pepper	1 mL
4	eggs	4
1 cup	milk	250 mL
1/3 cup	shredded Swiss cheese	75 mL
3 tbsp	freshly grated Parmesan cheese, divided	45 mL
1 tbsp	Dijon mustard	15 mL
1/2 tsp	dried thyme	2 mL

1. Unroll dough, separating into strips. Let rest for 5 minutes.

2. Coil one strip of dough into a spiral. Add a second strip of dough to the end of the first strip, pinching ends together to seal. Continue coiling dough into a spiral. Repeat with remaining dough strips. Let rest for 5 minutes.

3. Roll out dough into a solid 13-inch (33 cm) circle. Fit into prepared pie plate. Fold edges under and flute.

4. In a large nonstick skillet, heat oil over medium-high heat. Sauté potato, leeks, salt and pepper for 8 to 10 minutes or until potato is tender. Spread in prepared crust.

5. In blender, process eggs, milk, Swiss cheese, 2 tbsp (30 mL) of the Parmesan, mustard and thyme until smooth. Pour over potato mixture.

6. Bake in preheated oven for 35 minutes. Sprinkle with the remaining Parmesan and bake for 5 minutes or until bubbling. Let cool for 10 minutes before serving.

Spinach- and Ricotta-Stuffed Shells

With this recipe, I've actually persuaded my daughter, Kennedy, to eat spinach! She loves it, and she loves stuffing the shells with her mom.

Tips

For a bit more fire and heat, use a spicy marinara sauce, found in jars at the supermarket.

Squeeze thawed and drained spinach several times to remove excess moisture.

• Preheat oven to 350°F (180°C)
• 13- by 9-inch (33 by 23 cm) glass baking dish, greased

1	jar (26 oz/737 g) marinara sauce	1
½ tsp	dried oregano	2 mL
½ tsp	salt	2 mL
¼ tsp	freshly ground black pepper	1 mL
1	package (12 oz/375 g) jumbo pasta shells	1
1	package (10 oz/300 g) frozen chopped spinach, thawed and squeezed dry	1
1	egg, beaten	1
2 lbs	ricotta cheese	1 kg
2 tbsp	freshly grated Parmesan cheese	30 mL

1. In a small saucepan, combine marinara sauce, oregano, salt and pepper. Bring to a boil over medium-high heat. Reduce heat and simmer for about 5 minutes. Spread 2 cups (250 mL) of the sauce in prepared baking dish. Set the remaining sauce aside.

2. In a large pot of salted boiling water, cook pasta shells according to package directions. Immediately drain pasta and arrange on top of sauce.

3. In a medium bowl, combine spinach, egg, ricotta and Parmesan. Gently spoon mixture into pasta shells, dividing evenly. Pour the remaining sauce over shells.

4. Bake in preheated oven for 15 to 20 minutes or until bubbling. Serve shells with extra sauce from the dish drizzled on top.

Spinach, Zucchini and Sweet Onion Casserole

Here's a fresh and super-easy vegetable casserole. Steamed fresh green beans would be wonderful on the side.

- Preheat oven to 350°F (180°C)
- 8-cup (2 L) casserole dish

2	small sweet onions, sliced	2
2 lbs	fresh baby spinach	1 kg
1½ lbs	zucchini, thinly sliced	750 g
2 tsp	chopped fresh basil	10 mL
½ tsp	salt	2 mL
½ tsp	freshly ground black pepper	2 mL
¼ cup	olive oil	60 mL
½ cup	freshly grated Parmesan cheese	125 mL

1. In a large bowl, combine onions, spinach, zucchini, basil, salt and pepper. Add oil and toss to coat. Transfer to casserole dish.

2. Cover and bake in preheated oven for 45 minutes or until zucchini is tender. Uncover and sprinkle with cheese. Bake for 5 minutes or until cheese is melted.

Two-Squash Skillet Bake

Humble vegetables sometimes need a stylish presentation to get the attention they deserve. Serve with salsa on the side.

Tip

If you don't have an ovenproof skillet, transfer the zucchini mixture to a greased 13- by 9-inch (33 by 23 cm) glass baking dish after step 1.

- Preheat oven to 350°F (180°C)
- 10-inch (25 cm) ovenproof skillet

3 tbsp	butter	45 mL
2	small zucchini, cubed	2
2	small yellow summer squash (yellow zucchinl), cubed	2
1	small onion, chopped	1
2	eggs	2
½ cup	sour cream	125 mL
1 tsp	salt	5 mL
¾ tsp	freshly ground black pepper	3 mL
⅓ cup	chopped fresh basil	75 mL

1. In a skillet, melt butter over medium-high heat. Sauté zucchini, squash and onion for 5 to 7 minutes or until tender. Remove from heat.

2. In a large bowl, whisk together eggs, sour cream, salt and pepper. Pour over vegetable mixture.

3. Bake in preheated oven for 40 to 45 minutes or until edges are lightly browned and center is set. Sprinkle with basil.

Creamy Vegetable Bake with Swiss Cheese

Makes 8 to 10 servings

This casserole is perfect for crowds and kids of all ages.

Variation

For extra crunch, you can substitute seasoned dry bread crumbs for the onions on top.

- Preheat oven to 350°F (180°C)
- 13- by 9-inch (33 by 23 cm) glass baking dish, greased

2	packages (each 16 oz/500 g) frozen assorted vegetables (broccoli, cauliflower and carrots), thawed	2
2	cans (each 10 oz/284 mL) condensed cream of mushroom soup	2
1	can (6 oz/170 g) french-fried onions, divided	1
2 cups	shredded Swiss cheese, divided	500 mL
2/3 cup	sour cream	150 mL
1/2 tsp	freshly ground black pepper	2 mL

1. In a large bowl, combine vegetables, soup, half the onions, half the Swiss cheese, the sour cream and pepper. Pour into prepared baking dish.

2. Cover and bake in preheated oven for 40 minutes. Uncover and sprinkle with the remaining onions and cheese. Bake for 5 minutes or until onions and cheese are browned.

Harvest Gratin

Makes 6 servings

I simply love gratins. A casserole filled with fresh vegetables and topped with a simple bread crumb topping laced with a bit of Parmesan cheese — all I can say is, yum!

Tip

Visit your local farmers' market for fresh-picked vegetables, fruits and herbs. I am always amazed by the quality and price. Shop local and support local farmers!

- Preheat oven to 400°F (200°C)
- Large roasting pan
- 13- by 9-inch (33 by 23 cm) glass baking dish, greased

2	red bell peppers, cut into strips	2
1	yellow bell pepper, cut into strips	1
1	yellow summer squash (yellow zucchini), ends trimmed, halved lengthwise and cut crosswise into slices	1
1	zucchini, ends trimmed, halved lengthwise and cut crosswise into slices	1
1	large sweet onion, sliced	1
¼ cup	tomato sauce	60 mL
¼ cup	olive oil	60 mL
1 tbsp	chopped fresh basil	15 mL
1 tsp	chopped fresh thyme	5 mL
½ tsp	salt	2 mL
¼ tsp	freshly ground black pepper	1 mL
½ tsp	paprika	2 mL

Topping

2 cups	dry bread crumbs	500 mL
3 tbsp	freshly grated Parmesan cheese	45 mL
3 tbsp	olive oil	45 mL

1. In a large bowl, combine red peppers, yellow pepper, squash, zucchini, onion, tomato sauce, oil, basil, thyme, salt, pepper and paprika. Spread out in a single layer in roasting pan and roast in preheated oven for 45 to 60 minutes, stirring every 15 minutes, until vegetables are tender and lightly browned. Transfer vegetables to prepared baking dish.

2. *Topping:* In a medium bowl, combine bread crumbs, cheese and oil. Sprinkle over vegetables.

3. Bake for 20 minutes or until topping is golden brown. Let cool for 5 minutes before serving.

Cheesy Baked Vegetables

Makes 4 to 6 servings

Leeks and fresh greens combine beautifully in this delicious vegetable dish.

Tips

Wash the leeks carefully, removing all soil between shoots.

Use red or green Swiss chard or a combination.

- Preheat oven to 350°F (180°C)
- 8-cup (2 L) casserole dish, greased

4 cups	finely chopped leeks (white parts only)	1 L
4 cups	finely chopped baby spinach leaves	1 L
2 cups	finely chopped Swiss chard leaves	500 mL
3	eggs	3
2 tbsp	all-purpose flour	30 mL
1 tsp	salt	5 mL
½ tsp	freshly ground black pepper	2 mL
1 cup	shredded fontina cheese	250 mL
3 tbsp	butter	45 mL

1. In a large bowl, combine leeks, spinach and Swiss chard.

2. In a medium bowl, whisk together eggs, flour, salt and pepper. Pour over the vegetable mixture. Stir in cheese. Pour into prepared casserole dish and dot with butter.

3. Bake in preheated oven for 35 to 40 minutes or until set.

Harvest Lasagna with Infused Sage White Sauce

Fragrant sage infuses a delicate white sauce for the perfect combination of flavors with portobello mushrooms, sweet potatoes, spinach and creamy cheese.

Tip

You'll need to buy about 1½ lbs (750 g) of portobello mushrooms and 2½ lbs (1.25 kg) of sweet potatoes for this recipe.

- Preheat oven to 450°F (230°C)
- Rimmed baking sheet, coated with vegetable cooking spray
- 13- by 9- inch (33 by 23 cm) glass baking dish, greased

Infused Sage White Sauce

⅔ cup	all-purpose flour	150 mL
6 cups	milk	1.5 L
½ cup	finely chopped onion	125 mL
¼ cup	chopped fresh sage	60 mL
2 tbsp	finely chopped shallots	30 mL
1 tsp	salt	5 mL
1	dried bay leaf	1

Filling

8 cups	chopped portobello mushroom caps	2 L
6 cups	cubed peeled sweet potatoes (½-inch/1 cm cubes)	1.5 L
2 tbsp	olive oil, divided	30 mL
1½ tsp	salt, divided	7 mL
2½ cups	finely chopped onion	625 mL
2	cloves garlic, minced	2
1	package (10 oz/300 g) fresh baby spinach	1
1 cup	shredded Swiss cheese	250 mL
¾ cup	freshly grated Parmesan cheese	175 mL
12	oven-ready lasagna noodles	12

1. *White Sauce:* Place flour in a Dutch oven and gradually whisk in milk. Stir in onion, sage, shallots, salt and bay leaf. Bring to a boil over medium heat, stirring often, and cook for 1 minute or until thick. Strain through a sieve set over a bowl and discard solids. Set aside.

2. *Filling:* On prepared baking sheet, toss together mushrooms, sweet potatoes, half the oil and 1 tsp (5 mL) of the salt; spread out in a single layer. Roast in preheated oven for 20 minutes or until tender.

3. Meanwhile, in a large nonstick skillet, heat the remaining oil over medium-high heat. Sauté onion and garlic for 5 to 7 minutes or until onion is tender. Add spinach and the remaining salt; sauté for 2 minutes or until spinach wilts. Remove from heat.

4. In a small bowl, combine Swiss cheese and Parmesan.

5. Spread $^3/_4$ cup (175 mL) of the white sauce in bottom of prepared baking dish. Arrange 3 noodles over sauce. Top with half the mushroom mixture, $1^1/_2$ cups (375 mL) white sauce and $^1/_3$ cup (75 mL) cheese mixture. Top with 3 noodles, all of the onion filling, $1^1/_2$ cups (375 mL) white sauce and $^1/_3$ cup (75 mL) cheese mixture. Top with 3 noodles, the remaining mushroom mixture, $1^1/_2$ cups (375 mL) white sauce, then the last 3 noodles. Spread the remaining white sauce over noodles.

6. Bake in preheated oven for 30 minutes. Sprinkle with the remaining cheese and bake for 10 minutes or until cheese is melted. Let cool for 10 minutes before serving.

Layered Vegetable and Ziti Casserole

This baked ziti is packed with fresh vegetables and tons of flavor.

Tips

For a more hearty bite, substitute rigatoni, mostaccioli or penne for the ziti.

For the best flavor, when buying sun-dried tomatoes make sure they are soft and pliable.

- Preheat oven to 350°F (180°C)
- 13- by 9-inch (33 by 23 cm) glass baking dish

2 cups	ziti pasta	500 mL
1/4 cup	butter	60 mL
1 1/2 cups	heavy or whipping (35%) cream	375 mL
1 1/2 cups	freshly grated Parmesan cheese, divided	375 mL
3 tbsp	extra virgin olive oil	45 mL
2	cloves garlic, minced	2
1	small zucchini, sliced	1
1	small yellow summer squash (yellow zucchini), sliced	1
1	small green bell pepper, thinly sliced	1
1	small red bell pepper, thinly sliced	1
1	small carrot, diced	1
1/2 cup	finely chopped red onion	125 mL
1/2 cup	sliced mushrooms	125 mL
2 tbsp	finely chopped fresh oregano	30 mL
1/2 cup	dry-packed sun-dried tomatoes, chopped or julienned	125 mL
2 cups	tomato pasta sauce	500 mL
1/4 cup	dry red wine	60 mL
2 cups	shredded mozzarella cheese, divided	500 mL
2	plum (Roma) tomatoes, thinly sliced	2
1	can (14 oz/398 mL) artichoke hearts, drained and quartered	1
1/4 cup	fresh basil leaves, thinly sliced	60 mL

1. In a large pot of boiling water, cook ziti according to package directions. Drain and set aside.

2. In a medium saucepan, melt butter over medium-high heat. Whisk in cream and bring to a boil, whisking constantly. Reduce heat to low and stir in 1 cup (250 mL) of the Parmesan until thickened. Set aside.

3. In a large skillet, heat oil over medium-high heat. Sauté garlic, zucchini, squash, green pepper, red pepper, carrot, red onion, mushrooms and oregano for 5 to 7 minutes or until vegetables are tender-crisp. Stir in sun-dried tomatoes, pasta sauce, cream sauce and wine. Stir in ziti and half the mozzarella.

4. Spoon into baking dish and sprinkle with the remaining mozzarella. Arrange sliced tomatoes and artichokes across the top. Sprinkle with the remaining Parmesan.

5. Bake in preheated oven for 45 minutes or until bubbling. Let cool for 10 minutes. Top with sliced basil.

Baked Rigatoni

Makes 8 servings

This quick, easy, satisfying recipe is perfect for weeknight meals. Serve with a green salad and garlic bread.

Tip

You can often find finely chopped sun-dried tomatoes in packages. If you buy the larger halved ones, cut them into small pieces with kitchen scissors, wiping the blades with a hot, wet cloth when they get sticky.

- Preheat oven to 350°F (180°C)
- 13- by 9-inch (33 by 23 cm) glass baking dish

1 lb	rigatoni pasta	500 g
8 oz	mozzarella cheese, cut into cubes	250 g
3¾ cups	tomato pasta sauce	925 mL
1 cup	sliced mushrooms	250 mL
½ cup	finely chopped dry-packed sun-dried tomatoes	125 mL
½ cup	freshly grated Parmesan cheese	125 mL
2 tbsp	olive oil	30 mL
1 cup	shredded mozzarella cheese	250 mL

1. In a large pot of boiling water, cook rigatoni according to package directions. Drain.

2. In a large bowl, combine rigatoni, mozzarella cubes, pasta sauce, mushrooms, dried tomato bits, Parmesan and oil. Spoon into baking dish. Sprinkle with shredded mozzarella.

3. Cover and bake in preheated oven for 40 minutes. Uncover and bake for 5 minutes or until bubbling.

Ravioli Casserole

Makes 12 to 14 servings

I simply love ravioli, especially when it's homemade, but you can now find wonderful fresh or frozen selections in your local supermarket. This casserole has been a staple for years.

Tip

If you have your own homemade ravioli, by all means use it!

Variation

Ravioli comes stuffed with many types of fillings. For a non-vegetarian meal, try ravioli stuffed with beef or Italian sausage in this recipe.

- Preheat oven to 375°F (190°C)
- 13- by 9-inch (33 by 23 cm) glass baking dish, greased

3	packages (each 9 oz/255 g) cheese-stuffed ravioli	3
2 tbsp	butter	30 mL
1/4 cup	all-purpose flour	60 mL
2 cups	milk	500 mL
1/4 cup	dry white wine	60 mL
1/2 tsp	salt	2 mL
2	eggs, beaten	2
1 1/4 cups	freshly grated Parmesan cheese, divided	300 mL
4 cups	marinara sauce, divided	1 L
3 cups	shredded mozzarella cheese, divided	750 mL

1. In a large pot of boiling water, cook ravioli according to package directions. Drain and set aside.

2. In a medium saucepan, melt butter over medium heat. Stir in flour and cook, stirring constantly, for 2 minutes. Whisk in milk, wine and salt. Cook, stirring constantly, for 5 to 10 minutes or until thick and creamy. Remove from heat and let cool.

3. Whisk eggs, one at a time, into sauce. Stir in 1/2 cup (125 mL) of the Parmesan.

4. Spread 1/2 cup (125 mL) of the marinara sauce in bottom of prepared baking dish. Top with half the ravioli. Sprinkle with half the mozzarella and 1/4 cup (60 mL) Parmesan. Spread 1 1/2 cups (375 mL) marinara sauce over cheese. Drizzle with half the white sauce. Repeat layers with the remaining ravioli, mozzarella, marinara sauce and white sauce. Sprinkle with the remaining Parmesan.

5. Bake in preheated oven for 40 to 50 minutes or until bubbling.

Vegetarian Casserole with Indian Spices

Makes 6 to 8 servings

Fragrant Indian spices lend amazing flavor to this vegetarian casserole, which boasts a flaky homemade crust.

Tips

To enhance the flavor of spices, toast in a dry skillet over medium-high heat for 30 seconds or until fragrant.

For the best texture in this recipe, choose yellow-fleshed or russet potatoes and avoid waxy new potatoes.

- Preheat oven to 375°F (190°C)
- 9-inch (23 cm) glass pie plate

Dough

1/2 cup	all-purpose flour	125 mL
1/2 cup	whole wheat pastry flour	125 mL
1/4 tsp	salt	1 mL
2 tbsp	vegetable oil	30 mL
3 to 5 tbsp	cold water	45 to 75 mL

Filling

1 tbsp	yellow mustard seeds, toasted	15 mL
1 tsp	curry powder	5 mL
1 tsp	ground ginger	5 mL
1/2 tsp	ground cumin	2 mL
1/8 tsp	hot pepper flakes	0.5 mL
5	small potatoes (about 1 1/4 lbs/625 g), peeled and cut into quarters	5
1 1/2 tsp	olive oil	7 mL
3	cloves garlic, minced	3
1	onion, finely chopped	1
1	carrot, diced	1
1 cup	frozen peas	250 mL
1 cup	vegetable broth	250 mL
2 tsp	granulated sugar	10 mL
1/4 tsp	salt	1 mL
1/4 tsp	freshly ground black pepper	1 mL
1 tbsp	milk	15 mL

1. *Dough:* In a medium bowl, whisk together all-purpose flour, whole wheat flour and salt. Using a fork, stir in oil until clumps form. Add cold water, 1 tbsp (15 mL) at a time, stirring until dough holds together. Shape into a ball, cover with a damp towel and refrigerate until ready to use.

2. *Filling:* In a small bowl, combine mustard seeds, curry powder, ginger, cumin and hot pepper flakes. Set aside.

3. Place potatoes in a pot and add enough cold water to cover. Bring to a boil over high heat. Season water with salt, reduce heat and boil gently for 15 minutes or until tender. Drain, return to pot and mash with a potato masher, leaving small chunks.

4. In a large skillet, heat oil over medium heat. Add spice mixture and stir for 1 minute. Add garlic, onion and carrot; sauté for 3 to 5 minutes or until tender. Stir in peas and broth, scraping up bits stuck to pan.

5. Fold onion mixture into potatoes and stir in sugar, salt and black pepper. Spread in pie plate.

6. On a floured work surface, roll out dough to an 11-inch (28 cm) circle. Cover potato mixture with dough, pressing down to make sure no air pockets remain and pinching edge over rim of pie plate. Trim away excess dough and crimp edges. Prick crust with a fork to allow steam to vent. Brush crust with milk.

7. Place pie on a baking sheet and bake for 45 to 50 minutes or until crust is golden. Let cool for 5 minutes before serving.

Vegetable Tamale Pie

Makes 8 to 10 servings

You would never know by the richness and the flavor that this recipe is both vegan and gluten-free!

Tip

For flavor notes that range from savory to sweet, use a combination of green, yellow, red and/or orange bell peppers in this recipe, instead of just one color.

- 8-inch (20 cm) square baking dish

1/2 cup	polenta (yellow cornmeal)	125 mL
1/4 cup	shredded vegan Cheddar cheese alternative	60 mL
1 1/2 tsp	vegetable oil	7 mL
3	cloves garlic, minced	3
1	onion, finely chopped	1
1	small zucchini, diced	1
1/2	red, yellow or orange bell pepper, finely chopped	1/2
1 tbsp	chili powder	15 mL
1 tsp	ground cumin	5 mL
1 tsp	dried oregano	5 mL
1	can (14 to 19 oz/398 to 540 mL) pinto beans, drained and rinsed	1
1	can (14 1/2 oz/411 mL) tomato purée (or 1 3/4 cups/425 mL crushed tomatoes)	1
1/2 cup	frozen corn kernels	125 mL
2 tsp	brown rice flour	10 mL
1/4 cup	cold water	60 mL
1/2 tsp	salt	2 mL
1/2 tsp	freshly ground black pepper	2 mL

1. In a medium saucepan, bring 2 cups (500 mL) water to a boil over high heat. Stir in polenta, reduce heat and simmer, stirring often, for 30 minutes or until thick. Add cheese replacement and stir until melted. Remove from heat and set aside.

2. Preheat oven to 375°F (190°C).

3. In a large skillet, heat oil over medium-high heat. Sauté garlic and onion for 5 to 7 minutes or until tender. Add zucchini, red pepper, chili powder, cumin and oregano; sauté for 5 minutes. Stir in beans, tomato purée and corn.

Tip

This casserole freezes well. If you plan to freeze it, line the baking dish with foil, letting it overhang the sides, and lightly spray the foil with nonstick cooking spray. Prepare through step 4 and place in the freezer until solid. Using the foil overhang, remove casserole from pan, keeping foil intact. Place in a large plastic freezer bag and freeze for up to 3 months. When ready to cook, remove foil and place casserole in the original baking dish (or one the same size). Cover and thaw in the refrigerator, then bake as directed in step 5.

4. In a small bowl, whisk together rice flour and cold water to form a slurry. Stir into vegetable mixture and cook, stirring, for 3 minutes or until mixture thickens slightly. Season with salt and pepper. Spread filling in baking dish. Spread polenta mixture over filling.

5. Bake for 40 minutes or until bubbling. Let cool for 5 minutes before serving.

Ratatouille Casserole

Makes 6 to 8 servings

Our family friend Judy Colognesi, an excellent cook and baker who makes everything from scratch, shares her family's recipe for ratatouille casserole.

Tips

The juice drained from the tomatoes can be substituted for the vegetable broth, or you can save it for another use.

If you're preparing this dish for chicken-eaters, you can substitute chicken broth for the vegetable broth.

- Preheat oven to 350°F (180°C)
- 10-cup (2.5 L) casserole dish, greased

½ cup	long-grain white rice	125 mL
⅓ cup	olive oil	75 mL
4	cloves garlic, minced	4
2	onions, chopped	2
1	large eggplant, peeled and cut into ½-inch (1 cm) cubes	1
1 lb	zucchini, trimmed and cut into 1-inch (2.5 cm) thick rounds	500 g
2	red bell peppers, cut into thin strips	2
4 cups	canned diced tomatoes, drained	1 L
3 tbsp	chopped fresh parsley	45 mL
3 tbsp	chopped fresh basil	45 mL
1 tbsp	dried Italian seasoning	15 mL
2 tsp	salt	10 mL
½ tsp	freshly ground black pepper	7 mL
½ cup	vegetable broth	125 mL
½ cup	freshly grated Parmesan cheese	125 mL

1. In a medium saucepan, bring 8 cups (2 L) water to a boil over high heat. Add rice, reduce heat to medium and boil, uncovered, for 8 minutes. Drain and rinse under cold running water. Set aside.

2. In a Dutch oven, heat oil over medium-high heat. Sauté garlic and onion for 5 to 7 minutes or until onion is tender. Add eggplant and sauté for 2 minutes. Add zucchini, reduce heat to medium-low and cook, stirring occasionally, for 20 minutes. Remove from heat and stir in red peppers, tomatoes, parsley, basil, Italian seasoning, salt and pepper.

3. Place one-third of the eggplant mixture on bottom of prepared casserole dish. Top with half the rice. Layer with the remaining eggplant mixture and the remaining rice. Pour broth over top.

4. Cover and bake in preheated oven for 1 hour. Sprinkle with cheese, cover and bake for 20 minutes or until cheese is melted and casserole is bubbling. Uncover and place under the broiler for 1 minute.

Ratatouille Casserole (page 98)

Zucchini Squares (page 59)
and Corn Dip (page 60)

Black Bean Enchilada Casserole

Our family friend Stacia Hernstrom is a vegetarian. She and her mother worked together to convert her mother's chicken enchilada recipe into a vegetarian version, and they have graciously agreed to share it with you.

Variations

For non-vegetarians, you can substitute 1 lb (500 g) cooked lean ground beef or 4 boneless skinless chicken breasts, cooked and shredded, for the black beans.

You can replace the corn tortillas with flour tortillas.

- Preheat oven to 250°F (120°C)
- 13- by 9-inch (33 by 23 cm) glass baking dish, greased

2 tbsp	olive oil or butter	30 mL
1	onion, finely chopped	1
2	cans (each 14 to 19 oz/398 to 540 mL) black beans, drained and rinsed	2
1	can (4½ oz/127 mL) chopped mild green chiles	1
1	can (10 oz/284 mL) enchilada sauce	1
1 cup	sour cream	250 mL
30	6- or 7-inch (15 or 18 cm) corn tortillas	30
3 cups	shredded Cheddar cheese, divided	750 mL

1. In a large nonstick skillet, heat oil over medium-high heat. Sauté onion for 5 to 7 minutes or until tender. Stir in beans, chiles, enchilada sauce and sour cream; cook until heated through.

2. Tear tortillas into bite-size pieces. Layer half the tortilla pieces in prepared baking dish. Spoon in half the bean mixture and layer with half the cheese. Repeat layers, ending with cheese.

3. Bake in preheated oven for 40 to 45 minutes or until bubbling.

Easy Vegan Enchiladas

Makes 8 servings

I simply adore enchiladas and often serve Tex-Mex cuisine when I'm at home in Austin, Texas. This vegan alternative is loaded with the flavors I love.

Tip

Seitan is a chewy, protein-rich food made from wheat gluten and used as a meat substitute. Look for it at specialty food markets.

- Preheat oven to 350°F (180°C)
- 13- by 9-inch (33 by 23 cm) glass baking dish

1	onion, chopped	1
1 lb	seitan (see tip, at left)	500 g
4 oz	soy cream cheese alternative	125 g
2 cups	shredded vegan Cheddar cheese alternative, divided	500 mL
½ tsp	ground cumin	2 mL
3 cups	salsa, divided	750 mL
8	8- or 10-inch (20 or 25 cm) vegan flour tortillas	8

1. In a large nonstick skillet, over medium-high heat, cook onion and seitan for 8 to 10 minutes or until soft. Add cream cheese alternative, half the Cheddar cheese alternative and cumin; cook, stirring, until cheeses are melted. Stir in 1 cup (250 mL) of the salsa.

2. Spread 1 cup (250 mL) salsa in bottom of baking dish.

3. Spread ⅓ cup (75 mL) of the onion mixture down the center of a tortilla. Fold sides of tortilla over filling and roll up. Place seam side down in baking dish. Repeat with the remaining tortillas and onion mixture. Top with the remaining salsa and sprinkle with the remaining Cheddar cheese alternative.

4. Cover and bake in preheated oven for 30 minutes. Uncover and bake for 5 minutes or until golden brown.

Kidney Bean and Rice Casserole

Makes 8 to 10 servings

This tasty dish is a good choice for a potluck!

Tip

This recipe is so quick and easy as it is, but you can make it even more convenient by using instant rice.

- Preheat oven to 350°F (180°C)
- 13- by 9-inch (33 by 23 cm) glass baking dish

1	can (14 to 19 oz/398 to 540 mL) white, red or dark red kidney beans, drained and rinsed	1
2¼ cups	stewed tomatoes	550 mL
1½ cups	cooked rice	375 mL
¾ cup	chopped celery	175 mL
¾ cup	chopped onion	175 mL
¾ cup	chopped green bell pepper	175 mL
1 tsp	salt	5 mL
½ tsp	freshly ground black pepper	2 mL
1 cup	sliced mushrooms	250 mL
1 cup	shredded part-skim mozzarella cheese	250 mL

1. In a large bowl, combine beans, stewed tomatoes, rice, celery, onion, green pepper, salt and pepper. Spoon into baking dish and top with mushrooms.

2. Bake in preheated oven for 45 minutes or until vegetables are tender-crisp. Sprinkle with mozzarella and bake for 5 minutes or until cheese is melted.

Couscous Bake

Makes 8 servings

This casserole is great hot, cold or at room temperature, served alone or in a lettuce wrap. And it freezes easily.

Tip

If you plan to freeze this casserole, line the baking dish with foil, letting it overhang the sides, and lightly spray the foil with nonstick cooking spray. Prepare through step 3 and place in the freezer until solid. Using the foil overhang, remove casserole from pan, keeping foil intact. Place in a large plastic freezer bag and freeze for up to 3 months. When ready to cook, remove foil and place casserole in the original baking dish (or one the same size). Cover and thaw in the refrigerator, then bake as directed in step 4.

- Preheat oven to 375°F (190°C)
- 10-cup (2.5 L) casserole dish

1½ cups	vegetable broth	375 mL
1 cup	couscous	250 mL
½ tsp	salt	2 mL
¼ cup	olive oil	60 mL
3	cloves garlic, minced	3
1	large onion, finely chopped	1
1	can (28 oz/796 mL) diced tomatoes, drained and ⅓ cup (75 mL) juice reserved	1
2 cups	loosely packed fresh spinach leaves, sliced	500 mL
⅓ cup	pine nuts	75 mL
1 tsp	dried basil	5 mL
½ tsp	freshly ground black pepper	2 mL
1 cup	shredded Muenster cheese	250 mL

1. In a medium saucepan, bring broth to a boil over high heat. Add couscous and salt; cover, remove from heat and let stand for 5 minutes or until liquid is absorbed. Fluff with a fork.

2. In a large skillet, heat oil over medium-high heat. Sauté garlic and onion for 5 to 7 minutes or until tender. Add tomatoes and cook, stirring often, for 10 minutes. Stir in couscous, reserved tomato juice, spinach, pine nuts, basil and pepper.

3. Spread half the couscous mixture in casserole dish. Sprinkle with cheese. Spread the remaining couscous over cheese.

4. Cover and bake in preheated oven for 25 to 30 minutes or until bubbling.

Fish and Seafood Casseroles

Baked White Fish with Broccoli Rice
   and Lemon Butter Sauce 104
Tuna Noodle Casserole 105
Baked Tuna Mac 106
Fay's Tuna Casserole 107
Artichokes Stuffed with Tuna, Potato and Cheddar 108
Tuna Crab Bake 110
Creamy Seafood Bake 111
Oven Paella 112
Baked Sea Scallops 113
Cape Cod Casserole 114
Angel Hair Shrimp 115
Shrimp and Rice Casserole 116
Shrimp, Mushroom and Rice Casserole 117
Baked Macaroni with Fresh Shrimp and Mushrooms 118
Shrimp and Artichoke Divan 119
Crunchy Shrimp Casserole 120
Spicy Shrimp and Grits 121
Shrimp Enchilada Casserole 122
Crab and Shrimp Casserole 123
Sara's Mexican Seafood Casserole 124
Baked Crab with Sherry White Sauce 126
Seafood Spaghetti 128

Baked White Fish with Broccoli Rice and Lemon Butter Sauce

Makes 6 to 8 servings

The amazing flavor of fresh white fish is combined here with broccoli and rice in a buttery sauce.

Tip

In place of the white fish fillets, try trout, small salmon, char or grayling.

- Preheat oven to 375°F (190°C)
- 11- by 7-inch (28 by 18 cm) glass baking dish, greased

⅓ cup	butter	75 mL
⅓ cup	freshly squeezed lemon juice	75 mL
2 tsp	chicken-flavored instant bouillon granules	10 mL
1 tsp	hot pepper sauce	5 mL
1	package (10 oz/300 g) frozen chopped broccoli, thawed and drained	1
1 cup	cooked long-grain white rice	250 mL
1 cup	shredded sharp (old) Cheddar cheese	250 mL
6 to 8	fresh or frozen skinless white fish fillets (about 2 lbs/kg), thawed if frozen	6 to 8

1. In a small saucepan, melt butter over medium heat. Add lemon juice, bouillon and hot pepper sauce; heat, stirring, until bouillon dissolves. Remove from heat.

2. In a medium bowl, combine broccoli, rice, cheese and ¼ cup (50 mL) of the lemon butter sauce.

3. Place fish fillets on work surface with the skinned side down. Spread broccoli mixture evenly over top. Starting at narrowest end, roll up and place seam side down in prepared baking dish. Pour remaining sauce over roll-ups.

4. Bake in preheated oven for about 20 minutes or until fish is opaque and flakes easily when tested with a fork.

Tuna Noodle Casserole

This recipe defines comfort food in the home of the Harrisons, my dear friends and neighbors. Ellen makes a traditional tuna casserole, but adds some crunch with fresh vegetables.

Tip

Avoid overcooking the noodles when you boil them. You want them to be firm to the bite (al dente) so they don't get too mushy when baked with the sauce.

- Preheat oven to 350°F (180°C)
- 13- by 9-inch (33 by 23 cm) glass baking dish

12 oz	wide egg noodles	375 g
6 tbsp	butter, divided	90 mL
10 oz	mushrooms, sliced	300 g
1 tsp	salt, divided	5 mL
1 tsp	freshly ground black pepper, divided	5 mL
2	cans (each 6 oz/170 g) chunk light tuna packed in water, drained and flaked	2
1	can (10 oz/284 mL) condensed cream of mushroom soup	1
1 cup	frozen peas, thawed	250 mL
1/2 cup	freshly grated Parmesan cheese	125 mL
1/4 cup	chopped onion	60 mL
3 tbsp	chopped green bell pepper	45 mL
3 tbsp	chopped red bell pepper	45 mL
1/2 cup	mayonnaise	125 mL
1 tbsp	freshly squeezed lemon juice	15 mL
3/4 cup	dry bread crumbs	175 mL

1. In a large pot of boiling water, cook noodles according to package directions until just tender. Drain.

2. Meanwhile, in a skillet, melt 2 tbsp (30 mL) of the butter over medium-high heat. Cook mushrooms for 5 to 7 minutes or until tender. Season with half the salt and half the pepper.

3. In a large bowl, combine noodles, mushrooms, tuna, soup, peas, cheese, onion, green pepper, red pepper, mayonnaise, lemon juice and the remaining salt and pepper. Transfer to baking dish.

4. In the same skillet, melt the remaining butter over medium heat. Remove from heat and stir in bread crumbs. Sprinkle over noodle mixture.

5. Bake in preheated oven for 45 to 50 minutes or until bubbling.

Baked Tuna Mac

Makes 6 to 8 servings

Simple, easy and hearty, this recipe is the definition of comfort food!

Tip

Kids love fun pasta shapes. Look for wagon wheels, cartoon characters or geometric shapes when you plan to make a pasta dish for kids.

• Preheat oven to 375°F (190°C)
• 12-cup (3 L) casserole dish

4 cups	elbow macaroni	1 L
1½ cups	milk	375 mL
2	cans (each 10 oz/284 mL) condensed Cheddar cheese soup	2
1 tbsp	Worcestershire sauce	15 mL
2	cans (each 6 oz/170 g) chunk light tuna packed in water, drained and flaked	2
1	tomato, diced	1
¾ cup	dry bread crumbs	175 mL
¼ cup	butter, melted	60 mL

1. In a large pot of boiling water, cook macaroni according to package directions until just tender. Drain.

2. Meanwhile, in a saucepan, combine milk, soup and Worcestershire sauce. Heat over medium heat, stirring, until steaming.

3. In casserole dish, combine macaroni, tuna and tomato. Pour in milk mixture.

4. In a small bowl, combine bread crumbs and butter. Sprinkle over macaroni mixture.

5. Bake in preheated oven for 45 to 50 minutes or until bubbling.

Fay's Tuna Casserole

As a child, I absolutely loved this recipe — so much so that I listed it in my high school yearbook as my favorite food. My brother, Bud, and my daddy recently suggested that we get together and try to figure out Mom's recipe. We nailed it! Thanks, Mom, for serving this time after time!

Tip

Mom would vary the topping, sometimes using shredded cheese and sometimes crushed potato chips. Cheese is my favorite, but try the potato chips to discover yours!

- Preheat oven to 350°F (180°C)
- 13- by 9-inch (33 by 23 cm) glass baking dish

2 tbsp	butter	30 mL
1 cup	chopped onion	250 mL
1 cup	chopped celery	250 mL
2	cans (each 10 oz/284 mL) condensed cream of mushroom soup	2
½ cup	milk	125 mL
½ tsp	salt	2 mL
½ tsp	freshly ground black pepper	2 mL
12 oz	wide egg noodles	375 g
3	cans (each 6 oz/170 g) chunk light tuna packed in water, drained and flaked	3
½ cup	pimento-stuffed olives, sliced	125 mL
1 cup	shredded extra-sharp (extra-old) Cheddar cheese	250 mL

1. In a skillet, heat butter over medium heat. Sauté onion and celery for 5 to 7 minutes or until tender. Remove from heat and stir in soup, milk, salt and pepper.

2. Meanwhile, in a large pot of boiling water, cook noodles according to package directions until just tender. Drain.

3. In baking dish, combine noodles, onion mixture, tuna and olives. Sprinkle with cheese.

4. Bake in preheated oven for 45 to 50 minutes or until bubbling.

Artichokes Stuffed with Tuna, Potato and Cheddar

These beautiful artichokes filled with a savory tuna-potato mixture are such a treat and are great for entertaining or a fabulous first course for a special meal. My dear friend Lorinda from Orange County, California, taught me years ago how to prepare fresh artichokes with this amazing dipping sauce. Thank you for introducing me to such a fabulous delicacy.

- Preheat oven to 350°F (180°C)
- 11- by 7-inch (28 by 18 cm) glass baking dish

4	artichokes	4
1 tbsp	freshly squeezed lemon juice	15 mL
1 tsp	salt	5 mL
1½ cups	cubed potatoes (½-inch/1 cm cubes)	375 mL
¼ cup	chopped onion	60 mL
1 cup	sour cream	250 mL
1 cup	mayonnaise	250 mL
1 tsp	dried thyme, crushed	5 mL
½ tsp	paprika	2 mL
1	can (6 oz/170 g) chunk light tuna packed in water, drained and flaked	1
1½ cups	shredded Cheddar cheese	375 mL
⅓ cup	sweet pickle relish	75 mL

1. Rinse artichokes well and cut off stems, removing small bottom leaves. Trim tips of leaves and cut off about 1 inch (2.5 cm) of the tops of artichokes.

2. Stand artichokes upright in a deep saucepan large enough to hold them snugly. Add 2 to 3 inches (5 to 7.5 cm) of water, lemon juice and salt. Cover and bring to a gentle boil over medium-high heat. Reduce heat to medium and boil gently, adjusting heat as necessary, for 30 to 45 minutes or until base of artichokes can be pierced easily with a fork. Gently spread leaves and use a spoon to scrape choke from center of each artichoke. Turn artichokes upside down on paper towels to drain.

3. Meanwhile, combine potatoes and onions in a large pot and add cold water to cover. Bring to a boil over high heat. Season water with salt, reduce heat and boil gently for 10 minutes or until potatoes are tender. Drain.

Tip

To make the preparation easier when you're entertaining, cook the artichokes and prepare the stuffing the day ahead. Cover and refrigerate both separately. Just before serving, proceed with stuffing as directed in step 6.

4. In a medium bowl, stir together sour cream, mayonnaise, thyme and paprika.

5. In a large bowl, combine potato mixture, tuna, cheese, relish and half the sour cream mixture.

6. Gently spread center leaves of artichokes and fill with tuna mixture, dividing evenly. Place filled artichokes upright in baking dish.

7. Cover and bake in preheated oven for 15 minutes or until heated through.

8. Meanwhile, transfer the remaining sour cream mixture to a small saucepan and heat over low heat, stirring constantly, until heated through. Serve as a dip for the artichoke leaves.

Tuna Crab Bake

Here's a quick school-night dinner that's easy to sell to the whole family.

Tip

This recipe is great served with Chardonnay, which balances the flavor of the crab, tuna and Muenster.

- 8-cup (2 L) casserole dish, greased

1	can (6 oz/170 g) lump crabmeat, drained and flaked	1
1	can (6 oz/170 g) chunk light tuna packed in water, drained and flaked	1
4 cups	cubed French bread	1 L
2 cups	shredded Muenster, American, Swiss or provolone cheese	500 mL
2 tbsp	chopped fresh parsley	30 mL
4	eggs	4
3 cups	milk	750 mL
3 tbsp	butter, melted	45 mL
2 tsp	dry mustard	10 mL
1 tsp	grated onion	5 mL

1. In a small bowl, gently stir together crabmeat and tuna.

2. Place one-third of the bread cubes in bottom of prepared casserole dish. Cover with one-third of the crab mixture, one-third of the cheese and one-third of the parsley. Repeat layers two more times.

3. In a medium bowl, whisk together eggs, milk, butter, mustard and onion. Pour over layers in casserole dish. Cover and refrigerate for at least 6 hours or overnight.

4. Preheat oven to 350°F (180°C).

5. Uncover baking dish. Bake for 1 hour or until puffed and golden.

Creamy Seafood Bake

Makes 6 servings

This recipe delivers melt-in-your-mouth seafood in a creamy cheese sauce.

Tip

Substitute cod or tilapia for the orange roughy.

- Preheat oven to 400°F (200°C)
- 11- by 7-inch (28 by 18 cm) glass baking dish, greased

1½ lbs	skinless orange roughy fillets	750 g
¼ cup	dry white wine	60 mL
1 tbsp	freshly squeezed lemon juice	15 mL
¾ tsp	salt	3 mL
¼ tsp	hot pepper sauce	1 mL
3 tbsp	butter or margarine, divided	45 mL
1 cup	cooked lump crabmeat	250 mL
3 tbsp	all-purpose flour	45 mL
2	egg yolks	2
2 tbsp	half-and-half (10%) cream	30 mL
¼ cup	freshly grated Parmesan cheese	60 mL

1. Arrange fish in a single layer in prepared baking dish. Pour in wine and sprinkle with lemon juice, salt and hot pepper sauce. Dot with 1 tbsp (15 mL) of the butter.

2. Cover and bake in preheated oven for 20 to 25 minutes or until fish flakes easily when tested with a fork. Remove from oven and preheat broiler.

3. Carefully drain cooking liquid into a measuring cup, measure 1 cup (250 mL) and set aside. Top fish with crabmeat and set aside.

4. In a saucepan, melt the remaining butter over medium-low heat. Whisk in flour and cook, whisking, for 1 to 2 minutes or until smooth and bubbling. Gradually stir in cooking liquid and cook, stirring, for 3 to 5 minutes or until thickened and smooth. Remove from heat.

5. In a small bowl, beat egg yolks and cream. Whisk in 2 tbsp (30 mL) of the white sauce from the saucepan. Add egg mixture to the saucepan, whisking briskly. Return to medium-low heat and cook, stirring, for about 1 minute or until slightly thickened.

6. Pour sauce over fish and crab. Sprinkle with cheese. Broil about 5 inches (12.5 cm) from heat for about 10 minutes or until fish is hot and top is lightly browned.

Oven Paella

Many years ago, when we were visiting friends in Orange County, California, we had the opportunity to experience an outdoor paella party. We now often host our own version for friends at the beginning of spring. Although we love making this recipe outdoors on a barbecue burner, I've given you an oven version, which can be made in any season.

Tip

To clean and debeard mussels, first check to make sure the shells are tightly closed. Discard any with cracked shells. If any are open, tap them gently and discard any that don't close within a few seconds. Scrub each mussel, removing as much of the stringy bits clinging to the outside as you can. You will see a crack where the two shells meet, and you will see little threads of brown seaweed. This is the beard, some of which has been removed during processing. Pinching the beard, use a side-to-side motion to remove it.

- Preheat oven to 400°F (200°C)

2 cups	clam juice	500 mL
1 cup	chicken broth	250 mL
1/2 cup	dry white wine	125 mL
1/4 tsp	saffron threads, crushed	1 mL
1 lb	large shrimp, peeled and deveined	500 g
8 oz	skinless grouper fillet, cut into 1-inch (2.5 cm) pieces	250 g
1/4 tsp	salt	1 mL
3 tbsp	olive oil, divided	45 mL
1 lb	chorizo, cooked and cut into 1/2-inch (1 cm) slices	500 g
2	cloves garlic, minced	2
1/2 cup	chopped green bell pepper	125 mL
1/2 cup	chopped red bell pepper	125 mL
1/2 cup	chopped onion	125 mL
2 tsp	paprika	10 mL
1 cup	chopped tomato	250 mL
1 1/2 cups	short-grain white rice, such as Arborio	375 mL
1 lb	small mussels, scrubbed and debearded	500 g

1. In a Dutch oven, bring clam juice, broth, wine and saffron to a simmer over low heat. Keep warm.

2. In a medium bowl, combine shrimp and grouper. Sprinkle with salt and let stand for 5 minutes.

3. In a large skillet, heat 1 tbsp (15 mL) of the oil over medium-high heat. Sauté shrimp mixture and chorizo for 1 minute. Transfer to a bowl.

4. Add the remaining oil to skillet. Sauté garlic, green pepper, red pepper, onion and paprika for 3 minutes. Stir in tomato and sauté for 2 minutes. Stir in rice until well coated.

5. Add rice mixture to the Dutch oven, increase heat to high and bring to a boil. Reduce heat and simmer for 3 minutes. Add shrimp mixture and simmer for 2 minutes. Nestle mussels in rice mixture.

6. Bake in preheated oven for 15 minutes or until shells open. Discard any mussels that do not open. Remove from oven, cover and let stand for 10 minutes.

Baked Sea Scallops

Makes 4 servings

Sea scallops are a luxury that require very little effort to be fabulous. When properly cooked, they are delicate, soft and creamy to the bite. Happily, they cook quickly; just keep an eye on them.

Tip

Overdone scallops are rubbery, so watch carefully for doneness and test one if you're not sure. For the best taste and texture, I prefer to prep and bake this casserole just before serving.

- Preheat oven to 425°F (220°C)
- 8-cup (2 L) casserole dish

16	sea scallops, trimmed of hard side muscles	16
5	cloves garlic, minced	5
2	shallots, chopped	2
1/3 cup	butter, melted	75 mL
1/2 tsp	salt	2 mL
1/2 tsp	freshly ground black pepper	2 mL
1/4 tsp	ground nutmeg	1 mL
1 1/2 tbsp	freshly squeezed lemon juice	22 mL
1 cup	seasoned dry bread crumbs	250 mL
1/4 cup	olive oil	60 mL
1/4 cup	chopped fresh parsley	60 mL

1. Place scallops in casserole dish. Add garlic, shallots, butter, salt, pepper and nutmeg; stir gently to combine. Sprinkle with lemon juice.

2. In a medium bowl, combine bread crumbs and olive oil. Sprinkle over scallops.

3. Bake in preheated oven for 11 to 14 minutes or until scallops are firm and opaque and topping is browned. Serve sprinkled with parsley.

Cape Cod Casserole

Makes 10 to 12 servings

Fresh seafood is abundant on Cape Cod, so it's no surprise that this namesake casserole combines two types of shellfish — shrimp and bay scallops — for a great result.

- Preheat oven to 350°F (180°C)
- 12-cup (3 L) casserole dish

8 oz	thin egg noodles	250 g
1/2 cup	butter, divided	125 mL
1 lb	mushrooms, sliced	500 g
2 lbs	shrimp, peeled and deveined	1 kg
2 lbs	bay scallops, trimmed of hard side muscles	1 kg
6 tbsp	all-purpose flour	90 mL
1/2 tsp	salt	2 mL
1/8 tsp	freshly ground black pepper	0.5 mL
4 cups	milk	1 L
1/2 cup	dry sherry	125 mL
2 cups	shredded sharp (old) Cheddar cheese	500 mL
1/2 tsp	paprika	2 mL

1. In a large pot of boiling water, cook noodles according to package directions until just tender. Drain and transfer to casserole dish.

2. Meanwhile, in a large skillet, melt 2 tbsp (30 mL) of the butter over medium-high heat. Sauté mushrooms for 5 to 7 minutes or until tender. Spread over noodles, along with shrimp and scallops.

3. In a small saucepan, melt the remaining butter over medium heat. Whisk in flour, salt and pepper. Cook, stirring constantly, for about 2 minutes or until smooth. Gradually whisk in milk and cook, stirring constantly, until thickened. Add sherry and cook, stirring, until thickened. Pour over noodle mixture and sprinkle with cheese.

4. Cover and bake in preheated oven for 40 to 45 minutes or until hot and bubbly. Remove from oven and preheat broiler. Uncover casserole, sprinkle with paprika and broil for 3 to 5 minutes or until top is golden brown.

Angel Hair Shrimp

Makes 10 to 12 servings

This dish is great for entertaining and super-easy.

Tip

Substitute crawfish for the shrimp.

- Preheat oven to 350°F (180°C)
- 13- by 9-inch (33 by 23 cm) glass baking dish, greased

1 lb	angel hair pasta	500 g
1/2 cup	butter	125 mL
3	cloves garlic, minced	3
3	stalks celery, chopped	3
1	onion, chopped	1
1	bunch green onions, chopped	1
1	large green bell pepper, chopped	1
1/4 cup	all-purpose flour	60 mL
2 cups	half-and-half (10%) cream	500 mL
8 oz	pasteurized prepared cheese product, such as Velveeta, cubed	250 g
8 oz	Monterey Jack cheese, cubed	250 g
8 oz	small shrimp, peeled, deveined and cooked	250 g
1/2 tsp	salt	2 mL
1/2 tsp	freshly ground black pepper	2 mL
1/2 tsp	Creole seasoning	2 mL

1. In a large pot of boiling water, cook pasta according to package directions until just tender. Drain and transfer prepared baking dish.

2. Meanwhile, in a large skillet, melt butter over medium heat. Sauté garlic, celery, onion, green onions and green pepper for 5 to 7 minutes or until tender. Sprinkle with flour and cook, stirring constantly, for 3 to 5 minutes or until slightly thickened.

3. Gradually whisk in cream; reduce heat and simmer, stirring constantly, until sauce starts to thicken. Stir in pasteurized cheese, Monterey Jack, shrimp, salt, pepper and Creole seasoning; simmer, stirring constantly to make sure it doesn't scorch, for about 5 minutes or until cheese is melted. Add shrimp mixture to pasta and mix well.

4. Bake in preheated oven for 20 to 25 minutes or until bubbling.

Shrimp and Rice Casserole

Makes 4 servings

This recipe uses cost-effective canned shrimp, but it will taste even better if you decide to use fresh cooked shrimp.

Tip
This recipe freezes well. See page 13 for instructions.

- Preheat oven to 350°F (180°C)
- 9-inch (23 cm) square glass baking dish, greased

2 tbsp	butter	30 mL
1/2 cup	finely chopped onion	125 mL
1/2 cup	finely chopped green bell pepper	125 mL
2	cans (each 4 oz/114 g) small shrimp	2
2	cans (each 11 oz/312 mL) cream-style corn	2
2	eggs, beaten	2
1	can (6 oz/170 g) lump crabmeat, drained and flaked	1
2 cups	shredded Cheddar cheese, divided	500 mL
1 1/2 cups	instant white rice	375 mL

1. In a large skillet, melt butter over medium-high heat. Sauté onion and green pepper for 5 to 7 minutes or until tender. Stir in shrimp corn, eggs, crabmeat, 1/2 cup (125 mL) of the cheese and rice.

2. Pour into prepared baking dish and top with the remaining cheese. Bake in preheated oven for 30 minutes or until casserole is bubbling and rice is tender.

Shrimp, Mushroom and Rice Casserole

Makes 10 to 12 servings

I love the variety of flavors and textures in this hearty seafood recipe.

Tip

For a unique taste and texture, substitute a whole-grain blend for the wild rice blend.

- Preheat oven to 350°F (180°C)
- 13- by 9-inch (33 by 23 cm) glass baking dish, greased

2½ cups	long-grain and wild rice blend	625 mL
1 cup	long-grain white rice	250 mL
6 tbsp	butter, divided	90 mL
1	onion, chopped	1
4 oz	mushrooms, sliced	125 g
2	cans (each 10 oz/284 mL) condensed cream of mushroom soup	2
½ cup	dry white wine	125 mL
1 tbsp	freshly squeezed lemon juice	15 mL
1 tbsp	Worcestershire sauce	15 mL
¼ tsp	freshly ground black pepper	1 mL
2 lbs	small to medium shrimp, peeled, deveined and cooked	1 kg
1 cup	dry bread crumbs	250 mL
2 tbsp	freshly grated Parmesan cheese	30 mL

1. Cook wild rice blend and white rice separately according to package directions.

2. Meanwhile, in a large skillet, melt 2 tbsp (30 mL) of the butter over medium-high heat. Sauté onion and mushrooms for 5 to 7 minutes or until tender.

3. In a large bowl, whisk together mushroom soup, wine, lemon juice, Worcestershire sauce and pepper until smooth. Add onion mixture, wild rice and white rice; toss to coat. Gently stir in shrimp. Spread in prepared baking dish.

4. In a small skillet, melt the remaining butter over low heat. Stir in bread crumbs and remove from heat. Stir in cheese. Sprinkle over shrimp mixture.

5. Bake in preheated oven for 30 minutes or until casserole is bubbling and topping is golden brown.

Baked Macaroni with Fresh Shrimp and Mushrooms

Makes 8 servings

Elegant flambé is a show stopper, but this dish has amazing flavor to match the drama.

Tip

Freshly grated or shaved Parmesan cheese is always best right off the wedge, but prepackaged containers can be found in the refrigerated specialty cheese section of your local supermarket.

- Preheat oven to 400°F (200°C)
- 13- by 9-inch (33 by 23 cm) glass baking dish, greased

2 cups	elbow macaroni	500 mL
6 tbsp	butter, divided	90 mL
2 tbsp	all-purpose flour	30 mL
1¼ cups	milk	300 mL
½ tsp	salt, divided	2 mL
½ tsp	freshly ground black pepper, divided	2 mL
Pinch	ground nutmeg	Pinch
¾ cup	sliced mushrooms	175 mL
3	cans (each 4 oz/114 g) small shrimp	3
2 tbsp	brandy	30 mL
6 tbsp	freshly grated Parmesan cheese, divided	90 mL

1. In a large pot of boiling water, cook macaroni according to package directions until just tender. Drain and set aside.

2. In small saucepan melt 2 tbsp (30 mL) of the butter over medium heat. Whisk in flour. Gradually add milk, whisking constantly, until smooth and thickened. Remove from heat and season with half the salt, half the pepper and nutmeg. Keep warm.

3. In a skillet, melt the remaining butter over medium-high heat. Sauté mushrooms for 5 to 7 minutes or until tender. Season with the remaining salt and pepper. Add shrimp and cook until heated through.

4. Pour in brandy and flambé. When flames have subsided, stir in 3 tbsp (45 mL) of the cheese. Remove from heat.

5. Add the remaining cheese to the reserved white sauce. Stir in mushroom mixture. Add macaroni and toss to coat.

6. Pour into prepared baking dish. Bake in preheated oven for 20 to 25 minutes or until bubbling.

Shrimp and Artichoke Divan

This elegant shrimp dish is perfect for entertaining. Serve over rice or pasta.

Tip

For convenience, ask the clerk at the seafood counter to peel and devein shrimp and remove the tails. Or look for ready-to-use flash-frozen shrimp.

- Preheat oven to 375°F (190°C)
- 8-inch (20 cm) square glass baking dish, greased

1/2 cup	butter, divided	125 mL
1/4 cup	all-purpose flour	60 mL
1 1/2 cups	milk	375 mL
1/2 tsp	salt	2 mL
1/2 tsp	freshly ground black pepper	2 mL
1/4 cup	dry white wine	60 mL
1 tbsp	Worcestershire sauce	15 mL
8 oz	shrimp, peeled, deveined and tails removed	250 g
1	can (14 oz/398 mL) artichoke hearts, drained and quartered	1
4 oz	baby bella mushrooms, sliced	125 g
1/4 cup	freshly grated Parmesan cheese	60 mL
1/4 tsp	paprika	1 mL

1. In a saucepan, melt 6 tbsp (90 mL) of the butter over medium heat. Whisk in flour and cook, whisking constantly, for 5 minutes. Gradually add milk, whisking constantly, until smooth and thickened. Remove from heat and season with salt and pepper. Stir in wine and Worcestershire sauce. Keep warm.

2. Arrange shrimp and artichoke hearts in prepared baking dish.

3. In a large skillet, melt the remaining butter over medium-high heat. Sauté mushrooms for 5 to 7 minutes or until tender. Pour over shrimp and artichokes. Spoon white sauce over top and sprinkle with cheese and paprika.

4. Bake in preheated oven for 30 minutes or until bubbling.

Crunchy Shrimp Casserole

Water chestnuts give this creamy casserole crunch and an unexpected fresh flavor.

Tip

I usually use long-grain white rice for this recipe, but I substitute long-grain brown rice on occasion.

- Preheat oven to 350°F (180°C)
- 11- by 7-inch (28 by 18 cm) glass baking dish, greased

1½ lbs	shrimp, peeled and deveined	750 g
1	can (10 oz/284 mL) condensed cream of mushroom soup	1
⅓ cup	mayonnaise	75 mL
⅓ cup	milk	75 mL
1 tsp	Worcestershire sauce	5 mL
½ tsp	hot pepper sauce	2 mL
1	small onion, finely chopped	1
1	can (4 oz/114 mL) sliced mushrooms, drained (about ½ cup/125 mL)	1
1	can (8 oz/227 mL) sliced water chestnuts, drained	1
1	jar (2 oz/57 mL) sliced pimentos, drained	1
1 cup	thinly sliced celery	250 mL
2 tbsp	chopped fresh parsley	30 mL
1 tbsp	dry sherry	15 mL
2 cups	cooked rice (see tip, at left)	500 mL
1 cup	dry bread crumbs	250 mL
2 tbsp	melted butter	30 mL

1. Bring a large pot of water to a boil. Add shrimp, remove from heat and let stand for 5 minutes or until pink and opaque. Drain and set aside.

2. In a large bowl, combine soup, mayonnaise, milk, Worcestershire sauce and hot pepper sauce. Stir in onion, mushrooms, water chestnuts, pimentos, celery, parsley and sherry.

3. Spread rice in bottom of prepared baking dish. Evenly layer shrimp over rice. Pour soup mixture over shrimp.

4. In a small bowl, combine bread crumbs and butter. Sprinkle over shrimp mixture.

5. Bake in preheated oven for 30 minutes or until casserole is bubbling and bread crumbs are golden brown.

Spicy Shrimp and Grits

This casserole combines my passion for spicy foods with my love of North Carolina. It is amazingly rich and is a treat for breakfast, brunch or dinner.

Tip

Serve this dish as the star of a buffet-style brunch, along with fresh fruit, salad options and muffins.

- Preheat oven to 350°F (180°C)
- 13- by 9-inch (33 by 23 cm) glass baking dish, greased

4 cups	chicken broth	1 L
¾ tsp	salt, divided	3 mL
1 cup	regular grits	250 mL
1 cup	shredded pepper Jack cheese	250 mL
1 cup	shredded extra-sharp (extra-old) Cheddar cheese, divided	250 mL
2 tbsp	butter	30 mL
8	green onions, sliced	8
2	cloves garlic, minced	2
1 cup	chopped green bell pepper	250 mL
½ cup	chopped onion	125 mL
1	can (10 oz/284 mL) diced tomatoes and mild green chiles, drained	1
1 lb	small shrimp, peeled, deveined and cooked	500 g
¼ tsp	freshly ground black pepper	1 mL

1. In a large saucepan, bring broth and ½ tsp (2 mL) of the salt to a boil over high heat. Gradually stir in grits. Reduce heat to low, cover and simmer for 15 minutes. Stir in pepper Jack and ¾ cup (175 mL) of the Cheddar.

2. In a large skillet, melt butter over medium heat. Sauté green onions, garlic, green pepper and onion for 5 to 10 minutes or until tender.

3. Add onion mixture to grits mixture. Stir in tomatoes and chiles, shrimp, pepper and the remaining salt.

4. Spread in prepared baking dish and sprinkle with the remaining Cheddar. Bake in preheated oven for 30 to 45 minutes or until hot and bubbly.

Shrimp Enchilada Casserole

Double this recipe for a larger crowd or for very good, spicy leftovers.

Tips

Chipotle peppers are smoked jalapeño peppers in adobo sauce. They have a smoky flavor and are quite spicy.

This recipe doubles easily. Use a 13- by 9-inch (33 by 23 cm) dish and increase the baking time to 40 to 45 minutes. Uncover and bake for 5 minutes.

- Preheat oven to 375°F (190°C)
- 9-inch (23 cm) square glass baking dish

2 tbsp	olive oil	30 mL
5	cloves garlic, minced	5
3	red bell peppers, chopped	3
1	head broccoli, chopped	1
1	large onion, chopped	1
1	can (14 oz/398 mL) diced tomatoes, drained	1
1	chipotle pepper in adobo sauce, finely chopped	1
¼ tsp	salt	1 mL
3	6-inch (15 cm) corn tortillas, halved	3
1 lb	medium shrimp, peeled and deveined, chopped (about 2 cups/500 mL)	500 g
1 cup	shredded Cheddar cheese	250 mL

1. In a large skillet, heat oil over medium-high heat. Sauté garlic, red peppers, broccoli and onion for 5 to 7 minutes or until softened. Add tomatoes, chipotle peppers and salt; bring to a gentle boil. Remove from heat.

2. Spread half the broccoli mixture in baking dish. Place 3 tortilla halves on top, overlapping as necessary. Layer with half the shrimp and half the cheese. Repeat layers with broccoli, tortillas, shrimp and cheese.

3. Cover and bake in preheated oven for 25 to 30 minutes or until shrimp are pink and opaque. Uncover and bake for 5 minutes.

Crab and Shrimp Casserole

Makes 8 servings

My dear friend Carol Johnson loved the ease of this casserole, which uses canned shellfish, as fresh is often hard to find in her home state of Wisconsin.

Tip

If you can find fresh crab and shrimp, by all means substitute them for the canned. Use 3 cups (750 mL) flaked cooked fresh crabmeat and 2 cups (500 mL) cooked peeled shrimp.

- Preheat oven to 350°F (180°C)
- 13- by 9-inch (33 by 23 cm) glass baking dish, greased

4	cans (each 6 oz/170 g) lump crabmeat, drained and flaked	4
4	cans (each 4 oz/114 g) shrimp, drained	4
1	package (10 oz/300 g) frozen green peas, thawed	1
½	green bell pepper, chopped	½
3 cups	cooked long-grain white rice	750 mL
1½ cups	mayonnaise	375 mL
⅓ cup	chopped fresh parsley	75 mL
½ tsp	salt	2 mL
½ tsp	freshly ground black pepper	2 mL

1. In a large bowl, toss together crabmeat, shrimp, peas, green pepper, rice, mayonnaise, parsley, salt and pepper.

2. Spread in prepared baking dish. Cover and bake in preheated oven for 30 minutes or until bubbling.

Sara's Mexican Seafood Casserole

With roasted poblano peppers, fresh shrimp and Mexican cheeses, this casserole is an authentic Mexican delight.

Tip

To add a little more heat to this recipe, substitute pepper Jack cheese for the Monterey Jack. Pepper Jack is simply Monterey Jack with hot peppers (typically jalapeños) added.

- Preheat oven to 350°F (180°C)
- 13- by 9-inch (33 by 23 cm) glass baking dish, greased

2½ tbsp	cornstarch	37 mL
⅔ cup	cold water	150 mL
2 tbsp	butter	30 mL
1 cup	milk	250 mL
¾ cup	chicken broth	175 mL
3 tbsp	olive oil, divided	45 mL
2	cloves garlic, minced	2
½ cup	chopped onion	125 mL
8 oz	mushrooms, sliced	250 g
6 oz	spinach, trimmed and coarsely chopped or baby spinach	175 g
1 lb	medium shrimp, peeled, deveined and coarsely chopped	500 g
2 cups	shredded Monterey Jack cheese, divided	500 mL
1 cup	crumbled Mexican queso fresco	250 mL
½ tsp	salt	2 mL
½ tsp	freshly ground black pepper	2 mL
4	poblano peppers, roasted and peeled (see tip, at right)	4
12	6-inch (15 cm) white corn tortillas	12

1. In a small bowl, combine cornstarch and water. Set aside.

2. In a saucepan, melt butter over medium heat. Add milk, stirring constantly. Add broth and bring to a simmer, stirring constantly. Stir in cornstarch mixture and cook, stirring, for 3 to 5 minutes or until slightly thickened. Remove from heat and cover to keep warm.

3. In a large skillet, heat 2 tbsp (30 mL) of the oil over medium heat. Sauté garlic and onion for 5 to 7 minutes or until tender. Add mushrooms and sauté for 3 to 4 minutes or until just tender. Add spinach and sauté for 1 minute. Transfer to a large bowl.

4. Add the remaining oil to the skillet. Sauté shrimp for 2 to 3 minutes or until pink and opaque. Remove from heat and stir in white sauce.

5. Add the shrimp sauce to the spinach mixture, stirring lightly to combine. Stir in 1 cup (250 mL) of the Monterey Jack, queso fresco, salt and pepper.

6. Slice roasted poblanos lengthwise and remove stems and seeds.

7. Line bottom of prepared baking dish with 6 tortillas, overlapping as necessary. Spread half the shrimp mixture on top, then layer with half the poblanos. Repeat layers. Top with the remaining Monterey Jack.

8. Bake in preheated oven for about 30 minutes or until casserole is bubbling, top is golden and cheese is melted.

Baked Crab with Sherry White Sauce

My mother often used dry sherry when making a white sauce. This delicate recipe, featuring one of her white sauces, is one she would cook for elegant dinner parties.

Tips

Eggs separate more easily when they're cold, but are best warmed to room temperature before cooking or baking.

Since you're not using the egg whites in this recipe, freeze them to make meringues or angel food cake another time.

When whisking the hot sauce into the egg yolks in step 2, make sure to pour the sauce in a thin, steady stream while whisking constantly. This will gradually warm the eggs (temper them) without causing them to scramble. To keep the sauce silky smooth, keep whisking while you cook.

- Preheat oven to 450°F (230°C)
- 13- by 9-inch (33 by 23 cm) glass baking dish, greased

¼ cup	butter, divided	60 mL
2 tbsp	all-purpose flour	30 mL
1¼ cups	milk	300 mL
1	large clove garlic, smashed	1
2	egg yolks	2
⅓ cup	dry sherry	75 mL
½ tsp	dry mustard	2 mL
½ tsp	salt	2 mL
⅛ tsp	ground nutmeg	0.5 mL
⅛ tsp	cayenne pepper	0.5 mL
4	cans (each 8 oz/227 g) lump crabmeat, drained and flaked	4
2 tbsp	finely chopped fresh flat-leaf (Italian) parsley	30 mL
¼ cup	fine dry bread crumbs	60 mL
¼ cup	freshly grated Parmigiano-Reggiano cheese	60 mL

1. In a small saucepan, melt half the butter over medium-low heat. Whisk in flour and cook, whisking constantly, for 2 minutes. Gradually whisk in milk. Add garlic, increase heat to medium and bring to a boil, whisking constantly. Reduce heat and simmer, whisking, for about 3 minutes or until thickened. Remove from heat and discard garlic.

Tip

Freshly grated Parmigiano-Reggiano cheese creates wonderful flavor in this recipe.

2. In a medium bowl, whisk together egg yolks, sherry, mustard, salt, nutmeg and cayenne. While whisking briskly, gradually add $1/2$ cup (125 mL) of the white sauce to warm the yolks. Pour yolk mixture gradually into the remaining white sauce, whisking to combine. Return saucepan to very low heat and heat, whisking constantly, for 2 minutes. Remove from heat and gently stir in crabmeat and parsley. Pour into prepared baking dish.

3. In a small skillet, melt the remaining butter over low heat. Stir in bread crumbs and remove from heat. Stir in cheese. Sprinkle over crab mixture.

4. Bake in preheated oven for 15 to 20 minutes or until casserole is bubbling and topping is golden brown.

Seafood Spaghetti

My neighbors of many years, Jack and Nicole Williams, gave me this recipe. Jack, a native of southern Louisiana, explains that this dish is often called a "funeral casserole" because everyone seems to make it when there is a death in town. It is considered a comfort food.

Variation

Substitute 3 cups (750 mL) cooked shredded chicken for the shrimp and crabmeat. Try using a deli-roasted chicken from the supermarket. Remove the skin and bones and shred the chicken and you'll get the perfect amount for this recipe.

- Preheat oven to 350°F (180°C)
- 13- by 9-inch (33 by 23 cm) glass baking dish, greased

1 lb	spaghetti	500 g
¾ cup	butter	175 mL
1 cup	chopped onion	250 mL
½ cup	chopped green onions	125 mL
½ cup	chopped green bell pepper	125 mL
1	can (10 oz/284 mL) condensed cream of mushroom soup	1
1	can (12 oz or 370 mL) evaporated milk	1
8 oz	pasteurized prepared cheese product, such as Velveeta, cubed	250 g
6 oz	Mexican-flavor pasteurized prepared cheese product, such as Velveeta, cubed	175 g
2 lbs	small shrimp, peeled, deveined and cooked	1 kg
1 lb	cooked lump crabmeat	500 g
½ cup	dry bread crumbs	125 mL

1. In a large pot of boiling water, cook spaghetti according to package directions until just tender. Drain and set aside.

2. Meanwhile, in a large skillet, melt butter over medium heat. Sauté onion, green onions and green pepper for 5 to 7 minutes or until tender.

3. Reduce heat to low and stir in soup, evaporated milk, pasteurized cheese and Mexican pasteurized cheese, stirring until cheese is melted. Fold in shrimp, crabmeat and spaghetti.

4. Spread in prepared baking dish and sprinkle with bread crumbs. Bake in preheated oven for 30 minutes or until bubbling.

Chicken and Turkey Casseroles

Chicken Casserole D'Iberville 130
Mari's No Peeking Chicken 132
Chicken Apricot Bake 133
Tamale Pie 134
Chai Chipotle Chicken Casserole. 135
Chicken à la Candace 136
Spiced Chicken Casserole 137
Chicken Croquette Casserole 138
Chicken Florentine with Wild Rice 140
King Ranch Chicken Casserole .142
Chicken Pie 143
Crescent Chicken Casserole 144
Chicken and Dumpling Casserole 145
Brown Rice and Chicken Bake .146
À la King Chicken Casserole 146
Mom's Chicken Hot Dish. 147
Chicken and Artichoke Casserole 148
Tasty Chicken Casserole 149
Chicken Bell Pepper Bake. 150
Layered Chicken with Poblano Peppers and Cheese 151
Chicken, Sausage and Bean Cassoulet. 152
Mexican Chicken Lasagna 153
Southwestern Chicken Lasagna 154
Chicken Enchilada Casserole with Teriyaki Sauce 156
Verde Chicken Casserole 157
Jambalaya Casserole 158
Creamy Chicken Casserole. 159
Brunswick-Style Chicken Pot Pie. 160
Chicken Noodle and Green Pea Casserole 161
Classic Turkey Divan. 162
Turkey and Green Onion Phyllo Layer 163
Thanksgiving Leftover Casserole. 164
Turkey and Rice Enchiladas. 165
Baked Turkey and Ham Casserole. 166

Chicken Casserole D'Iberville

This amazingly savory chicken casserole, created by our dear family friend Patty Moncus, is so rich and yummy. It's a great choice for a potluck or when you're entertaining a large group. Thank you, Patty, for your inspiration!

Tip

For an easy, tidy and fun way to crush the crackers and fried onions, place them in a sealable plastic bag, seal and place the bag on the counter. Use a rolling pin, a meat mallet or the bottom of a saucepan to gently crush the crackers and onions into crumbs. Kids are a terrific help with this task!

- Preheat oven to 350°F (180°C)
- 16-cup (4 L) casserole dish

2	whole chickens (each 3 lbs/1.5 kg)	2
2	stalks celery	2
1	onion, quartered	1
1 cup	dry sherry	250 mL
1½ tsp	salt	7 mL
½ tsp	curry powder	2 mL
¼ tsp	freshly ground black pepper	1 mL
¼ tsp	poultry seasoning	1 mL
2 cups	long-grain and wild rice blend (12 oz/375 g)	500 mL
2 tbsp	butter	30 mL
1	bunch green onions, chopped (about 1 cup/250 mL)	1
1 lb	mushrooms, sliced	500 g
1 cup	sour cream	250 mL
1	can (10 oz/284 mL) condensed cream of chicken and mushroom soup	1
1	sleeve round buttery crackers, crushed (about 1½ cups/375 mL)	1
1	can (6 oz/170 g) french-fried onions, crushed	1
2 tbsp	butter, melted	30 mL
¼ tsp	paprika	1 mL
⅛ tsp	garlic powder	0.5 mL

1. Place chickens in a large Dutch oven and add enough water to cover. Add celery, onion, sherry, salt, curry powder, pepper and poultry seasoning; bring to a boil over high heat. Reduce heat to low, cover and simmer for 1 hour or until juices run clear when thigh is pierced and an instant-read thermometer inserted in the thickest part of a thigh registers 165°F (74°C). Remove chickens, reserving broth in Dutch oven. Let chickens cool.

This casserole freezes well.
Prepare through step 4,
let cool, cover tightly with
foil and freeze for up to
3 months. Thaw overnight
in the refrigerator, then
proceed with step 5,
adding 10 minutes to the
baking time.

2. Pour broth through a fine-mesh strainer into an 8-cup (2 L) glass measuring cup; discard solids. Measure 4½ cups (1.125 L) broth, adding water if necessary. Pour into a saucepan and bring to a boil over high heat. Stir in rice mix, reduce heat to low, cover and simmer for 25 minutes or until rice is tender and most of the liquid is absorbed. Remove from heat and let stand, covered, for 5 minutes. Fluff with a fork.

3. Meanwhile, remove skin and bones from chicken and discard. Coarsely chop or shred chicken.

4. In a clean large Dutch oven, melt 2 tbsp (30 mL) butter over medium-high heat. Sauté green onions and mushrooms for about 10 minutes or until tender. Stir in cooked rice, chicken, sour cream and soup. Spoon into casserole dish.

5. In a small bowl, combine crushed crackers and fried onions. Stir in melted butter, paprika and garlic powder. Sprinkle evenly over casserole.

6. Cover and bake in preheated oven for 20 to 30 minutes or until bubbling. Uncover and bake for 5 minutes.

Mari's No Peeking Chicken

Makes 4 servings

The title of this recipe says it all: no peeking! For perfect results, leave the dish covered throughout the entire baking time. My dear friend Gloria Mari McDonald from the Pineywoods of Texas shares this family favorite. Serve with a green salad and crusty bread for the perfect meal.

- Preheat oven to 350°F (180°C)
- 13- by 9-inch (33 by 23 cm) glass baking dish, greased

1½ cups	long-grain white rice	375 mL
1	envelope (1 oz/30 g) onion soup mix	1
1	can (10 oz/284 mL) condensed cream of mushroom soup	1
1	can (10 oz/284 mL) condensed cream of celery soup	1
1 cup	whole milk	250 mL
¼ cup	butter, melted	60 mL
4	boneless skinless chicken breasts (about 2 lbs/1 kg total)	4

1. In a medium bowl, combine rice, onion soup mix, mushroom soup, celery soup, milk and butter. Spoon into prepared baking dish. Place chicken breasts on top.

2. Cover and bake in preheated oven for 1½ hours or until rice is tender and chicken is no longer pink inside.

Chicken Apricot Bake

Apricot-pecan stuffing makes a great alternative to traditional dressing recipes, contributing both sweetness and crunch to this baked chicken dish.

Tip

Toast the pecans for the best flavor. In a dry skillet, over medium heat, toast chopped pecans, stirring constantly, for about 5 minutes or until lightly browned and fragrant. Immediately transfer to a bowl and let cool.

- Preheat oven to 350°F (180°C)
- 11- by 7-inch (28 by 18 cm) glass baking dish, greased

2 cups	seasoned stuffing mix	500 mL
2/3 cup	dried apricots, chopped	150 mL
1/3 cup	pecan halves, chopped	75 mL
1/4 cup	packed brown sugar	60 mL
1 tsp	dried thyme	5 mL
1/2 tsp	freshly ground black pepper	2 mL
1/4 tsp	salt	1 mL
2/3 cup	hot water	150 mL
4	boneless skinless chicken breasts	4
2 tbsp	apricot preserves	30 mL

1. In a large bowl, combine stuffing, apricots, pecans, brown sugar, thyme, pepper, salt and hot water. Spoon into prepared baking dish. Place chicken breasts on top. Top each chicken breast with preserves.

2. Bake in preheated oven for 45 to 50 minutes or until chicken is no longer pink inside.

Tamale Pie

Makes 6 servings

This recipe reminds me of holiday tamale-making gatherings at my hometown church, where we'd spend an entire day preparing delicate steamed tamales full of flavor. This creation takes a fraction of the time, but yields the same delicious results.

Tip
You can substitute boneless skinless chicken breasts for the chicken tenders.

- Preheat oven to 350°F (180°C)
- 13- by 9-inch (33 by 23 cm) glass baking dish, greased

1 cup	cornmeal	250 mL
1 tsp	salt	5 mL
1 cup	cold water	250 mL
2 tbsp	corn oil	30 mL
1/3 cup	chopped onion	75 mL
8 oz	chicken tenders, cut into 1-inch (2.5 cm) pieces	250 g
1/2	envelope (1 1/4 oz/37 g) taco seasoning mix	1/2
1 cup	salsa	250 mL
1/4 cup	drained sliced olives	60 mL
1	can (14 oz/398 mL) refried beans	1
2 cups	shredded Monterey Jack cheese	500 mL

1. In a medium bowl, combine cornmeal, salt and cold water. In a medium saucepan, bring 2 cups (500 mL) water to a boil over high heat. Slowly pour cornmeal mixture into boiling water, stirring constantly. Reduce heat to medium and boil gently, stirring often, for 8 to 10 minutes or until thickened. Reduce heat to low, cover and simmer for 5 minutes.

2. In a skillet, heat oil over medium heat. Sauté onions for about 5 minutes or until softened. Add chicken and sauté until browned and no longer pink inside. Add taco seasoning and 1/3 cup (75 mL) water; cook, stirring, until thickened. Stir in salsa and olives.

3. Spread cooked cornmeal evenly in prepared baking dish. Spread refried beans over cornmeal. Spread chicken mixture over bean layer. Sprinkle cheese over top.

4. Bake in preheated oven for 20 minutes or until bubbling.

Chicken Apricot Bake (page 133)

Spiced Chicken Casserole (page 137)

Chai Chipotle Chicken Casserole

My dear friend Michele Northrup, "the Saucy Queen," founded the Intensity Academy, an all-natural specialty sauce company, in 2007. I developed this recipe to showcase one of her fabulous barbecue sauces, but it is equally delicious with any sweet and smoky barbecue sauce.

Tips

Visit www.intensityacademy. com to find Chai Chipotle Q sauce and more!

In place of the chicken breasts, you can use 3 cups (750 mL) leftover cooked chicken or 1 deli-roasted chicken with the bones and skin removed.

- Preheat oven to 400°F (200°C)
- 13- by 9-inch (33 by 23 cm) glass baking dish, greased

1	package (20 oz/600 g) frozen shredded hash brown potatoes	1
1	onion, chopped	1
2 tsp	olive oil	10 mL
1 lb	boneless skinless chicken breasts	500 g
1½ cups	sweet and smoky barbecue sauce, such as Chai Chipotle Q barbecue sauce (see tip, at left)	375 mL
2 cups	shredded Monterey Jack cheese	500 mL

1. In a medium bowl, combine hash browns, onion and oil. Spread in prepared baking dish. Place chicken breasts on top. Spread barbecue sauce evenly over chicken. Sprinkle with Monterey Jack.

2. Bake in preheated oven for 45 minutes or until chicken is no longer pink inside.

Chicken à la Candace

Makes 8 servings

This recipe is the brilliant creation of my friend Candace. It's elegant yet easy and is great for entertaining Italian-style. Serve it with hot pasta and a beautiful glass of wine.

- Preheat oven to 350°F (180°C)
- 13- by 9-inch (33 by 23 cm) glass baking dish, greased

1 cup	dry bread crumbs	250 mL
1/4 cup	freshly grated Parmesan cheese	60 mL
2 tbsp	dried oregano	30 mL
1 tbsp	dried parsley	15 mL
Pinch	salt	Pinch
Pinch	freshly ground black pepper	Pinch
8	boneless skinless chicken breasts, pounded to 1/2 inch (1 cm) thick	8
8	thin slices cooked ham	8
8	slices mozzarella cheese (1/4-inch/0.5 cm thick slices)	8
1	jar (6 oz/175 mL) oil-packed julienne-cut sun-dried tomatoes, drained	1
	Juice of 1 lemon	
1 cup	milk	250 mL
	Lemon wedges	

1. In a medium bowl, combine bread crumbs, Parmesan, oregano, parsley, salt and pepper. Set aside.

2. Place chicken breasts on a work surface with the smooth side down. Place 1 slice of ham on top of each, then 1 slice of mozzarella and 2 to 3 sun-dried tomato slices. Sprinkle with lemon juice. Starting with the narrow end, roll up like a jelly roll, securing with toothpicks.

3. Dip rolls in milk, then in bread crumb mixture, coating evenly. Discard any excess milk and bread crumb mixture. Place rolls, seam side down, in prepared baking dish.

4. Bake in preheated oven for 45 minutes or until golden brown and chicken is no longer pink inside. Serve with lemon wedges on the side.

Spiced Chicken Casserole

Makes 6 servings

This dish, fragrant with cinnamon and ginger, includes many ingredients common to Indian cuisine, but with the addition of the optional phyllo dough, it detours to Greece for an East-West fusion twist.

Tips

Look for phyllo pastry in the freezer section of your local grocery. To keep phyllo dough from drying out, work quickly when brushing it with butter and keep extra sheets covered with plastic until you're ready for them.

Toast almonds in a dry skillet over medium heat, stirring and shaking pan constantly, for 3 to 4 minutes or until golden and fragrant. Immediately transfer to a bowl and let cool.

- Preheat oven to 400°F (200°C)
- 8-cup (2 L) casserole dish, greased

1½ lbs	boneless skinless chicken thighs, cut in half	750 g
1½ tsp	salt, divided	7 mL
½ tsp	freshly ground black pepper, divided	2 mL
1 tbsp	olive oil	15 mL
2	carrots, diced	2
1	onion, thinly sliced	1
1	clove garlic, finely chopped	1
2¼ cups	reduced-sodium chicken broth	550 mL
1 tbsp	finely grated gingerroot	15 mL
¼ tsp	ground cinnamon	1 mL
½ cup	plain yogurt	125 mL
1 cup	cooked basmati rice	250 mL
½ cup	golden raisins	125 mL
½ cup	toasted almonds, chopped	125 mL
6	sheets phyllo pastry, thawed (optional)	6
¼ cup	butter, melted (optional)	60 mL

1. Season chicken with ½ tsp (2 mL) of the salt and half the pepper. In a large Dutch oven or skillet, heat oil over medium-high heat. In batches, as necessary, cook chicken, turning once, for about 8 minutes or until browned on both sides. Transfer chicken to a plate.

2. Add carrots, onion and garlic to pan; sauté for 5 to 7 minutes or until softened. Add broth and bring to a boil, scraping up any brown bits from bottom of pan. Stir in ginger, cinnamon and the remaining salt and pepper. Remove from heat and stir in yogurt. Stir in rice, raisins, almonds and chicken.

3. Spoon into prepared casserole dish. If using phyllo, quickly brush each sheet with butter, stacking sheets on top of one another and place on casserole, molding to fit. Otherwise, cover casserole with lid or foil.

4. Bake in preheated oven for 25 to 30 minutes or until phyllo is golden and juices run clear when chicken is pierced.

Chicken Croquette Casserole

Makes 6 servings

My dear friend Cathy Sullivan is quite the cook, and she shares so many fabulous recipes. I couldn't resist adding this one to my book. It's an elegant choice when you're entertaining.

Tips

Freshly grated or shaved Parmesan cheese is always best right off the wedge, but prepackaged containers can be found in the refrigerated specialty cheese section of your local supermarket.

Liquid egg substitute works especially well in this recipe. It's a great ingredient to have on hand.

- Preheat oven to 375°F (190°C)
- 11- by 7-inch (28 by 18 cm) glass baking dish

$\frac{1}{2}$ cup	dry bread crumbs	125 mL
$\frac{1}{4}$ cup	freshly grated Parmesan cheese	60 mL
Pinch	salt	Pinch
Pinch	freshly ground black pepper	Pinch
Pinch	garlic powder	Pinch
1	egg, beaten	1
2 tbsp	milk	30 mL
$\frac{1}{2}$ cup	all-purpose flour	125 mL
6	boneless skinless chicken breasts, pounded to $\frac{1}{4}$ inch (0.5 cm) thick	6
3	slices prosciutto, cut in half lengthwise	3
3	shallots, chopped	3
3 oz	provolone cheese, cut into 6 slices	90 g
$\frac{1}{4}$ cup	butter or margarine	60 mL
1	red bell pepper, finely chopped	1
8 oz	mushrooms, sliced	250 g
$\frac{1}{2}$ tsp	minced garlic	2 mL
1 tsp	all-purpose flour	5 mL
$\frac{1}{2}$ cup	Marsala	125 mL
$\frac{1}{2}$ cup	chicken broth	125 mL
2	tomatoes, cut into wedges	2

1. In a shallow bowl, combine bread crumbs, Parmesan, salt, pepper and garlic powder. In another shallow bowl, whisk together egg and milk. Place $\frac{1}{2}$ cup (125 mL) flour in a shallow dish.

2. Place chicken breasts on a work surface with the smooth side down. Place 1 piece of prosciutto on top of each. Sprinkle evenly with shallots and top with a slice of provolone. Starting at one wide side, roll up to enclose filling, tucking in ends and pressing together firmly.

To neatly pound chicken breasts, work with one or two at a time and place them between large pieces of plastic wrap, leaving plenty of room between each breast and the edge of the wrap. Using a meat mallet or a rolling pin, start at the center of the breast and pound gently to flatten, moving out towards the edge and pounding to an even thickness. Flip the plastic wrap over and pound the other side to make sure it's even. You'll likely need to replace the plastic wrap for each batch, as it tends to tear as you pound.

3. Roll chicken in flour, coating evenly and shaking off excess. Dip in egg mixture, then in bread crumb mixture. Discard any excess flour, egg mixture and bread crumb mixture.

4. In a large skillet, melt butter over medium-high heat. Cook chicken rolls for 7 to 8 minutes or until chicken is no longer pink inside. Transfer chicken to a plate.

5. Add red pepper, mushrooms and garlic to fat remaining in skillet; sauté for 5 to 7 minutes or until softened. Sprinkle with 1 tsp (5 mL) flour and cook, stirring constantly, for 1 minute. Gradually stir in Marsala and broth; bring to a boil, stirring constantly. Reduce heat and simmer, stirring, until sauce thickens.

6. Place vegetables and tomatoes in bottom of baking dish and arrange chicken rolls on top. Pour sauce over top. Bake in preheated oven for 12 to 15 minutes or until bubbling.

Chicken Florentine with Wild Rice

Makes 4 servings

This beautiful dish features layers of long-grain and wild rice, chicken and spinach, covered with a fabulous cheesy, creamy sauce.

Tips

White rice works beautifully in this recipe in place of the long-grain and wild rice blend. Cook white rice according to package instructions before adding it to the baking dish in step 6.

If you like sharp cheese, use extra-sharp (extra-old) Cheddar.

- Preheat oven to 375°F (190°C)
- 13- by 9-inch (33 by 23 cm) glass baking dish, greased

1 cup	long-grain and wild rice blend (6 oz/175 g)	250 mL
¼ cup	all-purpose flour	60 mL
½ tsp	salt	2 mL
½ tsp	freshly ground black pepper	2 mL
4	boneless skinless chicken breasts	4
1 tbsp	olive oil	15 mL
1 tbsp	butter	15 mL
1 tbsp	all-purpose flour	15 mL
¼ cup	dry white wine	60 mL
½ cup	chicken broth	125 mL
½ cup	milk	125 mL
1 cup	shredded Cheddar cheese, divided	250 mL
1	bag (10 oz/300 g) fresh spinach, stems removed	1

1. In a medium saucepan, bring 2¼ cups (550 mL) water to a boil over high heat. Stir in rice mix, reduce heat to low, cover and simmer for 25 minutes or until rice is tender and most of the liquid is absorbed. Remove from heat and let stand, covered, for 5 minutes. Fluff with a fork. Set aside.

2. Meanwhile, in a medium bowl, combine ¼ cup (60 mL) flour, salt and pepper. Dredge chicken in seasoned flour, coating evenly and shaking off excess. Discard excess flour mixture.

3. In a large skillet, heat oil and butter over medium-high heat. Cook chicken, turning once, for about 8 minutes or until browned on both sides. Transfer chicken to a plate.

When you're assembling the casserole, the spinach will fill the dish and be slightly mounded. You may need to press it down a little to keep it from falling out, but it will wilt quickly in the oven, so you don't have to worry about the dish overflowing.

4. Stir 1 tbsp (15 mL) flour into fat remaining in skillet and cook, stirring constantly, for 1 minute. Reduce heat to low and gradually stir in wine, broth and milk, scraping up any brown bits from bottom of pan. Simmer, stirring constantly, until thick and bubbling. Add ¾ cup (175 mL) of the cheese, stirring until melted. Remove from heat and set aside.

5. Spoon cooked rice into prepared baking dish. Place chicken on top and cover with spinach. Pour cheese sauce over top and sprinkle with the remaining ¼ cup (60 mL) cheese.

6. Bake in preheated oven for 30 minutes or until chicken is no longer pink inside.

King Ranch Chicken Casserole

Here's my take on the famous King Ranch Casserole — classic, delectable comfort food with both a chicken version and a beef version (see page 194). Grilling the chicken first gives this dish its incredible flavor.

- Preheat barbecue grill to medium-high
- 13- by 9-inch (33 by 23 cm) glass baking dish, greased

2 lbs	boneless skinless chicken thighs	1 kg
2 tbsp	butter	30 mL
1	onion, sliced	1
1	can (10 oz/284 mL) diced tomatoes and mild green chiles	1
1	can (10 oz/284 mL) condensed cream of mushroom soup	1
1	can (10 oz/284 mL) condensed cream of chicken soup	1
10	6-inch (15 cm) flour tortillas, torn into bite-size pieces	10
2 cups	shredded Monterey Jack cheese	500 mL
1/4 cup	shredded Cheddar cheese	60 mL

1. Place chicken thighs on preheated barbecue and grill, turning once, for 5 to 7 minutes per side or until juices run clear when chicken is pierced. Let cool slightly, then cut into cubes.

2. Meanwhile, preheat oven to 350°F (180°C).

3. In a skillet, melt butter over medium heat. Sauté onion for 5 to 7 minutes or until softened. Stir in tomatoes and chiles, mushroom soup and chicken soup. Remove from heat.

4. Spread half the tortilla pieces in bottom of prepared baking dish. Layer with half the onion mixture, half the chicken and half the Monterey Jack. Repeat layers. Sprinkle Cheddar cheese over top.

5. Cover and bake in preheated oven for 20 minutes. Uncover and bake for 10 minutes or until bubbling.

Chicken Pie

Chicken pie is comfort food at its best, and one of my all-time favorites! Serve with your favorite green salad or fruit salad.

Tip

Look for puff pastry in the freezer section of your grocery store. The size of the package may vary from 14 to 18 oz (400 to 540 g). Just use half a package and roll out to fit the dish as necessary.

- Preheat oven to 350°F (180°C)
- 8-cup (2 L) casserole dish

3 tbsp	butter	45 mL
¼ cup	all-purpose flour	60 mL
2 cups	chicken broth	500 mL
¼ cup	light (5%) cream	60 mL
1 tsp	salt	5 mL
Pinch	freshly ground black pepper	Pinch
3 cups	cubed cooked chicken	750 mL
1	bag (16 oz/500 g) frozen mixed vegetables, thawed and drained	1
8 oz	frozen puff pastry, thawed	250 g

1. In a medium saucepan, melt butter over low heat. Sprinkle with flour and cook, stirring constantly, for 1 minute. Gradually whisk in broth, cream, salt and pepper. Increase heat to medium and cook, whisking constantly, for about 8 minutes or until thickened.

2. Pour enough sauce into casserole dish to just cover bottom. Add chicken and mixed vegetables. Cover with the remaining sauce. If necessary, on a floured surface, roll out puff pastry to about 1 inch (2.5 cm) larger than casserole dish. Place puff pastry on top of dish, pressing to seal edges. Cut a few ½-inch (1 cm) slits in pastry to vent steam.

3. Bake in preheated oven for 30 to 40 minutes or until pastry is golden.

Crescent Chicken Casserole

Makes 8 servings

This easy, delectable recipe uses leftover chicken or turkey, so it's ready in under 30 minutes. It's a great choice for bridal showers or baby showers, served with fresh fruit and mimosas.

- Preheat oven to 350°F (180°C)
- 13- by 9-inch (33 by 23 cm) glass baking dish, greased

2 tbsp	butter	30 mL
½ cup	chopped celery	125 mL
½ cup	chopped onion	125 mL
1	can (8 oz/227 mL) sliced water chestnuts, drained	1
1	can (10 oz/284 mL) condensed cream of chicken or mushroom soup	1
1	can (4 oz/114 mL) sliced mushrooms, drained (about ½ cup/125 mL)	1
3 cups	cubed cooked chicken or turkey	750 mL
⅔ cup	mayonnaise	150 mL
½ cup	sour cream	125 mL
1	can (8 oz/227 g) refrigerated crescent rolls	1
1 cup	shredded Swiss cheese	250 mL
½ cup	slivered almonds	125 mL
2 tbsp	melted butter	30 mL

1. In a large saucepan, melt 2 tbsp (30 mL) butter over medium heat. Sauté celery and onion for about 5 minutes or until softened. Stir in water chestnuts, chicken soup, mushrooms, chicken, mayonnaise and sour cream; cook, stirring constantly, until bubbling.

2. Pour into prepared baking dish. Separate crescent roll sheets into 2 squares and lay over mixture.

3. In a small bowl, combine cheese, almonds and melted butter. Sprinkle over dough.

4. Bake in preheated oven for 20 to 25 minutes or until topping is golden and filling is bubbling.

Chicken and Dumpling Casserole

This recipe reminds me of my grandmother's famous chicken and dumplings, but in a casserole. For me, it's the best of both worlds.

Tip

If you can't find buttermilk baking mix, use regular dry biscuit or baking mix and use buttermilk instead of plain milk.

- Preheat oven to 350°F (180°C)
- 13- by 9-inch (33 by 23 cm) glass baking dish, greased

1/4 cup	butter	60 mL
1/2 cup	chopped onion	125 mL
1/2 cup	chopped celery	125 mL
2	cloves garlic, minced	2
1/2 cup	all-purpose flour	125 mL
2	cans (each 10 oz/284 mL) condensed chicken broth	2
2 tsp	granulated sugar	10 mL
2 tsp	dried basil, divided	10 mL
1/2 tsp	freshly ground black pepper	2 mL
1/2 tsp	salt	2 mL
1	can (10 oz/284 mL) peas, drained	1
4 cups	cubed cooked chicken	1 L
2 cups	buttermilk baking mix	500 mL
2/3 cup	milk	150 mL

1. In a large saucepan, melt butter over medium heat. Sauté onion, celery and garlic for about 5 minutes or until softened. Sprinkle with flour and cook, stirring, for 1 minute. Gradually stir in broth, 1 cup (250 mL) water, sugar, half the basil, pepper and salt; bring to a boil. Stir in peas and chicken. Pour into prepared baking dish.

2. In a large bowl, combine buttermilk baking mix and the remaining basil. Using a fork, stir in milk until moistened. Drop by heaping spoonfuls on top of casserole.

3. Bake in preheated oven for 45 minutes or until dumplings are golden brown.

Brown Rice and Chicken Bake

Makes 8 to 10 servings

Nutrient-dense brown rice contributes wonderful flavor to this healthy dish, which is also low in fat, thanks to the use of breast meat and fat-free mayonnaise.

Tips

If you only have white rice on hand, feel free to substitute it for the brown rice.

If you're concerned about your salt intake, choose reduced-sodium soy sauce.

- Preheat oven to 350°F (180°C)
- 13- by 9-inch (33 by 23 cm) glass baking dish, greased

1	package (10 oz/300 g) frozen green peas (about 1½ cups/375 mL)	1
3 cups	cooked long-grain brown rice	750 mL
2 cups	cubed cooked chicken breasts	500 mL
½ cup	fat-free mayonnaise	125 mL
⅓ cup	slivered almonds (toasted if desired)	75 mL
1 tbsp	soy sauce	15 mL
¼ tsp	freshly ground black pepper	1 mL
¼ tsp	garlic powder	1 mL
¼ tsp	dried parsley	1 mL

1. In a large bowl, combine peas, rice, chicken, mayonnaise, almonds, soy sauce, black pepper, garlic powder and parsley. Spoon into prepared baking dish.

2. Cover and bake in preheated oven for 15 to 20 minutes or until bubbling.

À la King Chicken Casserole

Makes 4 to 6 servings

The combination of chicken, cream, mushrooms and peas gives this childhood favorite great flavor — and it's so filling! Serve over hot biscuits, English muffins or rice.

Tip

To lighten up this recipe, use reduced-fat cream of mushroom soup and sour cream and increase the flour to 2 tbsp (30 mL).

- Preheat oven to 350°F (180°C)
- 11- by 7-inch (28 by 18 cm) glass baking dish, greased

1 lb	boneless skinless chicken breasts, cut into 1-inch (2.5 cm) strips	500 g
1 tbsp	all-purpose flour	15 mL
1	can (10 oz/284 mL) condensed cream of mushroom soup	1
1	jar (2 oz/57 mL) diced pimentos, drained	1
1 cup	sour cream	250 mL
½ cup	frozen green peas	125 mL
½ tsp	salt	2 mL
¼ tsp	freshly ground black pepper	1 mL

1. In a large bowl, toss chicken with flour. Stir in soup, pimentos, sour cream, peas, salt and pepper. Pour into prepared baking dish.

2. Cover and bake in preheated oven for 40 to 45 minutes or until chicken is no longer pink inside.

Mom's Chicken Hot Dish

My two gal pals Jayna and Debra Judd have lovingly shared their mother, Marilyn's, recipe for a true Minnesota hot dish! Hot dishes were once the mainstay of farmers, as they were an economical way to feed both family and farm workers. Serve this dish as the Judd family did, with dinner rolls and dill pickles.

Tip

For added flavor, use leftover grilled chicken.

- Preheat oven to 350°F (180°C)
- 13- by 9-inch (33 by 23 cm) glass baking dish, greased

12 oz	wide egg noodles	375 g
2 tbsp	butter	30 mL
1	onion, chopped	1
1 cup	chopped celery	250 mL
2	cans (each 10 oz/284 mL) condensed cream of chicken soup	2
4 cups	diced cooked chicken	1 L
2 cups	chicken broth	500 mL
½ tsp	salt	2 mL
½ tsp	freshly ground black pepper	2 mL

1. In a large pot of boiling water, cook egg noodles according to package directions until just tender. Drain and set aside.

2. Meanwhile, in a skillet, melt butter over medium heat. Sauté onion and celery for 5 to 7 minutes or until softened.

3. In a large bowl, combine noodles, onion mixture, soup, chicken, broth, salt and pepper. Pour into prepared baking dish.

4. Bake in preheated oven for 35 to 40 minutes or until bubbling.

Chicken and Artichoke Casserole

Makes 8 to 10 servings

Our family friend Pat Schermerhorn loves to entertain and often serves this fabulous recipe, especially when throwing a party with a Greek theme. A Greek salad makes the perfect accompaniment.

Tips

This casserole freezes well. For instructions, see page 13.

Packages of wild rice with seasonings are sold in a variety of flavors, any of which will work well in this recipe.

- Preheat oven to 350°F (180°C)
- 13- by 9-inch (33 by 23 cm) glass baking dish, greased

2 tbsp	butter	30 mL
10	mushrooms, sliced	10
10	green onions, chopped	10
2	cans (each 10 oz/284 mL) condensed cream of chicken soup	2
½ cup	heavy or whipping (35%) cream	125 mL
½ cup	dry sherry	125 mL
1 tsp	salt	5 mL
10	thick slices bacon, cooked crisp and crumbled	10
2	cans (each 14 oz/398 mL) artichoke hearts, drained and quartered	2
4 cups	chopped cooked chicken	1 L
3 cups	shredded mozzarella cheese	750 mL
2 cups	julienned carrots	500 mL
4 cups	cooked wild rice with seasonings (see tip, at left)	1 L
	Freshly grated Parmesan cheese	

1. In a large skillet, melt butter over medium-high heat. Sauté mushrooms and green onions for about 7 minutes or until mushrooms are tender. Stir in soup, cream, sherry and salt; bring to a boil. Cook, stirring, until slightly thickened.

2. In a large bowl, combine mushroom mixture, bacon, artichokes, chicken, mozzarella and carrots.

3. Spread wild rice in bottom of prepared baking dish. Spread chicken mixture over rice and sprinkle with Parmesan cheese to taste.

4. Cover and bake in preheated oven for 30 minutes. Uncover and bake for 15 minutes or until bubbling.

Chicken and Artichoke Casserole (page 148)

Tuna Noodle Casserole (page 105)

Tasty Chicken Casserole

This is a good way to use up leftover chicken. Grilled chicken would make it even more flavorful.

Tips

Non-alcoholic substitutions for vermouth include white grape juice, white wine vinegar and non-alcoholic white wine.

To save time, you can use thawed frozen chopped broccoli instead of fresh.

- Preheat oven to 350°F (180°C)
- 13- by 9-inch (33 by 23 cm) glass baking dish, greased

2 tbsp	butter	30 mL
2 tbsp	all-purpose flour	30 mL
1 cup	chicken broth	250 mL
2 tbsp	vermouth	30 mL
2 cups	cubed cooked chicken	500 mL
2 cups	cooked long-grain white rice	500 mL
2 cups	chopped broccoli	500 mL
2 cups	shredded Cheddar cheese	500 mL
3	slices bacon, cooked crisp and crumbled	3

1. In a large skillet, melt butter over medium heat. Sprinkle with flour and cook, stirring constantly, for 1 minute. Gradually stir in broth and vermouth; cook, stirring constantly, until smooth, thickened and beginning to boil. Stir in chicken and rice.

2. Spread broccoli in bottom of prepared baking dish. Pour chicken mixture over top. Sprinkle with cheese and bacon.

3. Bake in preheated oven for 30 minutes or until bubbling.

Chicken Bell Pepper Bake

Makes 4 servings

When I was a child, one of my favorite meals was stuffed bell peppers, but as an adult I found them a bit tedious to make. So I figured out how to recreate my favorite dish the quick and easy way. Serve with a spicy ketchup or tomato sauce on the side. Enjoy!

Tip

This dish is a great make ahead, as the flavors will marry and mellow after refrigeration. Let the baked dish cool completely, then cover and refrigerate for up to 3 days. Cover and reheat in a 350°F (180°C) oven for 20 to 25 minutes or until heated through.

- Preheat oven to 350°F (180°C)
- 11- by 7-inch (28 by 18 cm) glass baking dish, greased

4	large green or red bell peppers	4
1	can (10 oz/284 mL) condensed chicken broth	1
1	can (8 oz/227 mL) tomato sauce	1
2 cups	diced cooked chicken	500 mL
1 cup	instant white rice	250 mL
1/2 cup	chopped onion	125 mL
1/4 cup	freshly grated Parmesan cheese	60 mL

1. Cut stem ends off bell peppers. Cut peppers in half lengthwise and scoop out seeds. Set aside.

2. In a medium bowl, combine broth, tomato sauce, chicken, rice and onion. Spread in an even layer in prepared baking dish. Arrange peppers, cut side down, on top.

3. Cover and bake in preheated oven for 45 minutes or until rice is tender. Uncover, sprinkle with Parmesan and bake for 5 minutes or until cheese is melted.

Layered Chicken with Poblano Peppers and Cheese

If you haven't tried poblano peppers, you are in for a treat with this recipe. The Cheddar cheese tames the mild heat of the poblanos.

Tip

Tortilla chips are a staple in my Texas home. I save the crushed chips from every bag for casserole recipes like this one.

- Preheat broiler
- Rimmed baking sheet, lined with foil
- 11- by 7-inch (28 by 18 cm) glass baking dish, greased

4	poblano chile peppers, cut in half and seeded	4
2	cloves garlic, minced	2
2 cups	chopped cooked chicken breasts	500 mL
1 cup	shredded Cheddar cheese	250 mL
1 cup	fresh corn kernels (about 2 ears)	250 mL
1/2 cup	chopped onion	125 mL
1/2 cup	chopped zucchini	125 mL
1/2 cup	chopped red bell pepper	125 mL
2 tbsp	finely chopped fresh cilantro	30 mL
1/2 tsp	salt	2 mL
1/2 tsp	ground cumin	2 mL
1/2 tsp	paprika	2 mL
1/2 tsp	freshly ground black pepper	2 mL
1/4 cup	salsa	60 mL
3/4 cup	crushed tortilla chips, divided	175 mL
	Nonstick cooking spray	

1. Place poblano peppers, skin side up, on prepared baking sheet and use your hand to flatten them. Broil for 8 minutes or until blackened. Transfer to a sealable plastic bag, seal and let stand for 15 minutes. Peel and discard skins.

2. Preheat oven to 375°F (190°C).

3. In a large bowl, combine garlic, chicken, cheese, corn, onion, zucchini, red pepper, cilantro, salt, cumin, paprika and pepper. Stir in salsa until well combined.

4. Place poblano peppers, cut side up, in prepared baking dish. Top evenly with 1/4 cup (60 mL) of the tortilla chips. Spoon chicken mixture evenly over chips. Sprinkle with the remaining chips and lightly coat chips with cooking spray.

5. Bake for 20 minutes or until cheese is melted and casserole is bubbling.

Chicken, Sausage and Bean Cassoulet

Cassoulet is a stew from the Languedoc region of France, named after the *cassole*, a distinctive deep, round earthenware pot with slanting sides. Cassoulet always contains meat and beans, but otherwise can be basically whatever you want it to be. I love the ease of this savory recipe.

Tips

If you cannot find canned great Northern beans, any canned white beans will work well in this recipe.

Look for a packaged cornbread mix with 4 g of sugar or less per 28- to 38-g serving. If your mix requires you to add oil, water and egg rather than just milk or water, use 1⅓ cups (325 mL) dry mix, 1 egg, ½ cup (125 mL) milk or water and 2 tbsp (30 mL) vegetable oil when making the batter as directed in step 3. If you cannot find a packaged cornbread mix, simply make 1½ cups (375 mL) of your favorite cornbread batter and pour it over the chicken mixture.

- Preheat oven to 400°F (200°C)
- 12-cup (3 L) casserole dish, greased

1 lb	smoked sausage, sliced	500 g
1 lb	boneless skinless chicken breasts, chopped	500 g
1	can (14 to 19 oz/398 to 540 mL) great Northern beans, drained and rinsed	1
1	can (14 oz/398 mL) diced tomatoes, drained	1
1	can (10 oz/284 mL) condensed chicken broth	1
1½ tsp	dried thyme	7 mL
1	package (6 oz/170 g) cornbread mix	1
⅔ cup	milk	150 mL

1. In a large skillet, over medium-high heat, cook sausage, stirring, for 8 minutes or until browned on all sides. Using a slotted spoon, transfer sausage to a plate lined with paper towels.

2. Add chicken to fat remaining in skillet. Cook, stirring, for 5 minutes or until browned on all sides. Return sausage to skillet. Stir in beans, tomatoes, broth and thyme; bring to a boil. Spoon into prepared casserole dish.

3. In a bowl, combine cornbread mix and milk. Pour evenly over chicken mixture.

4. Bake in preheated oven for 30 to 35 minutes or until topping is golden and chicken is no longer pink inside. Let cool for 10 minutes before serving.

Mexican Chicken Lasagna

My dear friend Jean Phillips often serves this yummy layered dish. We love our Tex-Mex — and we love how easy this is to assemble!

Tips

If you like heat, use spicy enchilada sauce.

This recipe makes great leftovers. Store in an airtight container in the refrigerator for up to 3 days. Reheat in a 350°F (180°C) oven or in the microwave on High until heated through.

- Preheat oven to 350°F (180°C)
- 13- by 9-inch (33 by 23 cm) glass baking dish, greased

8 oz	cream cheese, softened	250 g
2 cups	shredded Monterey Jack cheese, divided	500 mL
1/4 cup	chopped fresh cilantro	60 mL
1	can (28 oz/796 mL) enchilada sauce, divided	1
12	6-inch (15 cm) corn tortillas	12
3 cups	shredded cooked chicken	750 mL
1	onion, chopped	1
	Additional chopped fresh cilantro	

1. In a medium bowl, combine cream cheese, $1\frac{1}{2}$ cups (375 mL) of the Monterey Jack and cilantro. Set aside.

2. Spread $\frac{2}{3}$ cup (150 mL) of the enchilada sauce in bottom of prepared baking dish. Pour the remaining sauce into a bowl.

3. Dip four tortillas into enchilada sauce in bowl and arrange over sauce in baking dish, overlapping as necessary. Spread one-third of the cream cheese mixture over tortillas. Top with 1 cup (250 mL) of the chicken and one-third of the onion. Repeat layers once. Dip the remaining 4 tortillas in sauce and arrange over second layer. Top with the remaining chicken and onion. Pour the remaining enchilada sauce over lasagna and sprinkle with the remaining Monterey Jack.

4. Bake in preheated oven for 45 minutes or until bubbling. Let cool for 5 to 10 minutes before cutting into squares. Serve garnished with cilantro.

Southwestern Chicken Lasagna

Flavors of the Southwest make this casserole a big hit!

Tips

Eggs separate more easily when they're cold, but are best warmed to room temperature before cooking or baking.

Look for 99% fat-free condensed tomato soup.

- Preheat oven to 375°F (190°C)
- 13- by 9-inch (33 by 23 cm) glass baking dish, greased

8	lasagna noodles	8
4	egg whites, lightly beaten	4
1	can (4½ oz/127 mL) chopped mild green chiles	1
3 cups	fat-free cottage cheese	750 mL
⅓ cup	chopped fresh parsley	75 mL
2 tbsp	olive oil	30 mL
2	cloves garlic, minced	2
1	red or green bell pepper, chopped	1
1 cup	chopped onion	250 mL
2	cans (each 10 oz/284 mL) reduced-sodium condensed tomato soup	2
1	can (10 oz/284 mL) enchilada sauce	1
1 tbsp	chili powder	15 mL
1 tsp	ground cumin	5 mL
½ tsp	salt	2 mL
¼ tsp	freshly ground black pepper	1 mL
4 cups	chopped cooked chicken breasts	1 L
1½ cups	finely shredded reduced-fat sharp (old) Cheddar cheese	375 mL
1 cup	finely shredded reduced-fat Monterey Jack cheese	250 mL

1. In a large pot of boiling water, cook lasagna noodles according to package directions until just tender. Drain and set aside.

2. In a large bowl, whisk together egg whites, chiles, cottage cheese and parsley. Set aside.

3. In a large nonstick skillet, heat oil over medium heat. Sauté garlic, red pepper and onion for 5 to 7 minutes or until softened. Stir in soup, enchilada sauce, chili powder, cumin, salt and pepper; bring to a boil. Reduce heat and simmer, stirring occasionally, for 10 minutes.

4. Place 4 lasagna noodles in prepared baking dish. Spread half the cottage cheese mixture over noodles. Top with half the sauce mixture, 2 cups (500 mL) of the chicken and half each of the Cheddar and Monterey Jack. Repeat layers.

5. Cover and bake in preheated oven for about 45 minutes or until bubbling. Uncover and bake for 5 minutes or until cheese is browned. Let cool for 15 minutes before cutting into squares.

Chicken Enchilada Casserole with Teriyaki Sauce

Makes 6 servings

East meets West in this flavorful chicken enchilada dish. The added heat is tamed by the cheese and sour cream.

Tip

Visit www.intensityacademy. com to find Carrot Karma Hot Sauce, Chai Thai Teriyaki and more! They're absolutely fantastic in this dish.

- Preheat oven to 350°F (180°C)
- 13- by 9-inch (33 by 23 cm) glass baking dish, greased

1 tbsp	olive oil	15 mL
1	onion, chopped	1
2 cups	shredded cooked chicken breasts	500 mL
1/4 cup	spicy barbecue sauce, such as Carrot Karma Hot Sauce (see tip, at left)	60 mL
3/4 cup	teriyaki sauce, such as Chai Thai Teriyaki (see tip, at left)	175 mL
8	6-inch (15 cm) corn tortillas	8
1	can (14 to 19 oz/398 to 540 mL) kidney beans, drained	1
2 cups	shredded Cheddar cheese	500 mL
2 cups	salsa	500 mL
1/2 cup	sour cream	125 mL

1. In a large skillet, heat oil over medium heat. Sauté onion for 5 to 7 minutes or until softened. Remove from heat and stir in chicken, barbecue sauce and teriyaki sauce.

2. Arrange 4 tortillas in prepared baking dish, overlapping as necessary. Top with chicken mixture, beans and half the cheese. Arrange the remaining tortillas on top. Top with salsa and the remaining cheese.

3. Bake in preheated oven for 30 to 35 minutes or until cheese is melted. Serve topped with sour cream.

Verde Chicken Casserole

Makes 6 to 8 servings

Verde means "green" in Spanish, and green chiles are amazing in this recipe! Serve with your favorite salsa on the side.

Tip

Substitute flour tortillas for the corn if you prefer.

- Preheat oven to 350°F (180°C)
- 13- by 9-inch (33 by 23 cm) glass baking dish, greased

1 tbsp	vegetable oil	15 mL
2	cloves garlic, minced	2
1 cup	chopped onion	250 mL
2	cans (each 4$\frac{1}{2}$ oz/127 mL) chopped mild green chiles	2
2	cans (each 10 oz/284 mL) condensed cream of chicken soup	2
1$\frac{1}{3}$ cups	chicken broth	325 mL
1 cup	sour cream	250 mL
$\frac{3}{4}$ tsp	salt	3 mL
$\frac{1}{2}$ tsp	ground cumin	2 mL
$\frac{1}{2}$ tsp	freshly ground black pepper	2 mL
24	6-inch (15 cm) corn tortillas	24
4 cups	shredded cooked chicken breasts	1 L
2 cups	shredded sharp (old) Cheddar cheese	500 mL

1. In a large saucepan, heat oil over medium heat. Sauté garlic and onion for 5 to 7 minutes or until softened. Stir in chiles, soup, broth, sour cream, salt, cumin and pepper; bring to a boil, stirring constantly. Remove from heat.

2. Spread 1 cup (250 mL) of the soup mixture in bottom of prepared baking dish. Arrange 6 tortillas over soup mixture, overlapping as necessary. Top with 1 cup (250 mL) chicken and $\frac{1}{2}$ cup (125 mL) cheese. Repeat layers three more times, ending with cheese. Spread the remaining soup mixture over cheese.

3. Bake in preheated oven for 30 minutes or until bubbling.

Jambalaya Casserole

My book club friend Robyn Canard shared this amazing recipe, which I adore because it reminds me of my Louisiana family roots on my mother's side. Pass hot pepper sauce at the table, if desired.

Tip

If you want to tone down the spice, use mild Italian sausage.

- Preheat oven to 350°F (180°C)
- 13- by 9-inch (33 by 23 cm) glass baking dish

3 cups	shredded rotisserie chicken	750 mL
2 cups	long-grain white rice	500 mL
1 lb	hot Italian sausage, cut into 1-inch (2.5 cm) chunks	500 g
8 oz	mushrooms, sliced	250 g
3	green onions, sliced	3
2	stalks celery, cut into ½-inch (1 cm) pieces	2
2	bay leaves	2
½ tsp	dried thyme	2 mL
1	can (10 oz/284 mL) condensed French onion soup	1
1	can (10 oz/284 mL) condensed beef broth	1
1	can (6 oz/170 mL) tomato paste	1
2 tbsp	butter, cut into small pieces	30 mL

1. In a large bowl, combine chicken, rice, sausage, mushrooms, green onions, celery, bay leaves and thyme.

2. In a medium bowl, combine soup, broth and tomato paste. Pour over chicken mixture and toss to coat. Pour into baking dish and dot with butter.

3. Cover and bake in preheated oven for 45 to 60 minutes or until rice is tender. Discard bay leaves.

Creamy Chicken Casserole

Makes 4 to 6 servings

This easy recipe reminds me of a layered lasagna, but with a creamy chicken mixture. It's great for a family meal.

Tip

For ease of blending and mixing, always soften cream cheese. Unwrap it, cut it into cubes, place it in a bowl and let it soften at room temperature.

- Preheat oven to 350°F (180°C)
- 9-inch (23 cm) square glass baking dish

3	small boneless skinless chicken breasts (about 12 oz/375 g total)	3
1	chicken bouillon cube	1
1/4 cup	hot water	60 mL
8 oz	cream cheese, softened	250 g
2 cups	shredded mozzarella cheese, divided	500 mL
1	jar (26 oz/738 mL) tomato pasta sauce	1
6	oven-ready lasagna noodles	6

1. Place chicken in a medium saucepan and add enough water to cover. Bring to a simmer over medium heat. Simmer for 20 minutes or until no longer pink inside. Drain. Shred chicken with two forks.

2. In a large bowl, dissolve bouillon in hot water. Stir in shredded chicken, cream cheese and half the mozzarella.

3. Spread one-third of the pasta sauce in bottom of baking dish. Top with half the chicken mixture, then with 3 lasagna noodles, breaking to fit as necessary. Repeat layers. Top with the remaining sauce and sprinkle with the remaining mozzarella.

4. Bake in preheated oven for 45 minutes or until bubbling.

Brunswick-Style Chicken Pot Pie

Brunswick stew, a traditional dish from the southeast United States, is usually tomato-based and includes lima beans, corn and other vegetables. Authentic recipes often include squirrel or rabbit, but chicken, pork and beef are common too.

Tip

When draining tomatoes, freeze the liquid, then add it to soups, stews and sauces.

- Preheat oven to 350°F (180°C)
- 11- by 7-inch (28 by 18 cm) glass baking dish, greased

1/2 cup	all-purpose flour	125 mL
1/2 tsp	freshly ground black pepper	2 mL
6	boneless skinless chicken breasts	6
1/4 cup	butter	60 mL
1 cup	chopped onion	250 mL
1	can (10 oz/284 mL) condensed chicken broth	1
1	can (14 oz/398 mL) stewed tomatoes, drained	1
1	can (11 oz/312 mL) whole kernel corn, drained	1
1	package (10 oz/300 g) frozen baby lima beans, thawed	1
1 1/2 tsp	dried thyme	7 mL
1	can (10 oz/300 g) refrigerated biscuits	1

1. In a shallow bowl, combine flour and pepper. Dredge chicken in seasoned flour, coating evenly and shaking off excess. Discard excess flour mixture.

2. In a large skillet, melt butter over medium-high heat. In batches as necessary, cook chicken, turning once, for 8 to 10 minutes or until no longer pink inside. Transfer to a plate and let cool slightly.

3. Add onion to fat remaining in skillet; sauté for 3 to 5 minutes or until softened. Stir in broth, tomatoes, corn, beans and thyme; bring to a boil. Reduce heat to low, cover and simmer for 15 to 20 minutes or until beans are tender.

4. Shred chicken with a fork and stir into onion mixture. Pour into prepared baking dish. Cut biscuits into quarters and arrange over chicken mixture.

5. Bake in preheated oven for 15 to 20 minutes or until biscuits are golden brown.

Chicken Noodle and Green Pea Casserole

This easy recipe is made with readily available pantry ingredients, and it's ready in under 30 minutes, so it's a perfect dinner for those hectic weeknights.

Tips

Cook extra noodles when you're preparing another meal and save some for this dish. You'll need 2 cups (500 mL) cooked. Store them in the refrigerator for up to 2 days and give them a rinse in hot water before assembling the casserole.

If you have leftover shredded or diced chicken breast, by all means substitute it for the canned chicken. You'll need about 1½ cups (375 mL).

Use sharp (old) or even extra-sharp (extra-old) Cheddar cheese for a stronger cheese flavor.

- Preheat oven to 350°F (180°C)
- 8-inch (20 cm) square glass baking dish, greased

4 oz	wide egg noodles	125 g
2	cans (each 5 oz/142 g) chunk white chicken, drained	2
1	can (15 oz/425 mL) small green peas, drained	1
1¼ cups	shredded Cheddar cheese, divided	300 mL
¾ cup	mayonnaise	175 mL
1 tsp	dry mustard	5 mL
½ tsp	freshly ground black pepper	2 mL

1. In a large pot of boiling water, cook egg noodles according to package directions until just tender. Drain.

2. In a large bowl, combine chicken, peas, noodles, 1 cup (250 mL) of the cheese, mayonnaise, mustard and pepper. Spoon into prepared baking dish and sprinkle with the remaining cheese.

3. Bake in preheated oven for 25 minutes or until heated through.

Classic Turkey Divan

It is a tradition in my family to make this casserole on the Saturday or Sunday after Thanksgiving. We serve it over steaming hot white rice.

Variation

For an unusual twist, substitute curry powder for the nutmeg.

- Preheat broiler, with rack set 3 to 5 inches (7.5 to 12.5 cm) from heat source
- 11- by 7-inch (28 by 18 cm) glass baking dish

1½ lbs	broccoli, chopped	750 g
¼ cup	butter	60 mL
¼ cup	all-purpose flour	60 mL
1½ cups	chicken broth	375 mL
⅛ tsp	ground nutmeg	0.5 mL
½ cup	heavy or whipping (35%) cream	125 mL
1 cup	freshly grated Parmesan cheese, divided	250 mL
5	large slices cooked turkey breast	5

1. In a large pot of boiling salted water, cook broccoli for about 5 minutes or until tender-crisp. Drain and keep hot.

2. Meanwhile, in a medium saucepan, melt butter over low heat. Sprinkle with flour and cook, stirring constantly, for 1 minute. Gradually stir in broth and bring to a boil, stirring constantly. Boil, stirring, for 1 minute. Remove from heat and stir in nutmeg. Gently stir in cream and half the cheese.

3. Place hot broccoli in baking dish. Top with turkey slices. Pour sauce over meat and sprinkle with the remaining cheese.

4. Broil for 2 to 3 minutes or until cheese is golden brown.

Turkey and Green Onion Phyllo Layer

Makes 8 servings

This layered dish is extremely elegant, so it's a great choice when you're entertaining.

Tips

I use kitchen shears to slice green onions.

Look for phyllo pastry in the freezer section of your local grocery. To keep phyllo dough from drying out, work quickly when brushing it with butter and keep extra sheets covered with plastic until you're ready for them.

- Preheat oven to 400°F (200°C)
- 13- by 9-inch (33 by 23 cm) glass baking dish, greased

1 tbsp	butter	15 mL
1 cup	thinly sliced green onions	250 mL
4 cups	diced cooked turkey	1 L
¾ cup	chopped fresh parsley	175 mL
2 tsp	ground cumin	10 mL
1 tsp	minced garlic	5 mL
½ tsp	salt	2 mL
¼ tsp	freshly ground black pepper	1 mL
2	eggs, beaten	2
2	cans (each 4½ oz/127 mL) chopped mild green chiles	2
1½ cups	shredded Monterey Jack cheese	375 mL
½ cup	sliced black olives	125 mL
½ cup	golden raisins	125 mL
½ cup	chopped almonds	125 mL
10	sheets phyllo pastry, thawed	10
½ cup	melted butter	125 mL
	Sour cream and sliced black olives	

1. In a large skillet, melt 1 tbsp (15 mL) butter over medium heat. Sauté green onions for about 3 minutes or until tender. Remove from heat and stir in turkey, parsley, cumin, garlic, salt and pepper. Stir in eggs, chiles, cheese, olives, raisins and almonds.

2. Cut phyllo sheets in half widthwise. Working with one sheet at a time, brush each sheet with melted butter and layer it in prepared baking dish until 10 sheets are buttered. Spread turkey mixture evenly over phyllo. Working with one sheet at a time, brush 10 more phyllo sheets with butter and lay them over the filling. Using a serrated knife, cut through pastry into 8 squares.

3. Bake in preheated oven for 35 to 45 minutes or until crust is golden brown. Serve garnished with sour cream and olives.

Thanksgiving Leftover Casserole

When Thanksgiving is over, here is a unique way to combine all the leftovers into one casserole. My friend Carol Johnson always amazes me with how she can make a meal out of almost any ingredient lineup. Thank you, Carol, for this idea!

Tip

Be creative with this recipe and use your favorite Thanksgiving leftovers.

- Preheat oven to 350°F (180°C)
- 11- by 7-inch (28 by 18 cm) glass baking dish, greased

½ cup	butter	125 mL
1½ cups	chopped onion	375 mL
¼ cup	all-purpose flour	60 mL
1 tsp	salt	5 mL
½ tsp	freshly ground black pepper	2 mL
2 cups	chicken broth	500 mL
1 tbsp	heavy or whipping (35%) cream	15 mL
1 tbsp	cognac	15 mL
2 cups	leftover stuffing	500 mL
½ cup	cranberry sauce	125 mL
2 cups	shredded roast turkey	500 mL
1 cup	turkey gravy	250 mL
1 cup	cooked carrots	250 mL
1 cup	mashed potatoes	250 mL

1. In a medium saucepan, melt butter over medium heat. Sauté onion for 5 to 7 minutes or until lightly browned. Sprinkle with flour, salt and pepper; cook, stirring constantly, for 1 minute. Gradually stir in broth, cream and cognac; cook, stirring constantly, for 4 to 5 minutes or until thickened.

2. Spread stuffing in prepared baking dish. Add layers of cranberry sauce, turkey, gravy, carrots and mashed potatoes. Pour onion mixture over top.

3. Bake in preheated oven for 45 minutes or until bubbling.

Turkey and Rice Enchiladas

This is not your traditional enchilada recipe, but it's very pleasing nonetheless. Serve with your favorite toppings, such as shredded lettuce, chopped tomatoes, sliced black olives and green onions, sour cream and salsa.

Tips

I like to use a nonstick skillet when browning ground turkey, chicken or beef, as it eliminates the need for oil or butter.

Look for enchilada sauce in the international foods section of your local market.

- Preheat oven to 350°F (180°C)
- 13- by 9-inch (33 by 23 cm) glass baking dish, greased

1 lb	ground turkey	500 g
1	small onion, chopped	1
1	clove garlic, minced	1
1	can (6 oz/170 mL) tomato paste	1
3 cups	shredded Cheddar cheese, divided	750 mL
1 cup	cooked long-grain white rice	250 mL
1 cup	salsa	250 mL
1 tbsp	chili powder	15 mL
1½ tsp	dried oregano	7 mL
1 tsp	salt	5 mL
Pinch	hot pepper flakes	Pinch
12	6-inch (15 cm) flour tortillas	12
1	can (16 oz/454 mL) enchilada sauce	1

1. In a nonstick skillet, over medium-high heat, cook turkey, onion and garlic, breaking turkey up with the back of a spoon, for 8 to 10 minutes or until turkey is no longer pink. Stir in tomato paste, 2 cups (500 mL) of the cheese, rice, salsa, chili powder, oregano, salt and hot pepper flakes. Reduce heat and simmer, stirring often, for 5 minutes.

2. Place tortillas on a work surface. Spread ½ cup (125 mL) turkey mixture down the middle of each tortilla and roll up into a log.

3. Spread ½ cup (125 mL) enchilada sauce in bottom of prepared baking dish. Place rolled tortillas seam side down on top of sauce. Pour the remaining sauce over top. Sprinkle with the remaining cheese.

4. Bake in preheated oven for 25 to 30 minutes or until bubbling.

Baked Turkey and Ham Casserole

This recipe comes to you courtesy of my friend Beth Markin. Her grandmother created it back in the mid-1970s, when casseroles were at a peak in their popularity.

Tip

It's always a good idea to taste a dish before adding salt and pepper, then adjust the seasoning to your taste.

- Preheat oven to 375°F (190°C)
- 11- by 7-inch (28 by 18 cm) glass baking dish, greased

2 tbsp	butter	30 mL
2	green bell peppers, cut into thin strips	2
2 tbsp	all-purpose flour	30 mL
3 cups	chicken broth	750 mL
1 lb	cooked turkey, cut into thin strips	500 g
4 oz	smoked ham, cut into thin strips	125 g
1 tbsp	dried parsley	15 mL
1 tbsp	Worcestershire sauce	15 mL
½ tsp	salt	2 mL
¼ tsp	freshly ground white pepper	1 mL
1 cup	milk	250 mL
10 oz	thin egg noodles	300 g
6	saltine crackers, crushed	6
2 tbsp	freshly grated Parmesan cheese	30 mL

1. In a large saucepan, melt butter over medium heat. Sauté green peppers for about 5 minutes or until softened. Sprinkle with flour and cook, stirring constantly, for 1 minute. Gradually stir in broth and bring to a boil, stirring constantly. Reduce heat and simmer, stirring occasionally, for 5 minutes or until thickened.

2. Stir in turkey, ham, parsley, Worcestershire sauce, salt and pepper; increase heat to medium and bring to a boil. Gradually stir in milk; reduce heat and simmer, stirring constantly, for 5 minutes or until slightly thickened.

3. Meanwhile, in a large pot of boiling water, cook noodles according to package directions until just tender. Drain.

4. Place cooked noodles in prepared baking dish. Top with turkey mixture. Sprinkle with cracker crumbs and cheese.

5. Bake in preheated oven for 25 minutes or until lightly browned.

Pork Casseroles

Three-Cheese Ham Casserole. 168
Ham and Eggplant Parmigiana 169
Ham and Noodle Bake 170
Ham and Potato Bake. 171
Potato, Green Bean and Ham Casserole. 172
Southern Ham and Greens with Cornbread Crust 173
Bacon, Ham and Cheese Casserole 174
Pork Chops and Savory Stuffing 175
Roasted Butternut Squash and Bacon Pasta Bake 176
Latin Pork Chop Casserole 177
South of the Border Pork Chop Casserole. 178
Pork Chop and Potato Scallop .179
Pork, Apple and Sweet Potato Casserole 180
Pork and Creamed Cabbage Casserole. 181
Mu Shu Pork Casserole 182
Pork Rib Bake. 183
Leftover Pork and Baked Potato Casserole 184
Sausage, Sweet Pepper and Rice Casserole. 185
Carnitas Casserole with Mole .186
Spicy Sausage, Artichoke and Sun-Dried Tomato Bake 188
Sausage, Tomato and Rice Casserole 190
Topsy-Turvy Pizza Casserole. .191
Cheesy Spaghetti Casserole 192

Three-Cheese Ham Casserole

Ham and cheese is a classic through and through, and here you get *three* cheeses: mozzarella, Cheddar and cream cheese.

Tip

This casserole freezes well. For instructions, see page 13.

- Preheat oven to 400°F (200°C)
- 13- by 9-inch (33 by 23 cm) glass baking dish, greased

8 oz	wide egg noodles	250 g
1	can (10 oz/284 mL) condensed cream of mushroom soup	1
8 oz	cream cheese, softened	250 g
2/3 cup	milk	150 mL
6	baby carrots, chopped	6
4	green onions, thinly sliced	4
1	package (10 oz/300 g) frozen asparagus, thawed	1
2 cups	chopped cooked ham	500 mL
1 1/2 cups	broccoli florets	375 mL
2 cups	shredded mozzarella cheese, divided	500 mL
1 cup	shredded Cheddar cheese, divided	250 mL
1/2 cup	seasoned dry bread crumbs	125 mL

1. In a large pot of boiling water, cook egg noodles according to package directions until just tender. Drain and set aside.

2. In a large bowl, combine soup, cream cheese and milk. Stir in cooked noodles, carrots, green onions, asparagus, ham and broccoli.

3. Spread half the ham mixture in prepared baking dish. Sprinkle with half the mozzarella and half and the Cheddar. Top with the remaining ham mixture.

4. In a bowl, combine the remaining mozzarella, the remaining Cheddar and bread crumbs. Sprinkle over casserole.

5. Bake in preheated oven for 30 minutes or until lightly browned.

Ham and Eggplant Parmigiana

This recipe is prepared much like veal or chicken Parmesan, but with ham. It makes a nice change of pace.

Tip

Cornbread crumbs are a delicious substitute for the bread crumbs.

• 11- by 7-inch (28 by 18 cm) glass baking dish, greased

¾ cup	dry bread crumbs	175 mL
½ tsp	salt	2 mL
½ tsp	freshly ground black pepper	2 mL
1	egg	1
4	slices cooked ham (¼-inch/0.5 cm thick slices)	4
4	slices eggplant (½-inch/1 cm thick slices)	4
2 tbsp	olive oil, divided	30 mL
1	can (14 oz/398 mL) pasta-style stewed tomatoes	1
⅓ cup	sour cream	75 mL
¼ cup	freshly grated Parmesan cheese	60 mL
1 cup	shredded mozzarella cheese	250 mL

1. In a shallow bowl, combine bread crumbs, salt and pepper. In another shallow bowl, beat egg. Dip ham slices in egg, then in crumb mixture, coating evenly. Place breaded ham on a plate. Dip eggplant in egg, then in crumb mixture, coating evenly. Add to plate and refrigerate for 15 minutes.

2. Preheat oven to 350°F (180°C).

3. In a large skillet, heat half the oil over medium-high heat. Cook ham, turning once, for 4 to 5 minutes per side or until browned on both sides. Arrange in prepared baking dish.

4. Add the remaining oil to skillet. Cook eggplant, turning once, for 3 to 4 minutes per side or until golden brown on both sides. Arrange over ham.

5. In a medium bowl, combine tomatoes and sour cream. Spoon over eggplant and sprinkle with Parmesan.

6. Bake for 20 minutes. Sprinkle with mozzarella and bake for 5 minutes or until cheese is melted and bubbling.

Ham and Noodle Bake

Makes 4 to 6 servings

Here's an easy weeknight meal, ready in about 30 minutes!

Variation

Add 1 cup (250 mL) cooked broccoli florets or chopped spinach to the ham mixture with the cooked noodles.

- Preheat oven to 350°F (180°C)
- 13- by 9-inch (33 by 23 cm) glass baking dish, greased

12 oz	extra-wide egg noodles	375 g
1 tbsp	olive oil	15 mL
1	onion, chopped	1
2 cups	cubed cooked ham	500 mL
1	can (10 oz/284 mL) condensed cream of mushroom soup	1
2 cups	shredded extra-sharp (extra-old) Cheddar cheese, divided	500 mL
¾ tsp	freshly ground black pepper	3 mL

1. In a large pot of boiling water, cook egg noodles according to package directions until just tender. Drain.

2. Meanwhile, in a large saucepan, heat oil over medium heat. Sauté onion and ham for 5 to 7 minutes or until onion is softened. Stir in soup in and bring to a boil. Reduce heat to low and stir in half the cheese until melted.

3. Stir cooked noodles into ham mixture, then spread in prepared baking dish. Sprinkle with pepper and the remaining cheese.

4. Bake in preheated oven for 20 to 25 minutes or until bubbling.

Ham and Potato Bake

Makes 4 servings

This recipe is a treasured family heirloom — I found it tucked into one of my mother's cookbooks, handwritten on a sheet of paper with my great-grandmother's name.

Tips

The original recipe called for a ham steak, which I assume would have been about 1½ lbs (750 g). I substituted 4 cups (1 L) diced cooked ham, which works beautifully. You can find diced ham prepackaged in the meat section of your supermarket.

Can't find Yukon gold potatoes? No problem: the original recipe called for baking potatoes. I love the creaminess of Yukon gold, so I subbed them in.

- Preheat oven to 350°F (180°C)
- 13- by 9-inch (33 by 23 cm) glass baking dish, greased

2 cups	Yukon gold potatoes, thinly sliced	500 mL
½ tsp	salt	2 mL
½ tsp	freshly ground black pepper	2 mL
1	large white onion, thinly sliced	1
4 cups	diced cooked ham	1 L
2 tsp	dried thyme	10 mL
2 cups	milk	500 mL

1. Arrange potatoes in prepared baking dish and sprinkle with salt and pepper. Layer onion and ham on top. Sprinkle with thyme. Pour milk over ham.

2. Cover and bake in preheated oven for 1 hour or until potatoes are tender.

Potato, Green Bean and Ham Casserole

Makes 8 servings

I am so fortunate to have this in my recipe lineup for weeknight meals. My little girl, Kennedy, loves potatoes (of course), green beans and ham, so I put it all in a one-dish meal, and she savors it every single time!

- Preheat oven to 400°F (200°C)
- 13- by 9-inch (33 by 23 cm) glass baking dish, greased

2 lbs	small red-skinned potatoes, thinly sliced	1 kg
3	cloves garlic, thinly sliced	3
2	bay leaves	2
3 cups	whole milk	750 mL
4 oz	green beans, trimmed	125 g
½ cup	chopped deli-smoked ham	125 mL
1 cup	shredded Swiss cheese	250 mL
½ tsp	salt	2 mL
¼ tsp	freshly ground black pepper	1 mL
⅛ tsp	ground nutmeg	0.5 mL

1. In a large saucepan, combine potatoes, garlic, bay leaves and milk; bring to a boil over medium heat, stirring constantly. Reduce heat and simmer, stirring frequently, for 10 minutes. Remove from heat and let stand for 10 minutes. Drain in a colander set over a bowl, reserving 1 cup (250 mL) of the milk mixture. Discard bay leaves.

2. Meanwhile, in a pot of boiling water, cook green beans for 3 minutes or until tender-crisp. Rinse under cold water and drain.

3. Arrange half the potatoes in prepared baking dish. Layer green beans and ham over potatoes. Sprinkle with half each of the cheese, salt and pepper. Arrange the remaining potatoes on top. Sprinkle with remaining cheese, salt and pepper. Stir nutmeg into reserved milk mixture; pour over potatoes.

4. Cover with foil and cut three 1-inch (2.5 cm) slits in foil. Bake in preheated oven for 20 minutes. Uncover and bake for 20 minutes or until cheese begins to brown. Let cool for 10 minutes before serving.

Southern Ham and Greens with Cornbread Crust

From the Deep South of the United States comes a casserole rich with traditional ingredients.

Tips

If you can't find frozen mustard greens, use 2 lbs (1 kg) fresh, trim off the tough stems and cook in a large pot of boiling water for about 5 minutes or until tender. Drain well, then chop and add in step 2.

For a slightly different flavor, use collard greens instead of the mustard greens.

Instead of making the cornbread batter from scratch, you can substitute two 6-oz (170 g) packages (or 2⅔ cups/650 mL) of dry cornbread mix, prepared according to package directions.

- Preheat oven to 425°F (220°C)
- 13- by 9-inch (33 by 23 cm) glass baking dish, greased

2 tbsp	olive oil	30 mL
4 cups	chopped cooked ham	1 L
3 tbsp	all-purpose flour	45 mL
3 cups	chicken broth	750 mL
1	package (16 oz/500 g) frozen petite mixed vegetables, thawed	1
1	package (16 oz/500 g) frozen chopped mustard greens, thawed	1
1	can (14 to 19 oz/398 to 540 mL) black-eyed peas, drained and rinsed	1
½ tsp	hot pepper flakes	2 mL
1½ cups	white cornmeal	375 mL
½ cup	all-purpose flour	125 mL
2 tsp	baking powder	10 mL
1 tsp	granulated sugar	5 mL
½ tsp	salt	2 mL
2	eggs, lightly beaten	2
1½ cups	buttermilk	375 mL
¼ cup	melted butter or vegetable oil	60 mL

1. In a Dutch oven, heat oil over medium-high heat. Sauté ham for 5 minutes or until lightly browned. Sprinkle with 3 tbsp (45 mL) flour and cook, stirring constantly, for 1 minute. Gradually stir in broth and bring to a boil. Cook, stirring constantly, for 3 minutes or until thickened.

2. Stir in mixed vegetables and mustard greens; return to a boil. Cook, stirring often, for 5 minutes. Stir in peas and hot pepper flakes. Spoon into prepared baking dish.

3. In a large bowl, combine cornmeal, ½ cup (125 mL) flour, baking powder, sugar and salt. Stir in eggs, buttermilk and butter just until moistened. Pour batter evenly over ham mixture.

4. Bake in preheated oven for 20 to 25 minutes or until cornbread is golden brown and set.

Bacon, Ham and Cheese Casserole

Makes 8 servings

I love this dish because you can serve it at any time of day. If you serve it to guests, they'll badger you until you give them the recipe — don't say I didn't warn you!

Tips

I prefer center-cut bacon because it is leaner than regular side bacon, but regular bacon will do if you can't find center-cut.

If you have company for the weekend, this recipe can be prepared through step 3 the night before, covered and refrigerated overnight, then baked for breakfast the next morning. You'll need to increase the baking time by about 10 minutes.

Variation

Add 1 cup (250 mL) chopped fresh shrimp right before pouring the mixture into the baking dish.

- Preheat oven to 350°F (180°C)
- 13- by 9-inch (33 by 23 cm) glass baking dish, greased

8 oz	sliced bacon, preferably center-cut	250 g
8 oz	cooked ham, chopped	250 g
¾ cup	quick-cooking grits	175 mL
1 lb	pasteurized prepared cheese product, such as Velveeta, cubed	500 g
¼ cup	butter	60 mL
6	eggs, lightly beaten	6
½ cup	milk	125 mL
2 tsp	baking powder	10 mL
½ tsp	freshly ground black pepper	2 mL
Pinch	cayenne pepper	Pinch

1. In a large skillet, over medium-high heat, cook bacon until crisp. Using tongs, transfer to a plate lined with paper towels, reserving 1 tbsp (15 mL) drippings in the pan. Let cool, then crumble.

2. Add ham to drippings in pan, reduce heat to medium and sauté until browned. Remove from heat and set aside.

3. In a large saucepan, cook grits according to package directions. Remove from heat and stir in cheese and butter until melted. Stir in bacon, ham, eggs, milk, baking powder, black pepper and cayenne. Spread in prepared baking dish.

4. Bake in preheated oven for 45 minutes or until set.

Pork Chops and Savory Stuffing

This easy recipe results in succulent pork chops with a savory sausage stuffing.

Tip

Sweet pork has an affinity for fruit. You can substitute ¼ cup (60 mL) raisins, chopped dried plums or dried pears for the apricots.

- Preheat oven to 350°F (180°C)
- 13- by 9-inch (33 by 23 cm) glass baking dish, greased

4	boneless pork loin chops (about ½ inch/1 cm thick), trimmed of fat	4
½ tsp	salt	2 mL
½ tsp	freshly ground black pepper	2 mL
3 tbsp	olive oil, divided	45 mL
1 lb	mild Italian sausage (bulk or removed from casings)	500 g
2	stalks celery, chopped	2
1	onion, chopped	1
6	dried apricots, chopped	6
½	red bell pepper, chopped	½
1 cup	chicken broth	250 mL
¼ cup	chopped fresh parsley	60 mL
1 tsp	dried sage	5 mL
¼ cup	heavy or whipping (35%) cream	60 mL

1. Season pork chops with salt and pepper. In a large skillet, heat 2 tbsp (30 mL) of the oil over medium-high heat. Sear chops, turning once, for 1 to 2 minutes per side or until browned. Transfer to a plate and keep warm.

2. Add the remaining oil to skillet. Cook sausage, breaking it up with the back of a spoon, for 8 to 10 minutes or until no longer pink. Drain off fat. Add celery and onion; sauté for 5 minutes. Add apricots and red pepper; sauté for 3 minutes. Stir in broth, parsley and sage. Reduce heat to low and simmer for 5 to 6 minutes or until apricots are tender and plump. Stir in cream.

3. Spoon sausage mixture into prepared baking dish and arrange pork chops on top.

4. Cover and bake in preheated oven for 30 to 35 minutes or until just a hint of pink remains inside pork.

Roasted Butternut Squash and Bacon Pasta Bake

This hearty, fragrant and rich dish is wonderful at fall gatherings.

Tip

I simply love orecchiette ("little ears") pasta, which is very popular in the Apulia region of Italy. It is a small, round pasta with a cupped shape — perfect for holding sauce.

- Preheat oven to 425°F (220°C)
- Baking sheet, lined with foil, foil sprayed with nonstick cooking spray
- 11- by 7-inch (28 by 18 cm) glass baking dish, greased

¾ tsp	salt, divided	3 mL
½ tsp	dried rosemary	2 mL
¼ tsp	freshly ground black pepper	1 mL
¼ tsp	dried thyme	1 mL
3 cups	cubed peeled butternut squash (1-inch/2.5 cm cubes)	750 mL
6	slices bacon	6
1	onion, thinly sliced	1
3	cloves garlic, chopped	3
8 oz	orecchiette pasta	250 g
¼ cup	all-purpose flour	60 mL
2 cups	milk	500 mL
¾ cup	shredded provolone cheese	175 mL
⅓ cup	freshly grated Parmesan cheese	75 mL
	Nonstick cooking spray	

1. Combine ¼ tsp (1 mL) salt, rosemary, pepper and thyme. Spread squash in a single layer on prepared baking sheet and sprinkle with salt mixture. Bake in preheated oven for 45 minutes or until tender and lightly browned. Remove squash from oven and increase oven temperature to 450°F (230°C).

2. In a large nonstick skillet, over medium-high heat, cook bacon until crisp. Using tongs, transfer to a plate lined with paper towels, reserving 1½ tsp (7 mL) drippings in the pan. Let cool, then crumble.

3. Add onions and garlic to drippings in pan and reduce heat to medium; sauté for about 5 minutes or until tender.

4. In a large bowl, combine squash, bacon and onion mixture; set aside.

5. Meanwhile, in a large pot of boiling water, cook pasta according to package directions (omitting salt) until just tender. Drain and set aside.

Tip

Any type of mini pasta shapes will work in this recipe. I like elbow macaroni, mini shells and mini penne.

6. In another large skillet, combine flour and the remaining salt. Gradually whisk in milk and bring to a boil over medium-high heat, whisking constantly. Cook, whisking, for 1 minute or until slightly thickened. Remove from heat and stir in provolone until melted. Add pasta and toss well to combine.

7. Spoon pasta mixture into prepared baking dish. Top with squash mixture. Sprinkle evenly with Parmesan.

8. Bake for 15 minutes or until cheese is melted and beginning to brown.

Latin Pork Chop Casserole

Makes 4 servings

Serve this simple, speedy dish over Spanish rice, with guacamole salad and pinto beans on the side.

Tip

Look for Mexican white cheese dip in the dairy section of the grocery store. If you cannot find it, the traditional yellow cheese dip will work fine.

- Preheat oven to 375°F (190°C)
- 13- by 9-inch (33 by 23 cm) glass baking dish, greased

2½ cups	frozen roasted potatoes (about half a 20 oz/600 g bag)	625 mL
1	jar (15¼ oz/433 mL) Mexican white cheese dip, divided	1
4	boneless pork sirloin chops (about ½ inch/1 cm thick), trimmed of fat	4
1	can (10 oz/284 mL) Mexican-style diced tomatoes, drained	1

1. In a medium bowl, combine potatoes and cheese dip.

2. Arrange pork chops in prepared baking dish. Spoon potato mixture around the edges of pork chops. Pour diced tomatoes on top of pork chops.

3. Bake in preheated oven for 30 minutes or until just a hint of pink remains inside pork.

South of the Border Pork Chop Casserole

Makes 4 servings

This ridiculously easy casserole uses common pantry ingredients, for those nights when you just need to get something hearty and nutritious in the oven without thinking about it.

Tip

If pepper Jack cheese has too much spice for your taste, substitute Monterey Jack.

- Preheat oven to 350°F (180°C)
- 13- by 9-inch (33 by 23 cm) glass baking dish, greased

2 tbsp	olive oil	30 mL
4	thick-cut boneless pork loin chops (about 1 inch/2.5 cm thick), trimmed of fat	4
1	can (8 oz/227 mL) tomato sauce	1
1	envelope (1 1/4 oz/37 g) taco seasoning mix	1
1 1/2 cups	long-grain white rice	375 mL
1 cup	shredded pepper Jack cheese	250 mL

1. In a large skillet, heat oil over medium-high heat. Cook pork chops, turning once, for 3 to 4 minutes per side or until browned on both sides. Transfer to a plate and keep warm.

2. In a medium bowl, combine tomato sauce, taco seasoning, rice and 1 1/2 cups (375 mL) water. Pour into prepared baking dish. Arrange pork chops on top.

3. Cover and bake in preheated oven for 1 hour or until rice is tender and just a hint of pink remains inside pork. Sprinkle with cheese and bake, uncovered, for 5 minutes or until cheese is melted.

Pork Chop and Potato Scallop

This delicious recipe comes courtesy of my great friend Cathy Sullivan, who is a fabulous cook!

Tip

Add a 10-oz (300 g) package of frozen broccoli, thawed, with the potatoes for a complete meal in one dish. You'll need to switch to a 13- by 9-inch (33 by 23 cm) glass baking dish.

- Preheat oven to 375°F (190°C)
- 12-cup (3 L) shallow casserole dish, greased

1 tbsp	olive oil	15 mL
4	thick-cut boneless pork loin chops (about 1 inch/2.5 cm thick), trimmed of fat	4
1	can (10 oz/284 mL) condensed cream of mushroom soup	1
1/2 cup	sour cream	125 mL
2 tbsp	chopped fresh parsley	30 mL
4 cups	thinly sliced potatoes	1 L
1/2 tsp	salt	2 mL
1/2 tsp	freshly ground black pepper	2 mL

1. In a large nonstick skillet, heat oil over medium-high heat. Cook pork chops, turning once, for 3 to 4 minutes per side or until browned on both sides. Transfer to a plate and keep warm.

2. In a medium bowl, combine soup, sour cream, 1/4 cup (60 mL) water and parsley.

3. Arrange potatoes in casserole and sprinkle with salt and pepper. Pour in soup mixture. Top with pork chops.

4. Cover and bake in preheated oven for 1 hour or until potatoes and pork are tender.

Pork, Apple and Sweet Potato Casserole

This recipe is perfect for the beautiful days of fall, when the leaves are turning and there is a chill in the air. Serve with hot spiked apple cider.

Tip

Save a few minutes by tossing the potatoes and apples with the brown sugar and spreading the mixture on top of the pork. You'll lose the pretty layered effect but gain some time.

- Preheat oven to 350°F (180°C)
- 13- by 9-inch (33 by 23 cm) glass baking dish, greased

½ cup	all-purpose flour	125 mL
¾ tsp	salt, divided	3 mL
¾ tsp	freshly ground black pepper, divided	3 mL
6	thick-cut boneless pork loin chops (about 1 inch/2.5 cm thick), trimmed of fat	6
2 tbsp	vegetable oil	30 mL
4	sweet potatoes, peeled and sliced ¼ inch (0.5 cm) thick	4
½ cup	packed brown sugar	125 mL
3	apples, peeled, cored and cut into ½-inch (1 cm) rings	3
½ cup	dry white wine	125 mL

1. In a shallow dish, combine flour, ½ tsp (2 mL) salt and ½ tsp (2 mL) pepper. Dredge pork chops in seasoned flour, coating evenly and shaking off excess. Discard excess flour mixture.

2. In a large nonstick skillet, heat oil over medium-high heat until hot. Cook pork chops, turning once, for 3 to 4 minutes per side or until browned on both sides. Transfer to prepared baking dish.

3. Layer half the sweet potatoes over pork chops. Sprinkle with one-third of the brown sugar. Layer half the apples over sweet potatoes. Sprinkle with another third of the brown sugar. Layer with the remaining sweet potatoes, apples and brown sugar. Pour wine over mixture and sprinkle with the remaining salt and pepper.

4. Cover and bake in preheated oven for 1¼ hours or until just a hint of pink remains inside pork. Uncover and bake for 15 minutes or until apples are browned.

Pork and Creamed Cabbage Casserole

I have always loved creamed cabbage, and it is especially good in this pork casserole.

Tip

Save a few minutes by using a package of shredded cabbage or coleslaw mix.

- Preheat oven to 350°F (180°C)
- 9-inch (23 cm) square glass baking dish

1½ lbs	cabbage, shredded	750 g
2 tbsp	vegetable oil	30 mL
4	boneless pork loin chops (about ½ inch/1 cm thick), trimmed of fat	4
½ cup	heavy or whipping (35%) cream	125 mL
½ tsp	salt	2 mL
½ tsp	freshly ground black pepper	2 mL
½ tsp	caraway seeds	2 mL
½ tsp	paprika	2 mL
½ cup	shredded Swiss cheese	125 mL

1. In a large pot of boiling salted water, boil cabbage for 5 minutes. Drain and set aside.

2. Meanwhile, in a large nonstick skillet, heat oil over medium-high heat. Cook pork chops, turning once, for 3 to 4 minutes per side or until browned on both sides. Transfer to a plate and keep warm.

3. Add cream to skillet and bring to a boil. Reduce heat to medium and stir in cabbage, salt, pepper, caraway seeds and paprika. Cook, stirring occasionally, for 5 minutes.

4. Layer half the cabbage mixture in baking dish. Arrange pork chops on top. Spread the remaining cabbage mixture over pork chops and sprinkle with cheese.

5. Bake in preheated oven for 40 minutes or until just a hint of pink remains inside pork.

Mu Shu Pork Casserole

This recipe reminds me of the amazing mu shu pancakes from my favorite local Chinese restaurant.

Tips

Hoisin sauce is a Chinese barbecue sauce made from black beans. It adds a unique flavor that can't be duplicated with American barbecue sauce.

Prepare the pancake batter following the directions on a box of commercial pancake mix, or use your own recipe.

- Preheat oven to 350°F (180°C)
- 8-cup (2 L) casserole dish

½ cup	hoisin sauce	125 mL
¼ cup	orange juice	60 mL
2 tbsp	rice vinegar	30 mL
2 tbsp	reduced-sodium soy sauce	30 mL
1 tbsp	finely grated gingerroot	15 mL
1 lb	boneless pork loin chops (about ½ inch/1 cm thick), cut into ¼-inch (0.5 cm) thick strips	500 g
2 tbsp	cornstarch	30 mL
2 tbsp	olive oil, divided	30 mL
8 oz	shiitake mushrooms, stemmed and thinly sliced	250 g
2	carrots, shredded	2
1	small head savoy cabbage, shredded	1
1	can (8 oz/227 mL) sliced water chestnuts, drained	1
1 cup	whole fresh cilantro leaves	250 mL
1 cup	prepared pancake batter (see tip, at left)	250 mL
4	green onions, thinly sliced	4
1 tbsp	black sesame seeds	15 mL

1. In a small bowl, combine hoisin sauce, orange juice, vinegar, soy sauce and ginger; set aside.

2. Place pork in a medium bowl, sprinkle with cornstarch and toss to coat.

3. In a large skillet, heat half the oil over medium-high heat. Sauté pork for 5 to 7 minutes or until browned on all sides. Transfer to a plate.

4. Add the remaining oil to skillet and reduce heat to medium-low. Cook mushrooms, stirring occasionally, for about 5 minutes or until softened. Stir in carrots, cabbage, water chestnuts, cilantro and hoisin sauce mixture; cook, stirring occasionally, for 3 to 5 minutes or until cabbage begins to wilt. Stir in pork and any accumulated juices. Spoon into casserole dish.

5. In a small bowl, combine pancake batter and green onions. Pour over casserole. Sprinkle with sesame seeds.

6. Bake in preheated oven for 20 minutes or until pancake is golden brown.

Pork Rib Bake

Makes 6 servings

I simply love pork ribs, and I love this unique recipe with a bread crumb stuffing as a topping.

Tip

If the pan seems to be getting too dry before the ribs are done, add a little more broth to the bottom of the pan to maintain moisture.

- Preheat oven to 350°F (180°C)
- 13- by 9-inch (33 by 23 cm) glass baking dish

2 tbsp	butter	30 mL
2 cups	chopped celery	500 mL
1/2 cup	chopped onion	125 mL
8 cups	dry bread crumbs	2 L
1 cup	chicken broth	250 mL
1/2 cup	chopped fresh parsley	125 mL
1/2 tsp	salt	2 mL
1/2 tsp	freshly ground black pepper	2 mL
2	racks pork spareribs or side ribs (each about 3 lbs/1.5 kg)	2

1. In a large skillet, melt butter over medium heat. Sauté celery and onion for 5 to 7 minutes or until softened. Remove from heat and stir in bread crumbs, broth, parsley, salt and pepper.

2. Place 1 rack of ribs, meaty side up, in baking dish. Spread stuffing mixture on top. Cover with the remaining rack of ribs, meaty side up.

3. Cover and bake in preheated oven for 1 1/2 hours or until meat is falling off the bones.

Leftover Pork and Baked Potato Casserole

This recipe makes great use of leftover pork, but if you don't have any leftovers, you can purchase fully cooked pork in the meat or deli section of your local supermarket, then shred it. I love paprika in mashed potatoes, especially paired with the smoky flavor of barbecue sauce, as here.

Tips

If you don't have frozen mashed potatoes, use 3 cups (750 mL) homemade.

I particularly enjoy extra-sharp (extra-old) Cheddar cheese in this recipe.

Use your favorite smoky barbecue sauce, either store-bought or homemade.

- Preheat oven to 350°F (180°C)
- 13- by 9-inch (33 by 23 cm) glass baking dish, greased

6	slices bacon	6
1	package (22 oz/625 g) frozen mashed potatoes, thawed	1
3 oz	cream cheese, cut into cubes	90 g
3 cups	shredded Cheddar cheese, divided	750 mL
2 cups	milk	500 mL
1/2 tsp	salt	2 mL
1/2 tsp	freshly ground black pepper	2 mL
1/4 tsp	paprika	1 mL
1	can (4 1/2 oz/127 mL) chopped mild green chiles	1
1 cup	sour cream	250 mL
3 cups	shredded barbecued pork	750 mL
3/4 cup	smoky barbecue sauce	175 mL

1. In a large skillet, over medium-high heat, cook bacon until crisp. Using tongs, transfer to a plate lined with paper towels, reserving 2 tbsp (30 mL) drippings. Let cool, then crumble.

2. In a large bowl, combine reserved bacon drippings, mashed potatoes, cream cheese, 2 cups (500 mL) of the Cheddar, milk, salt, pepper and paprika. Stir in chiles and sour cream until well blended.

3. Spoon potato mixture into prepared baking dish. Sprinkle evenly with bacon and the remaining Cheddar. Top with shredded pork. Drizzle barbecue sauce evenly over pork.

4. Bake in preheated oven for 45 minutes or until bubbling.

Sausage, Sweet Pepper and Rice Casserole

This recipe is typical of the comfort food I had growing up. Today, I enjoy wrapping spoonfuls of this casserole in flatbread or a lettuce leaf.

Tip

If you like heat, use spicy pork sausage.

- Preheat oven to 350°F (180°C)
- 13- by 9-inch (33 by 23 cm) glass baking dish

1¾ lbs	pork sausage (bulk or removed from casings)	875 g
3	cloves garlic, minced	3
1	green bell pepper, chopped	1
1	red bell pepper, chopped	1
1 cup	long-grain white rice	250 mL
½ cup	diced onion	125 mL
1	can (28 oz/796 mL) diced tomatoes	1
1⅔ cups	chicken broth	400 mL
1 tsp	salt	5 mL
1 tsp	freshly ground black pepper	5 mL
¼ tsp	cayenne pepper	1 mL
1 cup	shredded mozzarella cheese	250 mL

1. In a large nonstick skillet, over medium-high heat, cook sausage, breaking it up with the back of a spoon, for 8 to 10 minutes or until no longer pink. Drain off fat. Add garlic, green pepper, red pepper, rice and onion; sauté for 5 minutes or until onion is softened. Stir in tomatoes, broth, salt, black pepper and cayenne. Pour into baking dish.

2. Cover and bake in preheated oven for 1 hour or until rice is tender and most of the liquid is absorbed. Sprinkle with cheese and bake, uncovered, for 10 minutes or until cheese is melted.

Carnitas Casserole with Mole

Makes 8 servings

Leftover carnitas, small pieces of slow-cooked pork, are practically a staple in Mexico. It is very common to layer the meat with corn tortillas and mole sauce. Dishes from the interior of Mexico often incorporate plantains, chiles and pumpkin seeds in a traditional mole flavored with Mexican chocolate.

Tips

If you can't find Mexican chocolate, substitute 1½ tsp (7 mL) unsweetened cocoa powder.

To make pulled pork, slow-cook, braise or roast a pork shoulder blade (butt) roast, then shred the meat. Serve it in sandwiches, tacos or enchiladas, then use the leftovers for rich casseroles such as this one.

Cotija cheese is an aged cow's milk cheese that is grated or crumbled over classic Mexican dishes. Substitute freshly grated Parmesan if you can't find Cotija.

- Preheat oven to 350°F (180°C)
- 13- by 9-inch (33 by 23 cm) glass baking dish, greased
- Blender

Mole

2	dried ancho chile peppers	2
1 cup	boiling water	250 mL
1 tbsp	olive oil	15 mL
1 cup	sliced ripe black plantains (½-inch/1 cm thick slices)	250 mL
2	cloves garlic, minced	2
½ cup	chopped onion	125 mL
½ tsp	salt	2 mL
½ tsp	ground cumin	2 mL
⅛ tsp	ground cinnamon	0.5 mL
1 cup	beef broth	250 mL
2 tbsp	dried cherries	30 mL
2 tbsp	salted green pumpkin seeds (pepitas)	30 mL
½ oz	Mexican chocolate, chopped	15 g

Casserole

12	6-inch (15 cm) corn tortillas	12
1½ cups	pulled pork (see tip, at left)	375 mL
½ cup	crumbled Cotija cheese (see tip, at left)	125 mL

1. *Mole:* Heat a large skillet over medium-high heat. Cook ancho chiles for 2 minutes per side or until fragrant.

2. In a small bowl, combine chiles and boiling water; cover and let stand for 10 minutes. Remove chiles from liquid, reserving liquid. Remove and discard stems and seeds from chiles. Set chiles and soaking liquid aside.

3. In the same skillet, heat oil over medium-high heat. Sauté plantains for 2 minutes or until lightly browned. Add garlic, onion, salt, cumin and cinnamon; sauté for about 3 minutes or until onion is softened. Stir in chiles, soaking liquid, broth, cherries and pumpkin seeds; bring to a boil. Reduce heat and simmer, stirring occasionally, for 10 minutes. Remove from heat and stir in chocolate until melted.

4. Transfer plantain mixture to a blender and add 1 cup (250 mL) water. Blend on medium speed until smooth.

5. *Casserole:* Spread 1 cup (250 mL) of the mole in bottom of prepared baking dish. Arrange 6 tortillas over mole, overlapping as necessary. Top with pork. Arrange the remaining tortillas over pork. Spread the remaining mole over tortillas. Sprinkle with Cotija cheese.

6. Bake in preheated oven for 30 minutes or until cheese begins to melt and casserole is heated through.

Spicy Sausage, Artichoke and Sun-Dried Tomato Bake

This recipe is an Italian delight, packed with authentic ingredients. Serve with crusty bread, a good-quality olive oil for dipping and a fabulous Italian wine.

Tips

For a milder version, use mild Italian sausages and omit the hot pepper flakes.

Thawed frozen artichoke hearts also work well. Use 14 hearts.

When cooking with wine, choose one you'd enjoy drinking. If it's not good enough for your glass, it's not good enough for your dish!

- Preheat oven to 350°F (180°C)
- 13- by 9-inch (33 by 23 cm) glass baking dish, greased

1 lb	hot Italian sausages (bulk or removed from casings)	500 g
2	cans (each 14 oz/398 mL) artichoke hearts, drained and cut into quarters	2
1	clove garlic, minced	1
1¾ cups	chicken broth	425 mL
¾ cup	julienne-cut oil-packed sun-dried tomatoes, drained and rinsed	175 mL
½ cup	dry white wine	125 mL
½ tsp	hot pepper flakes	2 mL
1 lb	cavatappi pasta	500 g
½ cup	freshly grated Parmesan cheese	125 mL
¼ cup	chopped fresh basil	60 mL
¼ cup	chopped fresh flat-leaf (Italian) parsley	60 mL
2 cups	shredded mozzarella cheese	500 mL

1. In a large nonstick skillet, over medium-high heat, cook sausage, breaking it up with the back of a spoon, for 8 to 10 minutes or until no longer pink. Drain off fat. Transfer sausage to a large bowl.

2. Add artichokes and garlic to skillet and reduce heat to medium; sauté for about 2 minutes or until garlic is tender. Add broth, sun-dried tomatoes, wine and hot pepper flakes; increase heat to medium-high and bring to a boil. Boil, stirring occasionally, for about 8 minutes or until sauce is slightly reduced.

3. Meanwhile, in a large pot of boiling salted water, cook pasta according to package directions until just tender. Drain and return to pot.

Rotini and radiatore pasta also work well with this sauce.

Freshly grated or shaved Parmesan cheese is always best right off the wedge, but prepackaged containers can be found in the refrigerated specialty cheese section of your local supermarket.

4. Add sausage, artichoke mixture, Parmesan, basil and parsley to the pasta, stirring until well combined. Pour into prepared baking dish and sprinkle with mozzarella.

5. Bake in preheated oven for 20 minutes or until cheese is melted and bubbling.

Sausage, Tomato and Rice Casserole

This combination of ingredients works so well together, adding up to a dish that's a great choice for a potluck!

Tip

Never throw away stale bread; instead, make fresh bread crumbs! Trim off the crusts, then tear bread into pieces. Process in a food processor to coarse crumbs. One slice of bread makes about $\frac{1}{3}$ cup (75 mL) crumbs.

- Preheat oven to 350°F (180°C)
- Baking pan, with a rack
- 13- by 9-inch (33 by 23 cm) glass baking dish

1 lb	small pork sausages	500 g
1 tbsp	olive oil	15 mL
$\frac{1}{2}$	green bell pepper, chopped	$\frac{1}{2}$
$\frac{1}{2}$	red bell pepper, chopped	$\frac{1}{2}$
1	can (28 oz/796 mL) diced tomatoes, drained	1
1	package (10 oz/300 g) frozen corn (about 2 cups/500 mL), thawed	1
3 cups	cooked long-grain white rice	750 mL
1 cup	shredded Cheddar cheese	250 mL
1 tbsp	chopped fresh parsley	15 mL
1 tbsp	Worcestershire sauce	15 mL
1 tsp	salt	5 mL
1 tsp	dried basil	5 mL
1 cup	fresh bread crumbs	250 mL
2 tbsp	butter, melted	30 mL

1. Place sausages on rack in baking pan. Bake in preheated oven for 15 minutes or until lightly browned. Remove from oven, leaving oven on, and cut into 1-inch (2.5 cm) pieces, set aside.

2. In a large skillet, heat oil over medium-high heat. Sauté green pepper and red pepper for 5 minutes or until softened.

3. In a large bowl, combine sautéed peppers, cooked sausage, tomatoes, corn, rice, cheese, parsley, Worcestershire sauce, salt and basil. Spoon into baking dish.

4. In a small bowl, combine bread crumbs and melted butter. Sprinkle on top of casserole.

5. Bake in preheated oven for 30 to 40 minutes or until bubbling and crumbs are golden.

Topsy-Turvy Pizza Casserole

Essentially, this is an upside-down pizza in a casserole dish. Use this method with your favorite pizza toppings.

Tip

You can use either a white or a whole wheat pizza crust.

Variation

Ground beef can be substituted for the pork sausage.

- Preheat oven to 425°F (220°C)
- 13- by 9-inch (33 by 23 cm) glass baking dish, greased

2 lbs	pork sausage (bulk or removed from casings)	1 kg
8 oz	mushrooms, sliced	250 g
1	onion, chopped	1
1/2 cup	chopped green bell pepper	125 mL
1 tbsp	dried basil, divided	15 mL
1 tsp	fennel seeds	5 mL
1/4 cup	all-purpose flour	60 mL
1	jar (26 oz/738 mL) tomato pasta sauce	1
2 cups	shredded mozzarella cheese, divided	500 mL
1	can (10 oz/300 g) refrigerated pizza crust	1
1 tbsp	olive oil	15 mL
2 tbsp	freshly grated Parmesan cheese	30 mL

1. In a large nonstick skillet, over medium-high heat, cook sausage, mushrooms, onion, green pepper, 2 tsp (10 mL) of the basil and fennel seeds, breaking sausage up with the back of a spoon, for 8 to 10 minutes or until sausage is no longer pink and onion is softened. Drain off fat.

2. Sprinkle flour over sausage mixture, stirring until blended. Stir in tomato sauce and bring to a boil, stirring constantly. Spoon into prepared baking dish. Sprinkle with 1 1/2 cups (375 mL) of the mozzarella.

3. Unroll pizza crust and place on top of sausage mixture, tucking edges into dish. Brush with olive oil and sprinkle with the remaining mozzarella, Parmesan and the remaining basil.

4. Bake in preheated oven for 20 minutes or until golden brown.

Cheesy Spaghetti Casserole

Makes 8 servings

I like making this simple casserole on the spur of the moment, as I usually have all the ingredients on hand.

Tip

Italian three-cheese blend is typically a combination of mozzarella, provolone and Parmesan. You can use any of the three cheeses if you can't find the blend.

- Preheat oven to 350°F (180°C)
- 13- by 9-inch (33 by 23 cm) glass baking dish, greased

12 oz	spaghetti	375 g
1 lb	mild pork sausage (bulk or removed from casings)	500 g
2 oz	pepperoni slices (about 30), cut in half	60 g
1	jar (26 oz/738 mL) tomato pasta sauce	1
2 cups	shredded Italian three-cheese blend (8 oz/250 g)	500 mL
¼ cup	freshly grated Parmesan cheese	60 mL

1. In a large pot of boiling water, cook spaghetti according to package directions until just tender. Drain well and pour into prepared baking dish.

2. Meanwhile, in a large nonstick skillet, over medium-high heat, cook sausage, breaking it up with the back of a spoon, for 8 to 10 minutes or until no longer pink. Drain off fat. Spread over spaghetti.

3. Wipe skillet clean and return to medium-high heat. Cook pepperoni, stirring occasionally, for 4 minutes.

4. Pour pasta sauce over sausage. Arrange half the pepperoni on top. Sprinkle evenly with Italian three-cheese blend and Parmesan. Arrange the remaining pepperoni over cheese.

5. Cover and bake in preheated oven for 30 minutes. Uncover and bake for 10 minutes or until cheese is melted.

Beef and Lamb Casseroles

King Ranch Casserole. 194
Beef, Brown Rice and Feta Cheese Casserole. 195
Beef Burgundy 196
The Reuben Casserole 197
Italian Beef Pie 198
Beef Pot Pie 199
Corn Pone Pie 200
Burrito Pie 201
Southwestern Shepherd's Pie. 202
Beef Stroganoff Casserole 203
Carry Along Casserole 204
Gammy's Delight. 205
Layered Beef and Zucchini Casserole 206
Busy Day Hamburger Casserole 207
Cabbage, Hamburger and Wild Rice Casserole. 208
Chai Chipotle Cheeseburger Casserole. 209
Kim's Mexican Casserole 210
Easy Taco-Mac. 211
Spectacular Beef Empanada Casserole 212
Enchilada Casserole 214
Easy Tamale Casserole. 215
Beef and Rice Keema. 216
Zucchini, Tomato and Beef Casserole with Polenta Crust . . . 217
Tater Nugget Casserole. 218
Beef and Beans 219
Beef Ziti with Silky Béchamel 220
Italian Macaroni Casserole 222
Baked Spaghetti. 223
Pasta Fazool Casserole. 224
Cavatini Casserole 225
My Very Favorite Lasagna. 226
Beef and Spinach Lasagna. 228
No-Pasta Lasagna 229
Baked Ziti. 230
Johnny Mazetti 231
Crunchy Chow Mein Casserole. 232
Santa Fe Stuffed Bell Peppers 233
Fragrant Lamb and Ziti Casserole 234
Stuffed Cabbage Rolls 236

King Ranch Casserole

Many King Ranch casserole recipes call for ground beef, but I prefer leftover shredded beef brisket, which makes this dish heartier and more flavorful. Serve with black bean and corn salsa and a guacamole salad. And don't forget the frozen margaritas!

Tips

Using red, green and yellow bell peppers adds beautiful color and flavor to this casserole. But if you only have one color on hand, that will be just fine!

Removing the ribs and seeds from a jalapeño lessens its heat.

- Preheat oven to 350°F (180°C)
- 13- by 9-inch (33 by 23 cm) glass baking dish, greased

2 tbsp	olive oil	30 mL
2	cloves garlic, minced	2
1 cup	chopped onion	250 mL
2/3 cup	chopped red bell pepper	150 mL
2/3 cup	chopped green bell pepper	150 mL
2/3 cup	chopped yellow bell pepper	150 mL
2 tbsp	chopped seeded jalapeño pepper	30 mL
1 tsp	salt	5 mL
1 tsp	freshly ground black pepper	5 mL
1 tsp	ground cumin	5 mL
1 tsp	garlic powder	5 mL
1 tsp	chili powder	5 mL
1	can (12 oz or 370 mL) evaporated milk	1
1	can (10 oz/284 mL) diced tomatoes with green chiles	1
1	can (10 oz/284 mL) condensed beef broth	1
5 cups	shredded cooked beef brisket	1.25 L
12	6-inch (15 cm) corn tortillas, cut into quarters	12
3 cups	shredded sharp (old) Cheddar cheese, divided	750 mL

1. In a large skillet, heat oil over medium heat. Sauté garlic, onion, red pepper, green pepper, yellow pepper and jalapeño for 5 to 7 minutes or until softened. Stir in salt, pepper, cumin, garlic powder and chili powder. Stir in evaporated milk, tomatoes with chiles and broth; increase heat to medium-high and bring to a boil. Reduce heat and simmer for 5 to 7 minutes or until slightly thickened. Remove from heat and stir in beef.

2. Arrange half the tortillas in prepared baking dish, overlapping as necessary. Top with half the beef mixture and half the cheese. Repeat layers, ending with cheese.

3. Cover and bake in preheated oven for 30 minutes. Uncover and bake for 5 minutes or until cheese is melted and bubbling.

King Ranch Casserole (page 194)

Pork, Apple and Sweet Potato Casserole (page 180)

Beef, Brown Rice and Feta Cheese Casserole

This recipe is a perfect way to use up any leftover cooked beef you might have on hand.

Tip

Feta is a crumbly salt-brined cheese most often produced in blocks and used in salads, pastries and sandwiches. It has a slightly grainy texture. I love Its salty flavor, especially In this recipe.

- Preheat oven to 400°F (200°C)
- 8-inch (20 cm) square glass baking dish, greased

1 tbsp	olive oil	15 mL
4 oz	mushrooms, sliced	125 g
1	onion, chopped	1
1	clove garlic, minced	1
1½ cups	canned diced tomatoes	375 mL
1 tsp	salt	5 mL
½ tsp	freshly ground black pepper	2 mL
2 cups	cooked brown rice	500 mL
1½ cups	chopped or shredded cooked beef	375 mL
3 oz	feta cheese, crumbled	90 g
6	kalamata olives, sliced	6
2 tbsp	freshly grated Parmesan cheese	30 mL

1. In a large skillet, heat oil over medium heat. Sauté mushrooms, onion and garlic for 5 to 7 minutes or until softened. Stir in tomatoes, salt and pepper; reduce heat and simmer, stirring often, for 10 minutes.

2. Spread half the rice in prepared baking dish. Top with cooked beef. Sprinkle with feta and olives. Pour in half the mushroom mixture. Layer with the remaining rice and the remaining mushroom mixture. Sprinkle Parmesan over top.

3. Bake in preheated oven for 25 to 30 minutes or until bubbling.

Beef Burgundy

Whenever my good friend Vicki Hansen makes her recipe for Beef Burgundy, it's always a huge hit — and it couldn't be easier! Serve it with hot rice, egg noodles or mashed potatoes.

Tip

When cooking with wine, choose one you'd enjoy drinking. If it's not good enough for your glass, it's not good enough for your dish!

- Preheat oven to 350°F (180°C)
- 13- by 9-inch (33 by 23 cm) glass baking dish

2	cans (each 10 oz/284 mL) condensed cream of celery soup	2
2	cans (each 10 oz/284 mL) condensed cream of mushroom soup	2
2	cans (each 4 oz/114 mL) sliced mushrooms, drained (about $\frac{1}{2}$ cup/125 mL)	2
2	envelopes (each 3 oz/90 g) dried onion soup mix	2
1 cup	Burgundy wine	250 mL
3 lbs	boneless stewing beef or sirloin tip, cut into bite-size pieces	1.5 kg

1. In a large bowl, combine celery soup, mushroom soup, mushrooms, onion soup mix and wine.

2. Layer beef in baking dish. Pour soup mixture over beef.

3. Cover and bake in preheated oven for 3 hours or until beef is fork-tender.

The Reuben Casserole

Those who love a Reuben sandwich will go nuts for this casserole. It's terrific for brunch or when you have the gang over to watch the big game.

Tip

For a less salty flavor, rinse the sauerkraut with cold water after draining it.

- Preheat oven to 400°F (200°C)
- 13- by 9-inch (33 by 23 cm) glass baking dish

8	slices rye bread, toasted and cubed	8
1	can (16 oz/454 mL) sauerkraut, drained	1
1 lb	deli-sliced corned beef, cut into thin strips	500 g
1 cup	Thousand Island salad dressing	250 mL
2 cups	shredded Swiss cheese	500 mL

1. Line bottom of baking dish with bread cubes. Spread sauerkraut evenly over bread cubes. Layer beef over sauerkraut. Pour dressing over beef.

2. Cover and bake in preheated oven for 20 minutes. Sprinkle with cheese and bake, uncovered, for 10 minutes or until cheese is melted and bubbling.

Italian Beef Pie

This rich, cheesy recipe evokes great childhood memories for my friend Mari Rohde, who continues to serve it to her family today.

Tip

I like to use a nonstick skillet when browning ground turkey, chicken or beef, as it eliminates the need for oil or butter.

Variation

Substitute 1 lb (500 g) frozen French-cut green beans, thawed, for the broccoli.

- Preheat oven to 350°F (180°C)
- 13- by 9-inch (33 by 23 cm) glass baking dish, greased

1½ lbs	lean ground beef	750 g
1 lb	frozen chopped broccoli, thawed and drained	500 g
1	can (10 oz/284 mL) condensed cream of mushroom soup	1
1 cup	sour cream	250 mL
2 tsp	dehydrated onion flakes	10 mL
1 tsp	salt	5 mL
½ tsp	freshly ground black pepper	2 mL
2 cups	shredded mozzarella cheese	500 mL

1. In a large nonstick skillet, over medium-high heat, cook beef, breaking it up with the back of a spoon, for 8 to 10 minutes or until no longer pink. Drain off fat.

2. Stir in broccoli, soup, sour cream, onion flakes, salt and pepper. Spread in prepared baking dish and sprinkle cheese on top.

3. Bake in preheated oven for 35 to 45 minutes or until bubbling.

Beef Pot Pie

Nothing is more comforting than savory pot pie on a cold, rainy day.

Tips

Brushing the crust with beaten egg creates a beautiful golden brown crust.

Two cups (500 mL) leftover cubed roast beef or steak works very well in this recipe in place of the cooked ground beef.

For the vegetables, I like to use petite-cut vegetables for soup. But there are many options available today; use what your family likes.

- Preheat oven to 425°F (220°C)
- 9-inch (23 cm) glass deep-dish pie plate

1 lb	lean ground beef	500 g
4 oz	mushrooms, sliced	125 g
1/2 cup	chopped onions	125 mL
3 cups	frozen mixed vegetables	750 mL
1 tsp	dried thyme	5 mL
3/4 tsp	salt	3 mL
3/4 tsp	freshly ground black pepper	3 mL
3 tbsp	cornstarch	45 mL
1	can (10 oz/284 mL) condensed consommé	1
1	9-inch (23 cm) refrigerated pie crust	1
1	egg, beaten	1

1. In a large nonstick skillet, over medium-high heat, cook beef, mushrooms and onions, breaking beef up with the back of a spoon, for 8 to 10 minutes or until beef is no longer pink. Drain off fat.

2. Stir in frozen vegetables, thyme, salt and pepper; reduce heat to medium and cook for 5 minutes or until vegetables are thawed.

3. In a bowl, whisk cornstarch into consommé until smooth. Add to beef mixture; increase heat to medium and cook, stirring, for about 3 minutes or until thickened.

4. Spoon beef mixture into pie plate. Place crust over mixture and crimp edges. Cut a few 1/2-inch (1 cm) slits in crust to vent steam. Brush with beaten egg.

5. Bake in preheated oven for 25 minutes or until crust is golden brown. Let cool for 5 to 10 minutes before serving.

Corn Pone Pie

My grandmother's corn pone pie was a regular weeknight recipe in my house when I was growing up. Now I see why, as the ingredients are affordable pantry staples.

Tips

The secret is in the simmer! For the best flavor and texture, simmer for 45 minutes.

For a richer flavor, you can replace the water in the sauce with reduced-sodium beef broth.

Look for a packaged cornbread mix with 4 g of sugar or less per 28- to 38-g serving. If your mix requires you to add oil, water and egg rather than just milk or water, use 1⅓ cups (325 mL) dry mix, 1 egg, ½ cup (125 mL) milk or water and 2 tbsp (30 mL) vegetable oil when making the batter as directed in step 3. If you cannot find a packaged cornbread mix, simply make 1½ cups (375 mL) of your favorite cornbread batter and pour it over the meat mixture.

- Preheat oven to 400°F (200°C)
- 11- by 7-inch (28 by 18 cm) glass baking dish

1 lb	lean ground beef	500 g
3	cloves garlic, chopped	3
1	onion, chopped	1
1	small jalapeño pepper, seeded and diced	1
1	can (14 to 19 oz/398 to 540 mL) pinto beans, drained and rinsed	1
2 cups	stewed tomatoes	500 mL
2 tbsp	chili powder	30 mL
½ tsp	salt (approx.)	2 mL
1	package (6 oz/170 g) cornbread mix	1

1. In a large nonstick skillet, over medium-high heat, cook beef, garlic, onion and jalapeño, breaking beef up with the back of a spoon, for 8 to 10 minutes or until beef is no longer pink. Drain off fat.

2. Stir in beans, tomatoes, chili powder, salt and 1 cup (250 mL) water. Cover, leaving lid slightly ajar, reduce heat to low and simmer, stirring occasionally, for 45 minutes or until thickened but still saucy. Season to taste with more salt, if necessary. Transfer to baking dish.

3. Meanwhile, prepare cornbread batter according to package directions. Pour over meat mixture.

4. Bake in preheated oven for 20 minutes or until cornbread is golden brown.

Burrito Pie

Makes 10 to 12 servings

Here, yummy beef and bean burrito flavors have migrated into a hearty casserole.

Tips

I like using lean ground beef to reduce the fat, especially when a recipe contains a lot of flavor, as this one does.

In my home state of Texas, we are fortunate to have a huge variety of taco sauces and salsas available. The consistency can range from chunky to thin. I prefer to use a chunky variety in this recipe.

- Preheat oven to 350°F (180°C)
- 16-cup (4 L) casserole dish

2 lbs	lean ground beef	1 kg
2	cloves garlic, minced	2
1	onion, chopped	1
2	cans (each 16 oz/454 mL) refried beans or refried black beans	2
1	can (2 oz/57 mL) sliced black olives, drained (about $1/4$ cup/60 mL)	1
1	can ($4\frac{1}{2}$ oz/127 mL) chopped mild green chiles	1
1	can (10 oz/284 mL) diced tomatoes with green chiles	1
1	jar (16 oz/454 mL) taco sauce	1
12	8- or 10-inch (20 or 25 cm) flour tortillas	12
2 cups	shredded Cheddar cheese	500 mL

1. In a large nonstick skillet, over medium-high heat, cook beef, garlic and onion, breaking beef up with the back of a spoon, for 8 to 10 minutes or until beef is no longer pink. Drain off fat.

2. Stir in beans, olives, chiles, tomatoes with chiles and taco sauce; reduce heat and simmer, stirring occasionally, for 15 to 20 minutes or until thickened.

3. Spread 1 cup (250 mL) of the beef mixture in casserole dish. Arrange half the tortillas on top, overlapping as necessary. Layer with half the beef mixture and half the cheese. Repeat layers of tortillas, beef and cheese.

4. Bake in preheated oven for 30 to 35 minutes or until bubbling.

Southwestern Shepherd's Pie

Traditional shepherd's pie is great, but shepherd's pie with a little kick of the Southwest? Terrific!

Tips

Yukon gold potatoes add extra flavor, but the butter and cilantro will enhance 2½ cups (375 mL) of your favorite instant mashed potatoes.

If you want to use canned corn, use a 14- or 15-oz (398 or 425 mL) can and drain first.

- Preheat oven to 350°F (180°C)
- 11- by 7-inch (28 by 18 cm) glass baking dish

1½ lbs	Yukon gold potatoes, cut into 1-inch (2.5 cm) cubes	750 g
½ cup	milk	125 mL
2 tbsp	butter	30 mL
2 tbsp	chopped fresh cilantro	30 mL
1 tsp	salt, divided	5 mL
1 tsp	freshly ground black pepper, divided	5 mL
1 lb	lean ground beef	500 g
2	cloves garlic, minced	2
½ cup	chopped onion	125 mL
1	can (14 to 19 oz/398 to 540 mL) black beans, drained and rinsed	1
1	can (14 oz/398 mL) diced tomatoes	1
1½ cups	corn kernels (thawed if frozen)	375 mL
½ cup	shredded Cheddar cheese	125 mL

1. Place potatoes in a large saucepan and add enough water to cover. Cover and bring to a boil over high heat. Reduce heat and simmer for about 15 minutes or until potatoes are just tender. Drain, return to the pot and add milk, butter, cilantro, half the salt and half the pepper; mash until smooth.

2. Meanwhile, in a large nonstick skillet, over medium-high heat, cook beef, garlic and onion, breaking beef up with the back of a spoon, for 8 to 10 minutes or until beef is no longer pink. Drain off fat.

3. Stir in beans, tomatoes and the remaining salt and pepper; bring to a boil. Reduce heat and simmer, stirring often, for 5 to 7 minutes or until heated through.

4. Spread beef mixture in baking dish. Spread corn evenly over meat. Spread mashed potatoes over corn. Sprinkle with cheese.

5. Bake in preheated oven for 20 minutes or until top is golden.

Beef Stroganoff Casserole

Beef stroganoff is so sinfully delicious, it embraces the body with comfort.

Tips

Too much garlic? Never! Feel free to use less, more or none at all.

For a richer flavor, use a 10-oz (284 mL) can of condensed beef consommé instead of the beef broth.

- Preheat oven to 350°F (180°C)
- 13- by 9-inch (33 by 23 cm) glass baking dish, greased

2 lbs	lean ground beef	1 kg
3	cloves garlic, minced	3
1	onion, chopped	1
2 cups	sliced cremini mushrooms	500 mL
1⅔ cups	beef broth	400 mL
2 tbsp	Worcestershire sauce	30 mL
1	can (10 oz/284 mL) condensed cream of mushroom soup	1
2 cups	sour cream	500 mL
¾ tsp	salt	3 mL
1 tsp	freshly ground black pepper	5 mL
8 oz	wide egg noodles	250 g
2 tbsp	butter	30 mL

1. In a large nonstick skillet, over medium-high heat, cook beef, garlic and onion, breaking beef up with the back of a spoon, for 8 to 10 minutes or until beef is no longer pink. Drain off fat.

2. Stir in mushrooms, broth and Worcestershire sauce; bring to a boil. Reduce heat and simmer, stirring occasionally, for 15 minutes. Stir in soup, sour cream, salt and pepper. Remove from heat.

3. Meanwhile, in a large pot of boiling water, cook egg noodles according to package directions until just tender. Drain and return to pot. Stir in butter until melted.

4. Pour beef mixture over noodles and stir to combine. Pour into prepared baking dish.

5. Bake in preheated oven for 30 minutes or until bubbling.

Carry Along Casserole

In the 1970s, casseroles were a hot trend, just as they're enjoying a resurgence in popularity today. My pal Tim Stamper shared a family casserole from back in the day.

Tip

I like to use a nonstick skillet when browning ground turkey, chicken or beef, as it eliminates the need for oil or butter.

- Preheat oven to 350°F (180°C)
- 13- by 9-inch (33 by 23 cm) glass baking dish, greased

2 lbs	lean ground beef	1 kg
½ cup	sliced green onions	125 mL
½ cup	chopped green bell pepper	125 mL
8 oz	wide egg noodles	250 g
2 tbsp	all-purpose flour	30 mL
1	can (8 oz/227 mL) tomato sauce	1
8 oz	cream cheese, softened	250 g
2 cups	small-curd cottage cheese	500 mL
1 cup	sour cream	250 mL
1 tsp	salt	5 mL
½ tsp	freshly ground black pepper	2 mL

1. In a large nonstick skillet, over medium-high heat, cook beef, green onions and green pepper, breaking beef up with the back of a spoon, for 8 to 10 minutes or until beef is no longer pink. Drain off fat.

2. Meanwhile, in a large pot of boiling water, cook egg noodles according to package directions until just tender. Drain and return to pot.

3. Sprinkle flour over beef mixture and stir to combine. Stir in tomato sauce, reduce heat and simmer for 10 minutes or until slightly thickened. Stir in cream cheese, cottage cheese, sour cream, salt and pepper. Stir in cooked noodles. Spread in prepared baking dish.

4. Bake in preheated oven for 20 minutes or until bubbling.

Gammy's Delight

Makes 10 to 12 servings

This recipe is from my dear friend Ruth Collins, also known as "Gammy," my daughter, Kennedy's, grandmother. I remember the first time this was served at a Collins family function — the dish was licked clean!

Tip

Use sharp (old) or extra-sharp (extra-old) Cheddar cheese for added bite.

- Preheat oven to 350°F (180°C)
- 12-cup (3 L) casserole dish, greased

1 cup	long-grain and wild rice blend (12 oz/375 g)	250 mL
3 lbs	lean ground beef	1.5 kg
1	large onion, chopped	1
1 tsp	salt	5 mL
1 tsp	freshly ground black pepper	5 mL
8 oz	cream cheese, cubed, softened	250 g
3 cups	shredded Cheddar cheese, divided	750 mL

1. In a medium saucepan, bring $4\frac{1}{2}$ cups (1.125 L) water to a boil over high heat. Stir in rice mix, reduce heat to low, cover and simmer for 25 minutes or until rice is tender and most of the liquid is absorbed. Remove from heat and let stand, covered, for 5 minutes. Fluff with a fork.

2. Meanwhile, in a very large nonstick skillet, over medium-high heat, cook beef, onion, salt and pepper, breaking beef up with the back of a spoon, for 8 to 10 minutes or until beef is no longer pink. Drain off fat.

3. Stir cream cheese into hot rice until melted. Spoon half the rice mixture into prepared casserole dish. Layer with 1 cup (250 mL) of the Cheddar and half the meat mixture. Repeat layers with the remaining rice mixture, another 1 cup (250 mL) Cheddar and the remaining meat mixture.

4. Cover and bake in preheated oven for 45 minutes. Sprinkle with the remaining Cheddar and bake, uncovered, for 5 minutes or until cheese is melted and bubbling.

Layered Beef and Zucchini Casserole

This dish resembles traditional lasagna but uses zucchini slices instead of pasta.

Tip

Lean ground beef and reduced-fat cheeses help make this casserole a bit lighter and healthier than a traditional lasagna.

- Preheat oven to 350°F (180°C)
- 13- by 9-inch (33 by 23 cm) glass baking dish, greased

6 cups	sliced zucchini (about 3 medium)	1.5 L
1 lb	lean ground beef	500 g
2	cloves garlic, minced	2
2 cups	marinara sauce	500 mL
½ tsp	salt	2 mL
½ tsp	dried basil	2 mL
½ tsp	dried oregano	2 mL
2	eggs, lightly beaten	2
2 cups	fat-free cottage cheese	500 mL
1 tbsp	dried parsley	15 mL
½ cup	seasoned dry bread crumbs, divided	125 mL
1¾ cups	shredded part-skim mozzarella cheese, divided	425 mL

1. In a large saucepan, bring 4 cups (1 L) water to a boil over high heat. Add zucchini and boil for 3 minutes or until tender-crisp. Drain and let cool.

2. In a large nonstick skillet, over medium-high heat, cook beef and garlic, breaking beef up with the back of a spoon, for 8 to 10 minutes or until beef is no longer pink. Drain off fat. Stir in marinara sauce, salt, basil and oregano; simmer for 1 minute. Remove from heat.

3. In a medium bowl, combine eggs, cottage cheese and parsley.

4. Arrange half the zucchini in prepared baking dish, overlapping as necessary. Sprinkle with half the bread crumbs. Spread half the cottage cheese mixture on top. Cover with half the beef mixture and 1 cup (250 mL) of the mozzarella. Repeat layers with the remaining zucchini, bread crumbs, cottage cheese mixture and beef mixture. Reserve the remaining mozzarella.

5. Bake in preheated oven for 45 minutes. Sprinkle with the reserved mozzarella and bake for 5 minutes or until cheese is melted.

Busy Day Hamburger Casserole

Makes 8 to 10 servings

My friend Jean Phillips, a successful realtor, knows recipes like this Midwest family favorite are a must on busy days. Thank you, Jean, for sharing your recipes and bringing over a favorite casserole when life brings hiccups.

Variation

Turn this into a cheeseburger casserole by topping it with 1 cup (250 mL) shredded Cheddar cheese instead of crushed potato chips.

- Preheat oven to 350°F (180°C)
- 13- by 9-inch (33 by 23 cm) glass baking dish, greased

1 lb	lean ground beef	500 g
1	large onion, chopped	1
1	green bell pepper, chopped	1
1	clove garlic, minced	1
2	cans (each 8 oz/227 mL) tomato sauce	2
1 tbsp	chili powder	15 mL
1 tsp	granulated sugar	5 mL
1 tsp	salt	5 mL
1/2 tsp	freshly ground black pepper	2 mL
8 oz	wide egg noodles, penne or rotini pasta	250 g
1 cup	crushed potato chips or tortilla chips	250 mL

1. In a large nonstick skillet, over medium-high heat, cook beef, onion, green pepper and garlic, breaking beef up with the back of a spoon, for 8 to 10 minutes or until beef is no longer pink. Drain off fat. Stir in tomato sauce, chili powder, sugar, salt and pepper.

2. Meanwhile, in a large pot of boiling water, cook egg noodles according to package directions until just tender. Drain and pour into prepared baking dish.

3. Spread meat mixture over noodles and top with potato chips.

4. Bake in preheated oven for 20 to 25 minutes or until bubbling.

Cabbage, Hamburger and Wild Rice Casserole

Family friend Jane Tollette, who hails from Wisconsin, shares this Midwestern comfort food that's especially wonderful on a cold winter day. Leftovers taste even better the next day!

Tip
Napa cabbage works well in this recipe.

- Preheat oven to 350°F (180°C)
- 13- by 9-inch (33 by 23 cm) glass baking dish, greased

1½ lbs	lean ground beef	750 g
1	onion, chopped	1
1	can (14 oz/398 mL) stewed tomatoes	1
1	can (10 oz/284 mL) diced tomatoes with green chiles	1
1	can (10 oz/284 mL) condensed tomato soup	1
½ cup	wild rice	125 mL
½ tsp	salt	2 mL
½ tsp	freshly ground black pepper	2 mL
1	head cabbage, cored and thinly sliced (about 6 cups/1.5 L)	1
1 cup	shredded Cheddar cheese	250 mL

1. In a large nonstick skillet, over medium-high heat, cook beef and onion, breaking beef up with the back of a spoon, for 8 to 10 minutes or until beef is no longer pink. Drain off fat.

2. Stir in stewed tomatoes, tomatoes with chiles, tomato soup, wild rice, salt and pepper; cook for 5 minutes or until heated through.

3. Line bottom of prepared baking dish with cabbage. Pour beef mixture over top.

4. Cover and bake in preheated oven for 1½ hours or until rice is tender. Sprinkle with cheese and bake, uncovered, for 10 minutes or until cheese is melted and bubbly.

Chai Chipotle Cheeseburger Casserole

My friend Michele Northrup — "the Saucy Queen" — started her company, the Intensity Academy, in her kitchen. Her amazing cheeseburger casserole features her Chai Chipotle Chup, Winner of the 2007 and 2009 Scovie Award for Best Condiment in the Nation.

Tip

Visit www.intensityacademy.com to find Chai Chipotle Chup and more. If you don't have Chai Chipotle Chup, substitute your favorite sweet and smoky barbecue sauce.

- Preheat oven to 350°F (180°C)
- 13- by 9-inch (33 by 23 cm) glass baking dish

2 lbs	lean ground beef	1 kg
1/2 cup	finely chopped onion	125 mL
1/2 cup	finely chopped green bell pepper	125 mL
1	can (16 oz/454 mL) tomato sauce	1
1/2 cup	Chai Chipotle Chup (see tip, at left)	125 mL
8 oz	American or Cheddar cheese slices	250 g
1	can (8 oz/227 g) refrigerated crescent rolls	1

1. In a large nonstick skillet, over medium-high heat, cook beef, breaking it up with the back of a spoon, for 8 to 10 minutes or until beef is no longer pink. Drain off fat.

2. Add onion and green pepper; sauté for 5 to 7 minutes or until softened. Add tomato sauce and Chup; cook, stirring, for 5 minutes or until heated through.

3. Spoon meat mixture into baking dish. Arrange cheese slices on top. Separate crescent roll sheets into 2 squares and lay over mixture.

4. Bake in preheated oven for 20 to 25 minutes or until dough is light brown.

Kim's Mexican Casserole

This dish would be great for a Mexican-themed party. Serve with dollops of sour cream and salsa, garnished with minced seeded jalapeños or finely chopped bell peppers for added crunch and color. On the side, serve a mixed green salad with orange sections.

Tip

I like to use a nonstick skillet when browning ground turkey, chicken or beef, as it eliminates the need for oil or butter.

- Preheat oven to 350°F (180°C)
- 13- by 9-inch (33 by 23 cm) glass baking dish, greased

1 lb	lean ground beef	500 g
1	envelope (1¼ oz/37 g) taco seasoning mix	1
6	6- or 7-inch (15 or 18 cm) flour tortillas	6
1	can (16 oz/454 mL) refried beans	1
8 oz	shredded Mexican-blend cheese (2 cups/500 mL)	250 g

1. In a large nonstick skillet, over medium-high heat, cook beef and taco seasoning, breaking beef up with the back of a spoon, for 8 to 10 minutes or until beef is no longer pink. Drain off fat.

2. Arrange tortillas in prepared baking dish, overlapping as necessary. Spread half the beans over tortillas, then half the beef mixture. Sprinkle with half the cheese. Repeat layers with the remaining beans, beef mixture and cheese.

3. Cover and bake in preheated oven for 45 minutes or until bubbling.

Easy Taco-Mac

Makes 6 to 8 servings

This recipe is crazy-simple and makes great leftovers. If you're making it for a large group, you can double or even triple the recipe — so long as you have a big enough baking dish! Increase the baking time as necessary.

Tips

Replace the macaroni with spiral pasta or any fun shape you like.

If your cornbread mix requires you to add oil, water and egg rather than just milk or water, use 1¾ cups (425 mL) dry mix, increase the milk to ¾ cup (175 mL) and add 3 tbsp (45 mL) vegetable oil with the egg when making the batter as directed in step 3. If you cannot find packaged mix, simply make 2 cups (500 mL) of your favorite cornbread batter (instead of mixing it with the egg and milk) and fold in the cheese.

- Preheat oven to 400°F (200°C)
- 10-cup (2.5 L) casserole dish

1 lb	lean ground beef	500 g
1	envelope (1¼ oz/37 g) taco seasoning mix	1
1	can (14 oz/398 mL) diced tomatoes	1
8 oz	elbow macaroni	250 g
½ cup	chopped celery	125 mL
1	box (8½ oz/241 g) cornbread mix	1
1	egg, lightly beaten	1
⅓ cup	milk	75 mL
½ cup	shredded Cheddar cheese	125 mL

1. In a large nonstick skillet, over medium-high heat, cook beef and taco seasoning, breaking beef up with the back of a spoon, for 8 to 10 minutes or until beef is no longer pink. Drain off fat.

2. Stir in tomatoes, macaroni, 1 cup (250 mL) water and celery; bring to a boil. Reduce heat to medium-low, cover and simmer, stirring occasionally, for 20 minutes.

3. In a medium bowl, combine cornbread mix, egg and milk, stirring with a fork until just combined. Fold in cheese.

4. Spoon beef mixture into casserole dish. Spoon dollops of batter on top.

5. Bake in preheated oven for 15 to 20 minutes or until bubbling.

Spectacular Beef Empanada Casserole

Makes 6 servings

I love empanadas, especially the ones served at a local dive in the Austin area. It was while I was savoring that delectable dish that the idea for this casserole popped into my head.

Tips

I like using lean ground beef to reduce the fat, especially when a recipe contains a lot of flavor, as this one does.

Any beer will work, but it's a nice touch to use a Mexican beer for this Mexican dish.

- Preheat oven to 350°F (180°C)
- 11- by 7-inch (28 by 18 cm) glass baking dish, greased

2 tbsp	olive oil	30 mL
3½ cups	diced potatoes	875 mL
1 cup	chopped onion	250 mL
1¼ lbs	lean ground beef	625 g
3	cloves garlic, minced	3
1½ tsp	dried oregano	7 mL
1½ tsp	chili powder	7 mL
1 tsp	ground cumin	5 mL
½ tsp	salt	2 mL
Pinch	freshly ground black pepper	Pinch
⅓ cup	all-purpose flour	75 mL
½ cup	beer, preferably Mexican	125 mL
1	can (10 oz/284 mL) condensed beef broth	1
1	can (14 oz/398 mL) diced tomatoes with green peppers and onions, drained	1
2 tbsp	chopped green olives	30 mL
1 tbsp	cider vinegar	15 mL
1	box (11 oz/312 g) refrigerated garlic-flavored bread sticks	1

1. In a large saucepan, heat oil over medium heat. Add potato and onion; cover and cook, stirring occasionally, for 7 to 9 minutes or until potato is softened.

2. Stir in beef, garlic, oregano, chili powder, cumin, salt and pepper; cook, breaking beef up with the back of a spoon, for 8 to 10 minutes or until beef is no longer pink. Drain off fat.

3. Sprinkle flour over beef mixture and cook, stirring constantly, for 1 minute. Gradually stir in beer, broth and tomatoes; bring to a boil. Remove from heat and stir in olives and vinegar. Spread in prepared baking dish.

4. Reserve the garlic spread packaged with the bread sticks. Unroll both sheets of dough, without separating them into bread sticks. Roll dough sheets together, forming a 12- by 10-inch (30 by 25 cm) rectangle. Place on top of dish, pressing to seal edges. Cut a few slits in the top to vent steam. Brush with the reserved garlic spread.

5. Bake in preheated oven for 25 to 30 minutes or until golden brown and bubbling around the edges. Let cool for 10 minutes before serving.

Enchilada Casserole

The layers of savory ingredients are so satisfying in this Latin-inspired recipe.

Tip

Look for enchilada sauce in the international foods section of your local supermarket.

- Preheat oven to 375°F (190°C)
- 13- by 9-inch (33 by 23 cm) glass baking dish

1½ lbs	lean ground beef	750 g
1	onion, finely chopped	1
5	drained pickled jalapeño peppers, chopped	5
2	cans (each 10 oz/284 mL) enchilada sauce, divided	2
1½ cups	shredded Colby-Jack cheese, divided	375 mL
1 tsp	chili powder	5 mL
1 tsp	ground cumin	5 mL
½ tsp	garlic powder	2 mL
	Vegetable oil	
12	6-inch (15 cm) corn tortillas	12

1. In a large nonstick skillet, over medium-high heat, cook beef and onion, breaking beef up with the back of a spoon, for 8 to 10 minutes or until beef is no longer pink. Drain off fat.

2. Stir in jalapeños, 1 can of enchilada sauce, 1 cup (250 mL) of the cheese, chili powder, cumin and garlic powder; cook, stirring, until cheese is melted. Remove from heat and keep warm.

3. In a small skillet, heat a thin layer of oil over medium-high heat. One at a time, dip tortillas in oil until pliable, about 15 seconds. Transfer to a plate lined with paper towels.

4. Arrange 6 tortillas in baking dish, overlapping as necessary. Spread beef mixture over tortillas. Arrange the remaining tortillas on top. Pour in the remaining enchilada sauce and sprinkle with the remaining cheese.

5. Bake in preheated oven for 25 to 30 minutes or until cheese is melted and bubbling.

Easy Tamale Casserole

This fantastic tamale casserole is perfect on a buffet!

Tip
Use 12 fresh tamales as a substitute for the canned.

- Preheat oven to 350°F (180°C)
- 13- by 9-inch (33 by 23 cm) glass baking dish

2	cans (each 15 oz/426 g) tamales	2
2	cans (each 15 oz/426 g) beef chili without beans	2
1	can (14 oz/398 mL) whole-kernel corn, drained	1
1	can (4½ oz/127 mL) chopped mild green chiles	2
2 cups	corn chips	500 mL
1½ cups	shredded Cheddar cheese	375 mL
½ cup	chopped onion	125 mL

1. Arrange tamales in baking dish.

2. In a large bowl, combine chili, corn and chiles. Pour over tamales. Top with corn chips, cheese and onion.

3. Bake in preheated oven for 30 to 35 minutes or until bubbling.

Beef and Rice Keema

Makes 6 servings

Keema, a spicy minced meat curry, is a traditional dish in India and Pakistan. It is usually made with lamb or goat, along with peas or potatoes. My ground beef casserole version features both peas and potatoes and has the added bonus of brown rice.

Tip

If you like heat, add a sprinkle of hot pepper flakes to each serving for traditional zing.

- Preheat oven to 350°F (180°C)
- 11- by 7-inch (28 by 18 cm) glass baking dish, greased

1½ lbs	lean ground beef	750 g
1 cup	chopped onions	250 mL
2 cups	canned crushed tomatoes	500 mL
1 cup	frozen peas	250 mL
1 cup	diced potatoes	250 mL
1 tbsp	curry powder	15 mL
½ tsp	ground cinnamon	2 mL
½ tsp	ground turmeric	2 mL
½ tsp	ground ginger	2 mL
½ tsp	salt	2 mL
½ tsp	freshly ground black pepper	2 mL
1 cup	cooked brown rice	250 mL

1. In a large nonstick skillet, over medium-high heat, cook beef and onions, breaking beef up with the back of a spoon, for 8 to 10 minutes or until beef is no longer pink. Drain off fat.

2. Stir in tomatoes, peas, potatoes, curry powder, cinnamon, turmeric, ginger, salt and pepper; bring to a boil. Reduce heat and simmer, stirring occasionally, for 25 minutes, adding water as necessary if mixture gets too thick (it should have the consistency of chili). Stir in cooked rice. Spread in prepared baking dish

3. Bake in preheated oven for 20 minutes or until bubbling.

Southwestern Shepherd's Pie (page 202)

Zucchini, Tomato and Beef Casserole
with Polenta Crust (page 217)

Zucchini, Tomato and Beef Casserole with Polenta Crust

I adore creamy polenta, especially when it's used as a crust for layered fresh vegetables and lean ground beef.

Tip

For added color, use a combination of zucchini and yellow summer squash.

- Preheat oven to 350°F (180°C)
- 11- by 7-inch (28 by 18 cm) glass baking dish, greased

1 tsp	salt	5 mL
1 cup	cornmeal	250 mL
½ tsp	steak seasoning	2 mL
1 cup	shredded Colby-Jack cheese, divided	250 mL
1 lb	lean ground beef	500 g
1 tbsp	olive oil	15 mL
1	onion, chopped	1
1	zucchini, cut in half lengthwise and sliced crosswise	1
1	can (28 oz/796 mL) diced tomatoes, drained	1
1	can (6 oz/170 mL) tomato paste	1
2 tbsp	chopped fresh flat-leaf (Italian) parsley	30 mL
	Cherry tomatoes, halved	

1. In a medium saucepan, bring 3 cups (750 mL) water and salt to a boil over medium-high heat. Gradually whisk in cornmeal, reduce heat and simmer, whisking constantly, for 3 minutes or until thickened. Remove from heat and stir in steak seasoning and ¼ cup (60 mL) of the cheese. Spread in prepared baking dish. Set aside.

2. In a large nonstick skillet, over medium-high heat, cook beef, breaking it up with the back of a spoon, for 8 to 10 minutes or until no longer pink. Drain off fat and transfer beef to a bowl.

3. In the same skillet, heat oil over medium heat. Sauté onion and zucchini for 5 to 7 minutes or until tender. Return beef to skillet and stir in tomatoes and tomato paste; bring to a simmer. Simmer, stirring often, for 8 to 10 minutes or until slightly thickened. Pour over polenta crust and sprinkle with the remaining cheese.

4. Bake in preheated oven for 30 minutes or until bubbling. Sprinkle with parsley just before serving and garnish with cherry tomatoes.

Tater Nugget Casserole

Every Nebraska resident knows this recipe and makes their own variation of it. Here's this Texas gal's take.

Tip

This is such a crowd pleaser, you may need to double the recipe. If you do, use two separate baking dishes and rotate them in the oven halfway through baking to make sure they bake evenly.

- Preheat oven to 350°F (180°C)
- 11- by 7-inch (28 by 18 cm) glass baking dish, greased

1 lb	lean ground beef	500 g
2	cans (each 10 oz/284 mL) condensed cream of mushroom soup	2
2	cans (each 16 oz/454 mL) French-style green beans, drained	2
1/2 cup	milk	125 mL
1/2 tsp	salt	2 mL
1/2 tsp	freshly ground black pepper	2 mL
2 cups	shredded Cheddar cheese	500 mL
1	bag (16 oz/454 g) frozen seasoned shredded potato nuggets, such as Tater Tots	1

1. In a large nonstick skillet, over medium-high heat, cook beef, breaking it up with the back of a spoon, for 8 to 10 minutes or until no longer pink. Drain off fat. Stir in soup, green beans, milk, salt and pepper.

2. Spread beef mixture in prepared baking dish and sprinkle with cheese. Arrange potato nuggets on top.

3. Bake in preheated oven for 25 to 30 minutes or until potato nuggets are brown and crispy.

Beef and Beans

This recipe is great any time, but I especially like serving it at July 4th celebrations.

Tip

If you can't find 28-oz (796 mL) cans of baked beans, use four 14-oz (398 mL) cans.

- Preheat oven to 375°F (190°C)
- Ovenproof Dutch oven

3 lbs	lean ground beef	1.5 kg
2	onions, chopped	2
2	cloves garlic, minced	2
2	stalks celery, chopped	2
2 tsp	beef bouillon granules	10 mL
⅔ cup	boiling water	150 mL
2	cans (each 28 oz/796 mL) baked beans in tomato sauce	2
8 oz	sliced bacon, cooked crisp and crumbled	250 g
1½ cups	ketchup	375 mL
2 tbsp	prepared mustard	30 mL
1½ tsp	salt	7 mL
½ tsp	freshly ground black pepper	2 mL

1. In Dutch oven, over medium-high heat, cook beef, onions, garlic and celery, breaking beef up with the back of a spoon, for 8 to 10 minutes or until beef is no longer pink. Drain off fat.

2. Dissolve bouillon in boiling water; stir into beef mixture. Stir in beans, bacon, ketchup, mustard, salt and pepper.

3. Cover and bake in preheated oven for 1 hour or until bubbling.

Beef Ziti with Silky Béchamel

With its savory meat sauce enhanced with aromatic herbs, layers of pasta and a silky béchamel sauce, this casserole boasts both spectacular beauty and divine flavor. No wonder we chose to feature it on the cover of the book!

Tips

I like using lean ground beef to reduce the fat, especially when a recipe contains a lot of flavor, as this one does.

I use a nonstick skillet when browning ground turkey, chicken or beef, as it eliminates the need for oil or butter.

Use a dry red wine, such as Merlot or Cabernet Sauvignon. Make sure to choose one you'd enjoy drinking. If it's not good enough for your glass, it's not good enough for your dish!

- Preheat oven to 350°F (180°C)
- 13- by 9-inch (33 by 23 cm) glass baking dish, greased

Meat Sauce

2 lbs	lean ground beef	1 kg
2	cloves garlic, chopped	2
1	onion, chopped	1
3	cans (each 14 oz/398 mL) diced tomatoes	3
¼ cup	tomato paste	60 mL
¼ cup	dry red wine	60 mL
1 tsp	salt	5 mL
1 tsp	dried oregano	5 mL
1 tsp	dried basil	5 mL
1 tsp	dried thyme	5 mL
½ tsp	hot pepper flakes	2 mL

Béchamel Sauce

⅓ cup	butter	75 mL
¼ cup	all-purpose flour	60 mL
4 cups	milk	1 L
½ cup	freshly grated Parmesan cheese	125 mL
2 tsp	salt	10 mL
1 lb	ziti pasta	500 g
1 cup	shredded mozzarella cheese	250 mL

1. *Meat Sauce:* In a large nonstick skillet, over medium-high heat, cook beef, garlic and onion, breaking beef up with the back of a spoon, for 8 to 10 minutes or until beef is no longer pink. Drain off fat.

2. Stir in tomatoes, tomato paste, wine, salt, oregano, basil, thyme and hot pepper flakes; bring to a boil. Cover, leaving lid ajar, reduce heat to low and simmer, stirring occasionally, for about 40 minutes or until some of the liquid has evaporated but sauce is still moist.

3. *Béchamel Sauce:* Meanwhile, in a medium saucepan, melt butter over medium heat. Sprinkle with flour and cook, whisking constantly, for about 6 minutes or until roux is golden.

4. In another medium saucepan, bring milk to the boiling point over medium heat. Gradually add to roux in a steady stream, whisking constantly until smooth. Bring to a boil over medium heat, whisking. Cook, whisking constantly, for 10 minutes. Remove from heat and stir in Parmesan and salt until cheese is melted. Keep warm.

5. In a large pot of boiling water, cook ziti according to package directions until just tender. Drain, transfer pasta to a large bowl and stir in 1 cup (250 mL) of the béchamel sauce.

6. Spread one-third of the ziti in prepared baking dish. Spread half the meat sauce evenly over top. Add another layer of ziti and top with the remaining meat sauce. Layer the remaining pasta on top. Pour the remaining béchamel sauce evenly over top.

7. Cover and bake in preheated oven for 40 to 45 minutes or until bubbling. Sprinkle with mozzarella and bake, uncovered, for 5 minutes or until cheese is melted.

Italian Macaroni Casserole

While this recipe tastes amazing to begin with, leftovers are even better the next day!

Tips

Instead of the macaroni, use any fun pasta shapes your kids like.

Never throw away stale bread; instead, make fresh bread crumbs! Trim off the crusts, then tear bread into pieces. Process in a food processor to coarse crumbs. One slice of bread makes about ⅓ cup (75 mL) crumbs.

- Preheat oven to 350°F (180°C)
- 13- by 9-inch (33 by 23 cm) glass baking dish, greased

1 lb	lean ground beef	500 g
1	onion, chopped	1
1	clove garlic, minced	1
4 oz	mushrooms, sliced	125 g
1	jar (26 oz/738 mL) tomato pasta sauce	1
1	can (8 oz/227 mL) tomato sauce	1
1	can (6 oz/170 mL) tomato paste	1
½ tsp	salt	2 mL
¼ tsp	freshly ground black pepper	1 mL
1¾ cups	elbow macaroni	425 mL
2	eggs, beaten	2
1 cup	shredded mozzarella cheese	250 mL
½ cup	fresh bread crumbs	125 mL

1. In a large nonstick skillet, over medium-high heat, cook beef, onion, garlic and mushrooms, breaking beef up with the back of a spoon, for 8 to 10 minutes or until beef is no longer pink. Drain off fat.

2. Stir in pasta sauce, tomato sauce, tomato paste, salt and pepper; reduce heat and simmer, stirring often, for 10 minutes.

3. Meanwhile, in a large pot of boiling water, cook macaroni according to package directions until just tender. Drain.

4. In a large bowl, combine eggs, cheese and bread crumbs. Stir in macaroni. Spread in prepared baking dish and top with meat sauce.

5. Bake in preheated oven for 35 to 30 minutes or until bubbling. Let cool for 10 minutes before serving.

Baked Spaghetti

Spaghetti's a classic, so how can it possibly be improved? Why, by baking it in a casserole, of course!

Tip

If you prefer, you can use linguini, angel hair or fettuccini pasta instead of the spaghetti.

- Preheat oven to 350°F (180°C)
- 13- by 9-inch (33 by 23 cm) glass baking dish, greased

1 lb	lean ground beef	500 g
1 cup	chopped onion	250 mL
1 cup	chopped green bell pepper	250 mL
1	can (28 oz/796 mL) diced tomatoes	1
1	can (10 oz/284 mL) condensed cream of mushroom soup	1
1	can (4 oz/114 mL) sliced mushrooms, drained ($\frac{1}{2}$ cup/125 mL)	1
1	can (2 oz/57 mL) sliced black olives, drained ($\frac{1}{4}$ cup cup/60 mL)	1
2 tsp	dried oregano	10 mL
12 oz	spaghetti	375 g
2 cups	shredded Cheddar cheese	500 mL
	Parmesan cheese (optional)	

1. In a large nonstick skillet, over medium-high heat, cook beef, onion and green pepper, breaking beef up with the back of a spoon, for 8 to 10 minutes or until beef is no longer pink. Drain off fat.

2. Stir in tomatoes, soup, mushrooms, olives and oregano; bring to a boil. Reduce heat and simmer, stirring occasionally, for 10 minutes.

3. Meanwhile, in a large pot of boiling water, cook spaghetti according to package directions until just tender. Drain.

4. Spread half the spaghetti in prepared baking dish. Top with half the beef mixture and sprinkle with half the Cheddar. Repeat layers.

5. Bake in preheated oven for 30 minutes or until bubbling. Serve sprinkled with Parmesan, if desired.

Pasta Fazool Casserole

This classic Italian dish of pasta and beans is both delicious and economical.

Tip

Mostaccioli is a smooth tube-shaped pasta that is great for casseroles. A ridged tube pasta, such as penne or ziti, works well too.

- Preheat oven to 400°F (200°C)
- 13- by 9-inch (33 by 23 cm) glass baking dish, greased

1 lb	lean ground beef	500 g
1 lb	hot or sweet Italian sausage (bulk or removed from casings)	500 g
2	cloves garlic, chopped	2
1	large onion, chopped	1
1 tsp	dried oregano, crumbled	5 mL
1/2 tsp	dried thyme, crumbled	2 mL
1	can (28 oz/796 mL) diced tomatoes, drained	1
2 tbsp	tomato paste	30 mL
1/2 tsp	salt	2 mL
1/2 tsp	freshly ground black pepper	2 mL
1/4 tsp	cayenne pepper	1 mL
1	can (14 to 19 oz/398 to 540 mL) kidney beans, drained and rinsed	1
1 lb	mostaccioli pasta	500 g
1/2 cup	freshly grated Parmesan cheese	125 mL
1/4 cup	chopped fresh flat-leaf (Italian) parsley	60 mL
12 oz	shredded Italian cheese blend (3 cups/750 mL)	375 g

1. In a large nonstick skillet, over medium-high heat, cook beef, sausage, garlic, onion, oregano and thyme, breaking meat up with the back of a spoon, for 8 to 10 minutes or until beef is no longer pink. Drain off fat.

2. Stir in tomatoes, tomato paste, salt, black pepper and cayenne; reduce heat and simmer, stirring often, for 5 minutes. Stir in beans and simmer until heated through.

3. Meanwhile, in a large pot of boiling water, cook pasta according to package directions until just tender. Drain and return to pot; stir in beef mixture.

4. Add Parmesan and parsley to beef mixture and toss to combine. Pour into prepared baking dish and sprinkle with Italian cheese.

5. Bake in preheated oven for about 30 minutes or until cheese is melted.

Cavatini Casserole

Makes 8 to 10 servings

When I was a teenager, I was a frequent patron of an international pizza chain, but I never ordered pizza — I couldn't get enough of their cavatini. For some reason, cavatini no longer appears on their menu, so to satisfy my craving, I had to create my own casserole version.

Tips

You can stir the pepperoni into the meat mixture, but I like having a separate layer in this casserole.

Substitute a 4½-oz (127 mL) can of sliced mushrooms, drained, for the fresh. Add with the tomatoes.

- Preheat oven to 375°F (190°C)
- 13- by 9-inch (33 by 23 cm) glass baking dish, greased

1 lb	lean ground beef	500 g
4 oz	mushrooms, sliced	125 g
½	green bell pepper, chopped	½
½	onion, chopped	½
1	jar (32 oz/909 mL) tomato pasta sauce	1
1	can (14 oz/398 mL) Italian-style stewed tomatoes, drained	1
2 cups	shredded mozzarella cheese, divided	500 mL
3 cups	assorted pasta wheels, shells and spirals	750 mL
4 oz	sliced pepperoni	125 g

1. In a large nonstick skillet, over medium-high heat, cook beef, mushrooms, green pepper and onion, breaking beef up with the back of a spoon, for 8 to 10 minutes or until beef is no longer pink. Drain off fat. Stir in pasta sauce, tomatoes, and half the cheese until cheese is melted.

2. Meanwhile, in a large pot of boiling water, cook pasta according to package directions until just tender. Drain and return to pot; stir in beef mixture.

3. Spread pasta mixture in prepared baking dish and layer pepperoni slices evenly on top.

4. Cover and bake in preheated oven for 20 minutes. Sprinkle with the remaining cheese and bake, uncovered, for 15 to 20 minutes or until cheese is melted and bubbling.

My Very Favorite Lasagna

I have tried many lasagna recipes, and this one is dense and perfect in every way. I have lightened it up by using lean ground beef and lower-fat dairy products.

Tips

This recipe works very well with extra-lean ground beef, if you want to lighten it up even more.

Instead of the dried herbs, you can use fresh; you'll need about twice as much of each. Stir fresh herbs into the sauce just before assembling the lasagna.

- Preheat oven to 350°F (180°C)
- 13- by 9-inch (33 by 23 cm) glass baking dish, greased

1 lb	lean ground beef	500 g
4	cloves garlic, minced	4
1	onion, chopped	1
1	can (28 oz/796 mL) diced tomatoes	1
1	can (14 oz/398 mL) Italian-style stewed tomatoes, chopped	1
1	can (8 oz/227 mL) tomato sauce	1
1	can (6 oz/170 mL) tomato paste	1
1/4 cup	chopped fresh parsley, divided	60 mL
2 tsp	dried oregano	10 mL
1 tsp	dried basil	5 mL
1 tsp	dried thyme	5 mL
1/2 tsp	dried rosemary, crumbled	2 mL
1/4 tsp	freshly ground black pepper	1 mL
1	egg white, lightly beaten	1
2 cups	non-fat ricotta cheese	500 mL
2 cups	non-fat cottage cheese	500 mL
1/2 cup	freshly grated Parmesan cheese	125 mL
12	oven-ready lasagna noodles	12
2 cups	shredded Italian cheese blend, divided	500 mL

1. In a large nonstick skillet, over medium-high heat, cook beef, garlic and onion, breaking beef up with the back of a spoon, for 8 to 10 minutes or until beef is no longer pink. Drain off fat.

2. Stir in diced tomatoes, stewed tomatoes, tomato sauce, tomato paste, half the parsley, oregano, basil, thyme, rosemary and pepper; bring to a boil. Reduce heat to low, cover and simmer, stirring occasionally, for 20 minutes. Uncover and simmer, stirring occasionally, for 20 minutes. Remove from heat.

3. In a medium bowl, combine egg white, ricotta, cottage cheese, Parmesan and the remaining parsley.

Try using lean ground veal, pork or turkey instead of the beef.

4. Spread $\frac{3}{4}$ cup (175 mL) of the meat sauce in bottom of prepared baking dish. Arrange 4 noodles over sauce. Top with half the ricotta mixture, $2\frac{1}{4}$ cups (550 mL) meat sauce and $\frac{2}{3}$ cup (150 mL) Italian cheese. Repeat layers with noodles, ricotta mixture, meat sauce and Italian cheese. Arrange the remaining noodles on top. Spread the remaining meat sauce over noodles.

5. Cover and bake in preheated oven for 1 hour. Sprinkle with the remaining Italian cheese and bake, uncovered, for 10 minutes or until cheese is melted. Let cool for 10 minutes before serving.

Beef and Spinach Lasagna

This unique, elegant lasagna really highlights the flavor of ground beef.

Tips

Oven-ready lasagna noodles are a tremendous time-saver. Of course, they will never be the same as fresh pasta, so if you're keen on fresh noodles, go for it! You can layer them into the lasagna without cooking them — they'll cook in the oven.

Feel free to substitute dried herbs for the fresh. I typically use half the amount. But fresh is so, well, *fresh*!

- Preheat oven to 350° (180°C)
- 11- by 7-inch (28 by 18 cm) glass baking dish, greased

1½ lbs	lean ground beef	750 g
2	cloves garlic, chopped	2
4 cups	tomato pasta sauce	1 L
1½ tsp	salt, divided	7 mL
¾ tsp	freshly ground black pepper, divided	3 mL
2	egg whites, beaten	2
2 cups	ricotta cheese	500 mL
¼ cup	freshly grated Parmesan cheese	60 mL
2 tbsp	chopped fresh basil	30 mL
2 tbsp	chopped fresh oregano	30 mL
9	oven-ready lasagna noodles	9
4 cups	loosely packed baby spinach	1 L
1½ cups	shredded mozzarella cheese	375 mL

1. In a large nonstick skillet, over medium-high heat, cook beef and garlic, breaking beef up with the back of a spoon, for 8 to 10 minutes or until beef is no longer pink. Drain off fat.

2. Stir in pasta sauce, 1 tsp (5 mL) of the salt and ½ tsp (2 mL) of the pepper; bring to a boil. Reduce heat and simmer for 5 minutes.

3. In a bowl, combine egg whites, ricotta, Parmesan, basil, oregano and the remaining salt and pepper.

4. Spread 1 cup (250 mL) of the meat sauce in bottom of prepared baking dish. Arrange 3 noodles over sauce. Top with half the ricotta mixture, half the spinach, ½ cup (125 mL) of the mozzarella and 1½ cups (375 mL) meat sauce. Repeat layers with noodles, ricotta mixture, spinach, mozzarella and meat sauce. Arrange the remaining noodles on top. Spread the remaining meat sauce over noodles.

5. Cover and bake in preheated oven for 45 minutes or until sauce is bubbling. Sprinkle with the remaining mozzarella and bake, uncovered, for 10 minutes or until cheese is melted. Let cool for 10 minutes before serving.

No-Pasta Lasagna

Makes 10 to 12 servings

This scrumptious recipe is low in carbohydrates and is gluten-free.

Tip

For an added kick of spice, use hot Italian sausage instead of mild.

- Preheat oven to 350°F (180°C)
- 13- by 9-inch (33 by 23 cm) glass baking dish, greased

4 cups	tomato sauce	1 L
½ tsp	dried oregano	2 mL
½ tsp	dried thyme	2 mL
½ tsp	salt	2 mL
½ tsp	freshly ground black pepper	2 mL
2 tbsp	butter or olive oil	30 mL
1	onion, chopped	1
3	cloves garlic, chopped	3
2 cups	sliced mushrooms	500 mL
2 lbs	lean ground beef	1 kg
1½ lbs	mild Italian sausage (bulk or removed from casings)	750 g
1 lb	bacon, chopped	500 g
3 lbs	zucchini, thinly sliced lengthwise	1.5 kg
2 cups	ricotta cheese	500 mL
½ cup	chopped fresh basil	125 mL
4 cups	shredded mozzarella cheese	1 L
1 cup	freshly grated Parmesan cheese	250 mL

1. In a large bowl, combine tomato sauce, oregano, thyme, salt and pepper.

2. In a large nonstick skillet, melt butter over medium heat. Sauté onion for 5 to 7 minutes or until softened. Add garlic and mushrooms; sauté for 5 minutes. Stir into tomato sauce mixture.

3. In the same skillet, over medium-high heat, cook beef, sausage and bacon, breaking beef and sausage up with the back of a spoon, for 8 to 10 minutes or until beef and sausage are no longer pink and bacon is cooked. Drain off fat.

4. Arrange one-third of the zucchini slices in bottom of prepared baking dish as if they were lasagna noodles. Top with one-third of the ricotta. Sprinkle with one-third of the basil. Layer with one-third each of the beef mixture, tomato sauce mixture, mozzarella and Parmesan. Repeat layers twice, ending with cheese.

5. Cover and bake in preheated oven for 45 minutes. Uncover and bake for 10 minutes or until cheese is browned. Let cool for 10 minutes before serving.

Baked Ziti

Oven-baked ziti with a combination of ground beef and pork makes for a very satisfying meal.

Tips

I like to use a nonstick skillet when browning ground turkey, chicken or beef, as it eliminates the need for oil or butter.

If you're trying to reduce your salt intake, you can substitute reduced-sodium or no-salt-added tomato sauce for the tomato pasta sauce.

- Preheat oven to 350°F (180°C)
- 8-cup (2 L) casserole dish, greased

8 oz	extra-lean ground beef	250 g
8 oz	mild pork sausage (bulk or removed from casings)	250 g
1	small onion, chopped	1
3 cups	tomato pasta sauce	750 mL
8 oz	ziti pasta	250 g
1	egg, lightly beaten	1
5 oz	frozen chopped spinach (about 1/2 package), thawed, drained and squeezed dry	150 g
2 cups	ricotta cheese	500 mL
2 tbsp	freshly grated Parmesan cheese	30 mL
1/2 tsp	garlic powder	2 mL
1/2 cup	shredded mozzarella cheese	125 mL

1. In a large nonstick skillet, over medium-high heat, cook beef, sausage and onion, breaking meat up with the back of a spoon, for 8 to 10 minutes or until beef and sausage are no longer pink. Drain off fat. Stir in pasta sauce and remove from heat.

2. Meanwhile, in a large pot of boiling water, cook ziti according to package directions until just tender. Drain.

3. In a large bowl, combine egg, spinach, ricotta, Parmesan and garlic powder. Add ziti and toss to coat.

4. Spread half the meat mixture in prepared casserole dish. Spoon ziti mixture over top. Spread the remaining meat mixture over ziti.

5. Cover and bake in preheated oven for 30 minutes. Sprinkle with mozzarella and bake, uncovered, for 5 minutes or until cheese is melted.

Johnny Mazetti

**Makes 10 to
12 servings**

When I was a child, this dish was served in my school cafeteria, but it wasn't until I was in culinary school that a fellow student told me it was called Johnny Mazetti. I hope you enjoy my version.

Tip

There are so many versions of this particular recipe that you really could substitute just about anything, creating a combination of flavors and textures your family enjoys.

- Preheat oven to 350°F (180°C)
- 13- by 9-inch (33 by 23 cm) glass baking dish, greased

1/4 cup	butter	60 mL
1 1/2 cups	chopped onions	375 mL
1 1/2 cups	chopped celery	375 mL
1 1/2 cups	chopped green bell pepper	375 mL
1 1/2 lbs	lean ground beef	750 g
1 1/2 lbs	lean ground pork	750 g
15	large stuffed olives, sliced	15
2	cans (each 8 oz/227 mL) tomato sauce	2
1	can (10 oz/284 mL) condensed tomato soup	1
1	can (10 oz/284 mL) diced tomatoes with green chiles	1
1	can (8 oz/227 mL) sliced mushrooms, with liquid	1
1 lb	wide egg noodles	500 g
1/3 cup	grated Parmesan cheese	75 mL

1. In a large skillet, melt butter over medium heat. Sauté onions, celery and green pepper for 5 to 7 minutes or until softened. Transfer vegetables to a plate.

2. Add beef and pork to skillet; increase heat to medium-high and cook, breaking meat up with the back of a spoon, for 8 to 10 minutes or until beef and pork are no longer pink. Drain off fat.

3. Return cooked vegetables to skillet and stir in olives, tomato sauce, soup, tomatoes with chiles and mushrooms. Spoon into prepared baking dish.

4. Meanwhile, in a large pot of boiling water, cook egg noodles according to package directions until just tender. Drain and gently stir into beef mixture. Sprinkle with cheese.

5. Bake in preheated oven for 45 minutes or until bubbling.

Crunchy Chow Mein Casserole

My dear friends Nancy and TC Farrington live in Arizona and were huge supporters of my first book, *200 Best Panini Recipes*. When Nancy heard about this book, she was eager to share one of her favorite casserole recipes, inspired by the flavors of Asian takeout.

Tip

Bean sprouts and chopped fresh cilantro make a crunchy and colorful garnish.

- Preheat oven to 350°F (180°C)
- 11- by 7-inch (28 by 18 cm) glass baking dish, greased

1 lb	lean ground beef	500 g
2	stalks celery, chopped	2
1	small onion, chopped	1
1	can (10 oz/284 mL) condensed cream of chicken soup	1
1 cup	cooked brown rice	250 mL
1/2 cup	slivered almonds	125 mL
3 tbsp	soy sauce	45 mL
5 oz	fried chow mein noodles	150 g

1. In a large nonstick skillet, over medium-high heat, cook beef, celery and onion, breaking beef up with the back of a spoon, for 8 to 10 minutes or until beef is no longer pink. Drain off fat.

2. In a large bowl, combine soup, rice, almonds, soy sauce and 1/2 cup (125 mL) water. Stir in beef mixture. Spoon into prepared baking dish and top with chow mein noodles.

3. Bake in preheated oven for 25 to 30 minutes or until bubbling.

Santa Fe Stuffed Bell Peppers

Makes 4 servings

These stuffed bell peppers with a Santa Fe twist of corn, chili powder and cumin are nutrient-dense thanks to lean beef and brown rice.

Tip

Choose any color bell peppers: green, red, yellow or orange.

- Preheat oven to 450°F (230°C)
- 13- by 9-inch (33 by 23 cm) glass baking dish

1 lb	lean ground beef	500 g
1	package (10 oz/300 g) frozen corn kernels (2⅓ cups/575 mL), thawed	1
1½ cups	salsa	375 mL
1½ cups	cooked brown rice	375 mL
¾ tsp	salt	3 mL
¾ tsp	freshly ground black pepper	3 mL
¾ tsp	chili powder	3 mL
¾ tsp	ground cumin	3 mL
4	large bell peppers, cut in half lengthwise, stems, cores and seeds removed	4
1 cup	shredded extra-sharp (extra-old) Cheddar cheese	250 mL

1. In a large nonstick skillet, over medium-high heat, cook beef, breaking it up with the back of a spoon, for 8 to 10 minutes or until no longer pink. Drain off fat. Stir in corn, salsa, rice, salt, pepper, chili powder and cumin.

2. Pierce peppers with a fork or sharp knife; place in baking dish. Fill each evenly with meat mixture.

3. Cover and bake in preheated oven for 20 minutes. Sprinkle evenly with cheese and bake, uncovered, for 5 minutes or until cheese is melted.

Fragrant Lamb and Ziti Casserole

This Greek dish has layers of ziti, meaty tomato sauce fragrant with spices and a silky béchamel sauce. Serve with a Greek salad to keep all the flavors humming together.

Tips

I like to use a nonstick skillet when browning ground meat, as it eliminates the need for oil or butter.

If you like to grind your own spices, a clean coffee grinder is perfect for the task. Just make sure to use that grinder only to grind spices. If you want to grind coffee beans too, you'll need a second grinder. You don't want the strong flavor of coffee tainting the taste of your spices!

- Preheat oven to 375°F (190°C)
- 16-cup (4 L) casserole dish, greased

Meat Sauce

2 lbs	lean ground lamb	1 kg
2	onions, chopped	2
2	cloves garlic, chopped	2
3	cans (each 14 oz/398 mL) diced tomatoes	3
4	sprigs fresh thyme	4
1½ tsp	salt	7 mL
1¼ tsp	ground cinnamon	6 mL
1¼ tsp	ground allspice	6 mL
1 tsp	ground nutmeg	5 mL
¼ tsp	ground cloves	1 mL

Béchamel Sauce

½ cup	butter	125 mL
⅓ cup	all-purpose flour	75 mL
7 cups	milk	1.75 L
1 cup	freshly grated Parmesan cheese	250 mL
1 tsp	salt	5 mL
¼ tsp	ground nutmeg	1 mL
5	egg yolks	5

2 lbs	ziti pasta	1 kg
1¾ cups	dry bread crumbs	425 mL
¼ cup	freshly grated Parmesan cheese	60 mL

1. *Meat Sauce:* In a large nonstick skillet, over medium-high heat, cook lamb, onions and garlic, breaking lamb up with the back of a spoon, for 8 to 10 minutes or until lamb is no longer pink. Drain off fat.

2. Stir in tomatoes, thyme, salt, cinnamon, allspice, nutmeg and cloves; bring to a boil. Cover, leaving lid ajar, reduce heat to low and simmer, stirring occasionally, for about 40 minutes or until some of the liquid has evaporated but sauce is still moist. Discard thyme.

Freshly grated or shaved Parmesan cheese is always best right off the wedge, but prepackaged containers can be found in the refrigerated specialty cheese section of your local supermarket.

3. *Béchamel Sauce:* Meanwhile, in a medium saucepan, melt butter over medium heat. Sprinkle with flour and cook, whisking constantly, for about 6 minutes or until roux is golden.

4. In another medium saucepan, bring milk to the boiling point over medium heat. Gradually add to roux in a steady stream, whisking constantly until smooth. Bring to a boil over medium heat, whisking. Cook, whisking constantly, for 10 minutes. Remove from heat and stir in cheese, salt and nutmeg until cheese is melted.

5. In a medium bowl, lightly beat egg yolks. Gradually whisk in 2 cups (500 mL) béchamel sauce. Gradually whisk yolk mixture into the remaining béchamel sauce. Keep warm.

6. In a large pot of boiling water, cook ziti according to package directions until just tender. Drain, transfer pasta to a large bowl and stir in 1 cup (250 mL) of the béchamel sauce..

7. Spread one-third of the ziti in prepared casserole dish. Spread half the meat sauce evenly over top. Add another layer of ziti and top with the remaining meat sauce. Layer the remaining pasta on top. Pour the remaining béchamel sauce evenly over top.

8. In a small bowl, combine bread crumbs and cheese. Sprinkle evenly over casserole.

9. Bake in middle of preheated oven for 45 to 50 minutes or until crumbs are golden brown and sauce is bubbling.

Stuffed Cabbage Rolls

While researching this dish, I learned that it is also called Polish Golumpki and can be prepared in a number of ways. Here is my version, which uses a combination of beef and pork.

Variation

Try ground lamb in place of either the beef or the pork.

- Preheat oven to 325°F (160°C)
- Steamer basket
- 13- by 9-inch (33 by 23 cm) glass baking dish

1	large head green cabbage, cored	1
2 tbsp	olive oil	30 mL
1	onion, chopped	1
1½ cups	cooked long-grain white rice	375 mL
1 tbsp	butter	15 mL
1½ tsp	salt, divided	7 mL
1 tsp	freshly ground black pepper, divided	5 mL
1½ lbs	lean ground beef	750 g
8 oz	lean ground pork	250 g
1	can (14 oz/398 mL) crushed tomatoes	1
½ cup	unsweetened apple juice	125 mL
1 tbsp	cider vinegar	15 mL

1. In a large pot fitted with a steamer basket, bring 2 inches (5 cm) of water to a boil over high heat. Place cabbage head in basket, reduce heat to low and steam for 8 minutes. Let cool slightly.

2. Remove 16 leaves from cabbage, saving any remaining cabbage for another use. Cut off raised portion of the center vein of each cabbage leaf, making sure to not cut the vein. Set leaves aside.

3. In a skillet, heat oil over medium heat. Sauté onion for 5 to 7 minutes or until softened. Let cool slightly.

4. In a large bowl, combine rice, butter, 1 tsp (5 mL) salt and ½ tsp (2 mL) pepper. Using your hands, work in sautéed onion, beef and pork.

5. Place cabbage leaves on a flat surface. Spoon rice mixture into the center of each cabbage leaf, dividing evenly. Fold in edges of leaves over rice mixture and roll up. Arrange cabbage rolls in baking dish.

6. In a medium bowl, combine tomatoes, apple juice, vinegar and the remaining salt and pepper. Pour evenly over cabbage rolls.

7. Cover and bake in preheated oven for 2½ hours or until cabbage is tender and filling is heated through.

Healthy Choices

Low-Fat Hash Brown Casserole 238

Asparagus, Bell Pepper and Cheese Frittata 239

Layered Artichokes and Potatoes 240

Chiles Rellenos Casserole 241

Quinoa-Stuffed Bell Peppers 242

Greek Spinach Pie 243

Southwest Butternut Squash Tortilla Bake 244

Quinoa and Mixed Veggie Bake 245

Layered Mexican Vegetable Bake
    with Red and Green Chile Sauce 246

Creamy Chipotle Black Bean Burrito Bake 247

Italian Baked Polenta 248

Lighten Up Tuna Casserole 249

Baked Shrimp Enchiladas 250

Cajun Shrimp and Rice Casserole 251

Easy Chicken Penne Pasta Bake 252

Baked Chicken Tetrazzini 253

My Very Favorite Sour Cream Chicken Enchiladas 254

Spinach, Chicken Sausage and Artichoke Casserole 255

Cremini Mushroom and Sausage Strata 256

Sloppy Joe Mac and Cheese 258

Layered Beef and Noodle Bake 260

Low-Fat Hash Brown Casserole

Breakfast casseroles are often loaded with fat and calories. I shaved the fat by using turkey bacon and low-fat dairy products in this creamy hash brown delight.

Tip

If you choose to splurge, you can use center-cut pork bacon instead of the turkey bacon.

• 11- by 7-inch (28 by 18 cm) glass baking dish, greased

6	slices turkey bacon	6
2	cloves garlic, minced	2
1 cup	chopped onion	250 mL
2 lbs	frozen hash brown potatoes	1 kg
1	can (10 oz/284 mL) reduced-sodium, fat-free condensed cream of mushroom soup	1
1 cup	shredded reduced-fat extra-sharp (extra-old) Cheddar cheese, divided	250 mL
1/2 cup	chopped green onions	125 mL
1/2 cup	fat-free sour cream	125 mL
1/2 tsp	salt	2 mL
1/2 tsp	freshly ground black pepper	2 mL

1. In a large nonstick skillet, over medium-high heat, cook bacon, turning once, until crisp. Using tongs, transfer to a plate lined with paper towels. Let cool, then crumble.

2. Drain any fat from skillet and spray with cooking spray. Reduce heat to medium; sauté garlic and onion for 5 to 7 minutes or until softened. Stir in hash browns; reduce heat to low, cover and cook, stirring occasionally, for 15 minutes.

3. In a large bowl, combine crumbled bacon, soup, 1/4 cup (60 mL) of the cheese, green onions, sour cream, salt and pepper. Gently stir in hash brown mixture. Spoon into prepared baking dish and sprinkle with remaining cheese. Cover and refrigerate for at least 6 hours or overnight.

4. Preheat oven to 350°F (180°C).

5. Bake, covered, for 45 minutes. Uncover and bake for 15 minutes or until golden brown.

Asparagus, Bell Pepper and Cheese Frittata

The pairing of nutrient-dense asparagus with vibrant red peppers makes for a colorful, flavorful frittata.

Tip

Try making frittatas in an ovenproof skillet for an authentic look.

- Preheat oven to 325°F (160°C)
- 10-inch (25 cm) glass deep-dish pie plate, greased

2 tbsp	dry bread crumbs	30 mL
1 lb	asparagus	500 g
1 tbsp	extra virgin olive oil	15 mL
2	onions, chopped	2
2	cloves garlic, chopped	2
1/2 cup	chopped red bell pepper	125 mL
1/2 cup	chopped yellow bell pepper	125 mL
1/2 tsp	salt, divided	2 mL
4	eggs	4
2	egg whites	2
1 cup	part-skim ricotta cheese	250 mL
1 tbsp	chopped fresh parsley	15 mL
1/4 tsp	freshly ground black pepper	1 mL
1/2 cup	shredded Swiss cheese	125 mL

1. Sprinkle prepared pie plate with bread crumbs. Set aside.

2. Snap tough ends off asparagus. Slice off the top 2 inches (5 cm) and reserve. Cut the stalks into 1/2-inch (1 cm) slices.

3. In a large nonstick skillet, heat oil over medium heat. Sauté onions, garlic, red pepper, yellow pepper and 1/4 tsp (1 mL) salt for 5 to 7 minutes or until softened. Add asparagus stalks and 1/2 cup (125 mL) water. Reduce heat and simmer, stirring, for 5 to 7 minutes or until asparagus is tender and liquid has evaporated. Arrange in an even layer in pie plate.

4. In a large bowl, whisk eggs and egg whites. Whisk in ricotta, parsley, pepper and the remaining salt. Pour over vegetables. Arrange the reserved asparagus tips on top and sprinkle with Swiss cheese.

5. Bake in preheated oven for about 35 minutes or until a knife inserted in the center comes out clean. Let cool for 5 minutes before serving.

Layered Artichokes and Potatoes

Fresh artichokes and potatoes combine with Parmesan cheese in this tasty casserole.

Tip

Never throw away stale bread; instead, make fresh bread crumbs! Trim off the crusts, then tear bread into pieces. Process in a food processor to coarse crumbs. One slice of bread makes about $1/3$ cup (75 mL) crumbs.

- Preheat oven to 375°F (190°C)
- 11- by 7-inch (28 by 18 cm) glass baking dish, greased

2	cloves garlic, chopped	2
$2/3$ cup	freshly grated Parmesan cheese	150 mL
6 tbsp	freshly squeezed lemon juice, divided	90 mL
4	artichokes (each about 12 oz/375 g)	4
$1\frac{1}{2}$ lbs	potatoes, peeled and cut into $1/4$-inch (0.5 cm) thick slices	750 g
$1/2$ tsp	salt	2 mL
$1/4$ tsp	freshly ground black pepper	1 mL
$1/2$ cup	vegetable broth	125 mL
$1/3$ cup	fresh bread crumbs	75 mL

1. In a small bowl combine garlic and Parmesan. Set aside.

2. Fill a large bowl with water and add $1/4$ cup (60 mL) of the lemon juice. For each artichoke, peel away all outer leaves. Remove leaves at the base until the fuzzy choke is visible. Trim the leaves with a paring knife, removing any fibrous green portions. Trim the bottom $1/4$ inch (0.5 cm) from the stem and pare away the tough outer skin. Remove the choke. Cut the stem and heart into thin slices and place in lemon water while you continue preparing the remaining artichokes.

3. Arrange half the potatoes in prepared baking dish. Drain artichokes and layer on top of potatoes. Sprinkle with the remaining lemon juice, salt, pepper and half the garlic mixture. Arrange the remaining potatoes on top. Pour broth over potatoes.

4. Cover and bake in preheated oven for 1 to $1\frac{1}{4}$ hours or until potatoes are tender.

5. In a bowl, combine bread crumbs and the remaining garlic mixture. Sprinkle over potatoes. Bake, uncovered, for 10 to 15 minutes or until topping is golden.

Chiles Rellenos Casserole

Makes 6 servings

If you love chiles rellenos, you will love this casserole! Serve with salsa or fresh pico de gallo.

Tip

Liquid egg substitute works wonderfully well in this recipe, but feel free to use 6 eggs instead.

- Preheat oven to 350°F (180°C)
- 11- by 7-inch (28 by 18 cm) glass baking dish, greased

3	cans (each 4½ oz/127 mL) whole mild green chiles, drained	3
4	6- or 7-inch (15 or 18 cm) flour tortillas, cut into 1-inch (2.5 cm) strips	4
1 cup	shredded part-skim mozzarella cheese	250 mL
1 cup	shredded reduced-fat Cheddar cheese	250 mL
1½ cups	liquid egg substitute	375 mL
⅓ cup	skim milk	75 mL
¼ tsp	garlic powder	1 mL
¼ tsp	ground cumin	1 mL
¼ tsp	chili powder	1 mL
¼ tsp	salt	1 mL
¼ tsp	freshly ground black pepper	1 mL

1. Cut along one side of each chile and open it to lie flat. Layer half each of the chiles, tortilla strips, mozzarella and Cheddar in prepared baking dish. Repeat layers.

2. In a medium bowl, whisk together egg substitute, milk, garlic powder, cumin, chili powder, salt and pepper. Pour over casserole.

3. Bake in preheated oven for 40 to 45 minutes or until a knife inserted 2 inches (5 cm) from the edge of the pan comes out clean. Let cool for 10 minutes before slicing and serving.

Quinoa-Stuffed Bell Peppers

My mom always made stuffed bell peppers with rice and ground beef, topped with a tomato sauce. I took a bit of a different approach, using a sauté of fresh vegetables and quinoa. I love both recipes!

Tip

Toast almonds in a dry skillet over medium heat, stirring and shaking pan constantly, for 3 to 4 minutes or until golden and fragrant. Immediately transfer to a bowl and let cool.

- Preheat oven to 350°F (180°C)
- 13- by 9-inch (33 by 23 cm) glass baking dish, greased

1 tbsp	olive oil	15 mL
1	red onion, chopped	1
1	red bell pepper, chopped	1
1 cup	shredded carrots	250 mL
8 oz	mushrooms, chopped	250 g
1 cup	packed baby spinach, thinly sliced	250 mL
2 tbsp	chopped fresh parsley	30 mL
1 cup	cooked quinoa	250 mL
1 tsp	paprika	5 mL
¾ tsp	ground cumin	3 mL
½ tsp	salt	2 mL
½ tsp	freshly ground black pepper	2 mL
6	green bell peppers, tops removed, cored and seeded	6
¼ cup	toasted chopped almonds	60 mL

1. In a large skillet, heat oil over medium-high heat. Sauté onion, red pepper and carrots for 5 minutes or until softened. Add mushrooms and sauté for 5 minutes or until softened. Add spinach and parsley; sauté for 2 to 3 minutes or until spinach is wilted. Stir in quinoa, paprika, cumin, salt and pepper.

2. Stuff green peppers with quinoa mixture, dividing equally and gently packing the mixture down. Arrange upright in prepared baking dish. Sprinkle with almonds.

3. Cover and bake in preheated oven for about 1 hour or until peppers are tender.

Quinoa-Stuffed Bell Peppers (page 242)

Cheesy Baked Vegetables (page 87)

Greek Spinach Pie

Here, classic Greek flavors, including spinach, feta and mint, are layered between sheets of delicate phyllo pastry.

Tip

Work quickly with phyllo dough to keep it from drying out.

- Preheat oven to 350°F (180°C)
- 13- by 9-inch (33 by 23 cm) glass baking dish, greased

	Nonstick cooking spray	
2	onions, chopped	2
2	cloves garlic, minced	2
½ cup	minced green onions	125 mL
10 oz	fresh baby spinach, sliced	300 g
¼ cup	chopped fresh parsley	60 mL
2 tbsp	finely chopped fresh mint	30 mL
3	egg whites	3
4 oz	crumbled reduced-fat feta cheese	125 g
½ cup	freshly grated Parmesan cheese	125 mL
½ tsp	salt	2 mL
¼ tsp	freshly ground black pepper	1 mL
10	sheets frozen phyllo pastry, thawed	10

1. Spray a large nonstick skillet with cooking spray and heat over medium-high heat. Sauté chopped onions for 8 minutes or until browned. Add garlic and green onions; sauté for 1 minute. Add spinach, a handful at a time, and sauté for 1 to 2 minutes or until wilted. Add parsley and mint; sauté for 1 minute. Transfer to a large bowl and let cool slightly.

2. In a medium bowl, whisk together egg whites, feta, Parmesan, salt and pepper. Stir into spinach mixture.

3. Place one phyllo sheet on a large cutting board. (Keep remaining phyllo sheets covered with a damp cloth.) Spray pastry with cooking spray. Place in center of prepared baking dish, allowing phyllo to extend up long sides of dish. Layer 4 more phyllo sheets in dish, spraying each with cooking spray before adding the next. Spread spinach mixture evenly over phyllo. Layer the remaining 5 phyllo sheets on top, spraying each with cooking spray before adding the next. Carefully fold edges of pastry into center. Spray with cooking spray. Score phyllo with 2 lengthwise cuts and 3 crosswise cuts, forming 12 rectangles.

4. Bake in preheated oven for 40 minutes or until golden brown.

Southwest Butternut Squash Tortilla Bake

This easy casserole, filled with traditional flavors of the Southwest, is a wonderful way to showcase butternut squash.

Tips

For more heat, use 2 jalapeños and leave in the seeds. But be careful — the ribs and seeds really add to the heat!

Butternut squash is easier to dice if you microwave it on High for about 2 minutes before peeling.

If you want to use canned corn, use a 14 or 15 oz (398 or 425 mL) can and drain before using.

- Preheat oven to 400°F (200°C)
- 8-cup (2 L) round casserole dish

2 tbsp	olive oil, divided	30 mL
1	onion, thinly sliced	1
2	cloves garlic, minced	2
1	jalapeño pepper, seeded and minced	1
1 tsp	paprika	5 mL
1 tsp	ground cumin	5 mL
1 tsp	dried oregano	5 mL
1	can (16 oz/454 mL) crushed tomatoes	1
1 lb	butternut squash, peeled, seeded and diced	500 g
1 cup	vegetable broth	250 mL
1	can (14 to 19 oz/398 to 540 mL) black beans, drained and rinsed	1
1½ cups	corn kernels (thawed if frozen)	375 mL
¼ tsp	salt	1 mL
¼ tsp	freshly ground black pepper	1 mL
8	6-inch (15 cm) corn tortillas, cut into ¾-inch (2 cm) strips	8
½ cup	shredded reduced-fat sharp (old) Cheddar cheese	125 mL

1. In a large nonstick skillet, heat half the oil over medium heat. Sauté onion for 5 to 7 minutes or until softened. Add garlic and jalapeño; sauté for 1 minute. Add paprika, cumin and oregano; sauté for 1 minute. Add tomatoes, squash and broth; bring to a simmer. Reduce heat to low, cover and simmer for about 10 minutes or until squash is just tender. Stir in beans, corn, salt and pepper.

2. Spoon squash mixture into casserole dish. Layer tortilla strips over top. Brush with the remaining oil.

3. Bake in preheated oven for 25 to 30 minutes or until topping is golden brown and filling is bubbling. Sprinkle with cheese and bake for 3 minutes or until cheese is melted.

Quinoa and Mixed Veggie Bake

I love how the texture of the quinoa complements the beautiful array of fresh vegetables in this dish, but leftover brown or white rice would work well too.

Tips

When draining tomatoes, freeze the liquid, then add it to soups, stews and sauces.

Use your favorite mushrooms in place of the baby bellas. I like the meaty flavor of baby bellas, and they are often sold already sliced, which is certainly convenient.

Quinoa is not technically a grain, but it can be used in place of grains in almost any dish.

- Preheat oven to 350°F (180°C)
- 13- by 9-inch (33 by 23 cm) glass baking dish, greased

1 tbsp	extra virgin olive oil	15 mL
2	cloves garlic, finely chopped	2
1	large onion, chopped	1
1	red bell pepper, chopped	1
1	zucchini, chopped	1
1	yellow summer squash, chopped	1
8 oz	baby bella mushrooms, sliced	250 g
1	can (14 oz/398 mL) diced fire-roasted tomatoes, drained	1
½ tsp	salt	2 mL
½ tsp	freshly ground black pepper	2 mL
2	eggs, beaten	2
4 cups	cooked quinoa	1 L
⅓ cup	freshly grated Parmesan cheese	75 mL
2 tbsp	chopped fresh parsley	30 mL

1. In a large nonstick skillet, heat oil over medium heat. Sauté garlic and onion for 5 to 7 minutes or until softened. Add red pepper, zucchini, squash and mushrooms; sauté for about 5 minutes or until just tender. Stir in tomatoes and cook for 2 minutes. Season with salt and pepper.

2. Transfer vegetable mixture to a large bowl and stir in eggs, quinoa, cheese and parsley. Spread in prepared baking dish.

3. Bake in preheated oven for 20 to 25 minutes or until golden brown.

Layered Mexican Vegetable Bake with Red and Green Chile Sauce

This colorful dish is bursting with true Latin flavor.

Tips

Chipotle peppers in adobo sauce, green chile sauce and red chile sauce are found in the international foods section of your supermarket.

Salsa verde, also called green chile sauce or tomatillo sauce, is typically made with tomatillos, green chiles and cilantro. Red chile sauce is made with ground roasted or dried red chiles, tomatoes and garlic. Both sauces vary in their heat level depending on the amount of chiles used. I like to use mild sauces in my recipes.

There are usually a number of peppers in each can of chipotles. I use what I need and freeze the remainder in ice cube trays to drop into sauces, soups and stews for added heat and smoky flavor.

- Preheat oven to 350°F (180°C)
- 11- by 7-inch (28 by 18 cm) glass baking dish, greased

2 tsp	olive oil	10 mL
2 cups	fresh corn kernels (about 4 ears)	500 mL
2 cups	diced zucchini	500 mL
1 cup	chopped red bell pepper	250 mL
1 cup	chopped onion	250 mL
2	chipotle peppers in adobo sauce, chopped	2
2	cloves garlic, minced	2
1 tsp	dried oregano	5 mL
2 cups	baked tortilla chips	500 mL
1 cup	shredded part-skim Monterey Jack cheese	250 mL
2 cups	salsa verde, heated	500 mL
2 cups	red chile sauce, heated	500 mL

1. In a large nonstick skillet, heat oil over medium-high heat. Sauté corn, zucchini, red pepper and onion for 5 to 7 minutes or until softened. Add chipotle peppers, garlic and oregano; sauté for 2 minutes.

2. Arrange half the tortilla chips in a single layer in prepared baking dish. Spread half the corn mixture on top. Sprinkle with half the cheese. Repeat layers with the remaining tortilla chips, corn mixture and cheese.

3. Bake in preheated oven for 20 minutes or until hot and bubbly. Top each serving with $1/4$ cup (60 mL) green chile sauce and $1/4$ cup (60 mL) red chile sauce.

Creamy Chipotle Black Bean Burrito Bake

Authentic Mexican flavors abound in this vegetarian recipe, with smoky chipotle peppers in adobo sauce, black beans, corn and creamy Monterey Jack cheese. Serve garnished with avocado slices and chopped fresh cilantro.

Tips

You can adjust the heat in the recipe by choosing mild, medium or hot salsa. Turn it up a little bit more by adding another chipotle pepper or two.

Look for canned chipotle peppers in adobo sauce in the international foods section of your supermarket. They're a great addition to soups, stews, sauces and dressings — anywhere you want to add heat and smoky flavor.

- Preheat oven to 350°F (180°C)
- 11- by 7-inch (28 by 18 cm) glass baking dish, greased

½ cup	reduced-fat sour cream	125 mL
1	chipotle pepper in adobo sauce, finely chopped	1
1	can (14 to 19 oz/398 to 540 mL) black beans, drained and rinsed	1
1 cup	frozen corn kernels, thawed	250 mL
4	8- to 10-inch (20 to 25 cm) reduced-fat flour tortillas	4
1 cup	salsa	250 mL
½ cup	shredded part-skim Monterey Jack cheese	125 mL

1. In a medium bowl, combine sour cream and chipotle pepper. Stir in beans and corn.

2. Spoon ½ cup (125 mL) of the sour cream mixture down the center of each tortilla. Roll up and place seam side down in prepared baking dish. Spread salsa evenly over tortillas. Sprinkle with cheese.

3. Cover and bake in preheated oven for 20 minutes or until bubbling.

Italian Baked Polenta

Makes 6 servings

This quick, easy recipe is great for entertaining.

Tip

Button mushrooms are affordable and work well in this recipe, but baby bellas are a wonderful substitution.

- Preheat oven to 400°F (200°C)
- 13- by 9-inch (33 by 23 cm) glass baking dish, greased

2 tsp	olive oil	10 mL
2 cups	chopped onions	500 mL
2	cloves garlic, chopped	2
3 cups	coarsely chopped mushrooms (about 12 oz/375 g)	750 mL
1½ tsp	salt, divided	7 mL
½ tsp	freshly ground black pepper	2 mL
⅓ cup	dry red wine	75 mL
1 tbsp	chopped fresh rosemary	15 mL
1 tbsp	tomato paste	15 mL
1	can (14 oz/398 mL) diced tomatoes	1
1 cup	instant polenta	250 mL
½ cup	freshly grated Parmesan cheese	125 mL
½ cup	part-skim ricotta cheese	125 mL

1. In a large nonstick skillet, heat oil over medium-high heat. Sauté onions for 3 to 5 minutes or until softened. Add garlic, mushrooms, ½ tsp (2 mL) of the salt and pepper; sauté for 4 minutes. Stir in wine, rosemary and tomato paste; reduce heat to medium and cook, stirring, for 3 minutes. Stir in tomatoes and bring to a boil; reduce heat and simmer, stirring occasionally, for 7 to 10 minutes or until thickened. Remove from heat.

2. Meanwhile, in a medium saucepan, bring 4 cups (1 L) water to a boil over high heat. Gradually stir in polenta and the remaining salt. Reduce heat to low and simmer, stirring frequently, for about 5 minutes or until thick.

3. Spread one-third of the polenta in prepared baking dish. Spread half the tomato sauce over polenta and sprinkle with 2 tbsp (30 mL) Parmesan. Drop half the ricotta cheese by spoonfuls on top of the Parmesan. Repeat layers once. Spread the remaining polenta on top and sprinkle with the remaining Parmesan.

4. Bake in preheated oven for 30 minutes or until bubbling.

Lighten Up Tuna Casserole

I love tuna casserole, especially this lighter version made with skim milk, tuna packed in water, Parmesan cheese and dry bread crumbs for the topping.

Tip

When cooking with wine, choose one you'd enjoy drinking. If it's not good enough for your glass, it's not good enough for your dish!

- Preheat oven to 350°F (180°C)
- 8-inch (20 cm) square glass baking dish, greased

2 tsp	extra virgin olive oil	10 mL
1	onion, chopped	1
8 oz	mushrooms, sliced	250 g
½ cup	dry white wine	125 mL
⅓ cup	all-purpose flour	75 mL
3 cups	skim milk	750 mL
½ tsp	salt	2 mL
½ tsp	freshly ground black pepper	2 mL
8 oz	wide egg noodles	250 g
2	cans (each 6 oz/170 g) water-packed chunk light tuna, drained	2
1 cup	frozen peas, thawed	250 mL
1 cup	freshly grated Parmesan cheese, divided	250 mL
½ cup	dry bread crumbs	125 mL

1. In a large nonstick skillet, heat oil over medium-high heat. Sauté onion and mushrooms for 5 to 7 minutes or until softened. Add wine and cook for 4 to 5 minutes or until evaporated. Sprinkle with flour and cook, stirring, for 1 minute. Gradually stir in milk, salt and pepper; bring to a simmer, stirring constantly. Reduce heat and simmer, stirring, for 4 to 6 minutes or until thickened.

2. Meanwhile, in a large pot of boiling salted water, cook noodles according to package directions until just tender. Drain and return to pot.

3. Remove onion mixture from heat and stir in tuna, peas and half the cheese. Add to noodles and stir gently to coat. Spoon into prepared baking dish and sprinkle with bread crumbs and the remaining cheese.

4. Bake in preheated oven for 30 to 35 minutes or until bubbling.

Baked Shrimp Enchiladas

Makes 8 servings

This easy casserole makes an excellent weeknight meal. It's loaded with flavor and has much less fat than traditional shrimp enchiladas.

Tip

Precooked shrimp is a great time-saver in this recipe.

- Preheat oven to 425°F (220°C)
- 13- by 9-inch (33 by 23 cm) glass baking dish, greased

2	cans (each 4½ oz/127 mL) chopped mild green chiles	2
1 lb	cooked medium shrimp, diced	500 g
2 cups	enchilada sauce, divided	500 mL
1 cup	frozen corn kernels, thawed	250 mL
12	6-inch (15 cm) corn tortillas	12
1	can (15 oz/426 mL) fat-free refried beans	1
1 cup	shredded reduced-fat Mexican-blend cheese	250 mL
½ cup	chopped fresh cilantro	125 mL

1. In a medium bowl, combine chiles, shrimp, ½ cup (125 mL) of the enchilada sauce and corn. Set aside.

2. Spread ½ cup (125 mL) of the remaining enchilada sauce in prepared baking dish. Arrange 6 tortillas on top, overlapping as necessary. Spread refried beans evenly over tortillas. Top with shrimp mixture. Arrange the remaining 6 tortillas on top and pour the remaining sauce over tortillas.

3. Cover and bake in preheated oven for about 30 minutes or until bubbling. Sprinkle with cheese and bake for about 5 minutes or until cheese is melted. Serve garnished with cilantro.

Cajun Shrimp and Rice Casserole

Makes 8 to 10 servings

The creamy baked mixture of wild rice, long-grain rice, cheese and shrimp is so satisfying.

Tips

The wild rice adds flavor and texture to this recipe, but it can also be made with white rice alone.

If your skillet isn't big enough to hold all of the ingredients, transfer the shrimp mixture to a large bowl once the cheese is melted.

- Preheat oven to 350°F (180°C)
- 13- by 9-inch (33 by 23 cm) glass baking dish, greased

2 tsp	olive oil	10 mL
1 cup	chopped onion	250 mL
1 cup	chopped green bell pepper	250 mL
2 lbs	cooked medium shrimp	1 kg
4 oz	light pasteurized prepared cheese product, such as Velveeta, cubed	125 g
6 oz	light garlic-and-herb-flavored spreadable cheese, such as Boursin	175 g
1	can (10 oz/284 mL) reduced-sodium, fat-free condensed cream of mushroom soup	1
3 cups	cooked wild rice	750 mL
2 cups	cooked long-grain brown rice	500 mL
1 cup	chopped green onions	250 mL
½ tsp	salt	2 mL
¼ tsp	freshly ground black pepper	1 mL

1. In a large nonstick skillet, heat oil over medium heat. Sauté onion and green pepper for 5 to 7 minutes or until softened. Add shrimp, pasteurized cheese, spreadable cheese and soup and cook, stirring occasionally, until cheese is melted. Stir in wild rice, brown rice, green onions, salt and pepper. Spoon into prepared baking dish.

2. Bake in preheated oven for 30 to 35 minutes or until bubbling.

Easy Chicken Penne Pasta Bake

This casserole is one of my daughter's favorite recipes. I love it too, and I am not sure Kennedy realizes she is eating spinach. It's a perfect way to get protein, veggies, dairy and whole grains in her diet.

Tips

Fire-roasted canned tomatoes add a fabulous smoky flavor to recipes. I substitute them for regular canned tomatoes whenever possible!

I grill or roast extra chicken breasts on Sunday evenings to add to weeknight casseroles. Store chopped cooked chicken in an airtight container in the refrigerator for easy meals during the week.

- Preheat oven to 400°F (200°C)
- 13- by 9-inch (33 by 23 cm) glass baking dish, greased

1 lb	whole wheat penne pasta	500 g
1	can (28 oz/796 mL) tomato sauce	1
1	can (14 oz/398 mL) fire-roasted diced tomatoes	1
1	can (2¼ oz/64 mL) sliced black olives, drained (about ¼ cup/60 mL)	1
4 cups	cubed cooked chicken breasts	1 L
2 cups	packed fresh spinach, thinly sliced	500 mL
¼ cup	chopped red onion	60 mL
¼ cup	chopped green bell pepper	60 mL
1 tsp	dried basil	5 mL
1 tsp	dried oregano	5 mL
½ cup	shredded part-skim mozzarella cheese	125 mL
½ cup	crumbled reduced-fat feta cheese	125 mL

1. In a large pot of boiling water, cook pasta according to package directions until just tender. Drain.

2. In a large bowl, combine cooked pasta, tomato sauce, tomatoes, olives, chicken, spinach, onion, green pepper, basil and oregano. Spoon into prepared baking dish and sprinkle with mozzarella and feta.

3. Bake in preheated oven for 30 minutes or until heated through and cheese is melted.

Baked Chicken Tetrazzini

Makes 6 servings

My friend Meg Plotsky makes the most fabulous chicken tetrazzini I've ever tasted. We decided to lighten it up a bit by using low-fat milk and reducing the butter and oil. We also chose whole wheat pasta to add flavor and nutrition. Voila! A healthy recipe that's just as delicious as the original.

Tip

Whenever you grill chicken, cook up some extra breasts, then chop or shred the meat and refrigerate it in an airtight container for up to 3 days. That way, you'll have it on hand for casserole recipes such as this one, simplifying your meal preparation another night.

- Preheat oven to 375°F (190°C)
- 11- by 7-inch (28 by 18 cm) glass baking dish, greased

8 oz	whole wheat angel hair pasta	250 g
1½ tsp	butter	7 mL
½	onion, finely chopped	½
8 oz	mushrooms, sliced	250 g
1 tsp	salt, divided	5 mL
1 tsp	freshly ground black pepper, divided	5 mL
1 cup	frozen peas	250 mL
1 tbsp	olive oil	15 mL
2½ tbsp	all-purpose flour	37 mL
1 cup	reduced-sodium chicken broth	250 mL
¼ cup	low-fat (1%) milk	60 mL
2 cups	chopped cooked chicken breasts	500 mL
6 tbsp	grated Romano cheese, divided	90 mL
¼ cup	finely chopped fresh chives, divided	60 mL

1. In a large pot of boiling water, cook pasta according to package directions until just tender. Drain and set aside.

2. In a large nonstick skillet, melt butter over medium-high heat. Sauté onion, mushrooms, and half each of the salt and pepper for 5 to 7 minutes or until softened. Stir in peas and sauté for 2 minutes. Transfer to a large bowl, stir in pasta and set aside.

3. In a small saucepan, heat oil over medium heat. Stir in flour until smooth. Gradually stir in broth and cook, stirring constantly, for about 3 minutes or until thickened. Stir in milk and the remaining salt and pepper. Cook, stirring, until thickened.

4. Add milk mixture to pasta mixture, along with chicken, 4 tbsp (60 mL) of the cheese and half the chives; toss gently to combine. Pour into prepared baking dish and sprinkle with the remaining cheese and chives.

5. Bake in preheated oven for 30 minutes or until golden brown and bubbling.

My Very Favorite Sour Cream Chicken Enchiladas

Makes 8 servings

I love chicken enchiladas with sour cream sauce, but they do have an awful lot of calories and fat. Here, I have lightened up my traditional recipe by using lower-fat versions of a few key ingredients. Now, for a splurge, I go all out, but for weeknights this is the ticket!

Tip

In the deli section of the supermarket, you can often find rotisserie chicken. Remove the skin and bones, and you are left with about 3 cups (750 mL) meat.

- Preheat oven to 350°F (180°C)
- 13- by 9-inch (33 by 23 cm) glass baking dish, greased

1	can (10 oz/284 mL) fat-free condensed cream of chicken soup	1
2 cups	light sour cream	500 mL
1 tbsp	chopped fresh cilantro	15 mL
2 tsp	olive oil	10 mL
1 cup	chopped onion	250 mL
1	can (10 oz/284 mL) diced tomatoes with green chiles	1
1	can (4 1/2 oz/127 mL) chopped mild green chiles	1
3 cups	shredded cooked chicken breasts	750 mL
16	6-inch (15 cm) corn tortillas	16
2 cups	shredded reduced-fat pepper Jack cheese, divided	500 mL

1. In a medium saucepan, combine soup, sour cream and cilantro; heat over medium-high heat, stirring, until steaming. Remove from heat and keep warm.

2. In a large nonstick skillet, heat oil over medium heat. Sauté onion for 5 to 7 minutes or until softened. Stir in tomatoes with chiles, chiles and chicken; cook until heated through. Remove from heat.

3. On a griddle or in another skillet, over medium-high heat, warm tortillas until pliable, about 30 seconds per side. Fill each tortilla with 3 tbsp (45 mL) chicken mixture and 1 tbsp (15 mL) of the shredded cheese. Roll up tortillas and place seam side down in prepared baking dish. Pour sour cream sauce over tortillas and sprinkle with the remaining cheese.

4. Bake in preheated oven for 30 minutes or until bubbling.

Spinach, Chicken Sausage and Artichoke Casserole

Makes 6 servings

I love the savory ingredients in this recipe, which is perfect for brunch or any time you are entertaining special guests.

Tips

For the artichokes, you can use thawed frozen or drained canned.

I am lucky to live in Austin, where we have a wealth of high-end supermarkets and specialty stores that feature a huge variety of fresh gourmet sausages. Just about any sausage will work in this recipe, so experiment with what you like.

- 11- by 7-inch (28 by 18 cm) glass baking dish, greased

4	egg whites	4
4	eggs	4
1 cup	skim milk	250 mL
1/2 cup	sliced fresh basil	125 mL
2 tbsp	Dijon mustard	30 mL
1/4 tsp	salt	1 mL
1/4 tsp	freshly ground black pepper	1 mL
5 cups	packed fresh spinach, trimmed and thinly sliced	1.25 L
4 cups	cubed whole-grain bread (1-inch/ 2.5 cm cubes)	1 L
1 cup	diced cooked chicken sausage (about 5 oz/150 g)	250 mL
3/4 cup	chopped artichoke hearts (see tip, at left)	175 mL
3/4 cup	shredded part-skim mozzarella cheese	175 mL

1. In a medium bowl, whisk together egg whites, eggs and milk. Stir in basil, mustard, salt and pepper.

2. In a large bowl, combine spinach, bread cubes, sausage and artichokes. Add egg mixture and toss to coat. Pour into prepared baking dish. Cover and refrigerate for at least 6 hours or overnight.

3. Preheat oven to 375°F (190°C).

4. Bake, covered, for 40 to 45 minutes or until set. Sprinkle with cheese and bake, uncovered, for 15 to 20 minutes or until puffed and golden on top. Transfer to a wire rack and let cool for 15 to 20 minutes before serving.

Cremini Mushroom and Sausage Strata

Makes 12 servings

Many years ago, I met Lia Huber through the International Association of Culinary Professionals. Lia told me her dream of establishing a place where people could explore how we nourish ourselves, each other and the earth we share through the food we eat. She wanted to create a site with solid articles on sound nutrition, eating with an "eco-clean conscience" and being mindful about meals, along with scrumptious recipes that put the concepts into practice. She envisioned a library of videos to help people get more comfortable in the kitchen and a "Facebook for food lovers" area for people to get into deeper conversations. With Nourish Network, she fulfilled her dream. I am thrilled to present to you this fabulous recipe and an amazing website: www. nourishnetwork.com.

- 13- by 9-inch (33 by 23 cm) glass baking dish, greased

1 lb	mild Italian sausage (bulk or removed from casings)	500 g
1	onion, chopped	1
4 cups	sliced cremini mushrooms	1 L
	Sea salt	
	Freshly ground black pepper	
5	eggs	5
2 cups	1% or 2% milk	500 mL
1 tbsp	Dijon mustard	15 mL
1 tsp	dry mustard	5 mL
1/8 tsp	ground nutmeg	0.5 mL
1 lb	whole-grain bread (preferably day-old), cut into 1/2-inch (1 cm) thick slices	500 g
3/4 cup	shredded Gruyère cheese, divided	175 mL

1. In a large nonstick skillet, over medium-high heat, cook sausage, breaking it up with the back of a spoon, for 8 to 10 minutes or until no longer pink. Drain off all but 2 tsp (10 mL) fat. Add onion and mushrooms; sauté for 8 to10 minutes or until golden brown. Season to taste with salt and pepper. Remove from heat.

2. In a medium bowl, whisk together eggs, milk, Dijon mustard, dry mustard, nutmeg and a pinch each of salt and pepper.

Spinach, Chicken Sausage
and Artichoke Casserole (page 255)

Cape Cod Casserole (page 114)

3. Arrange half the bread slices along bottom of prepared baking dish, overlapping as necessary. Spoon half the sausage mixture evenly over top. Sprinkle with $1/4$ cup (60 mL) of the cheese. Repeat layers with the remaining bread, the remaining sausage mixture and $1/4$ cup (60 mL) cheese. Pour egg mixture evenly over top. With the back of a spatula, press down to moisten everything with liquid. Cover and refrigerate overnight.

4. Preheat oven to 350°F (180°C).

5. Top strata with the remaining cheese. Bake, uncovered, for 40 minutes or until hot and bubbly. Let cool for 10 minutes before slicing and serving.

Sloppy Joe Mac and Cheese

One of my daughter's favorite meals is mac and cheese. Another is sloppy Joes on wheat buns. I combined the best of both worlds (according to Kennedy) in this light, flavorful recipe.

Tips

I like to use a nonstick skillet when browning ground turkey, chicken or beef, as it eliminates the need for oil or butter.

Because the vegetables in this recipe are finely chopped — or even shredded, in the case of the carrots — fussy kids may never realize they're there!

- Preheat oven to 350°F (180°C)
- 13- by 9-inch (33 by 23 cm) glass baking dish, greased

4 cups	elbow macaroni	1 L
12 oz	extra-lean ground beef	375 g
½ cup	finely diced celery	125 mL
½ cup	shredded carrot	125 mL
1	can (14 oz/398 mL) diced tomatoes	1
1	can (6 oz/170 mL) tomato paste	1
1	envelope (1¼ oz/37 g) sloppy Joe seasoning mix	1
1 tbsp	butter	15 mL
1	small onion, finely chopped	1
⅓ cup	all-purpose flour	75 mL
½ tsp	grainy mustard	2 mL
¾ tsp	salt	3 mL
¼ tsp	freshly ground black pepper	1 mL
4 cups	2% milk	1 L
2 tsp	Worcestershire sauce	10 mL
8 oz	reduced-fat pasteurized prepared cheese product, such as Velveeta, cubed	250 g
2 cups	shredded reduced-fat Cheddar cheese, divided	500 mL

1. In a large pot of boiling water, cook macaroni according to package directions until just tender. Drain and set aside.

2. Meanwhile, in a large nonstick skillet, over medium-high heat, cook beef, celery and carrot, breaking beef up with the back of a spoon, for 8 to 10 minutes or until beef is no longer pink. Drain off fat. Stir in tomatoes, tomato paste, sloppy Joe seasoning and ½ cup (125 mL) water; bring to a boil. Reduce heat to low, cover and simmer, stirring occasionally, for 10 minutes.

Avoid overcooking the pasta when you boil it. You want it be firm to the bite (al dente) so is doesn't get too mushy when baked with the sauce.

3. In another large nonstick skillet, melt butter over medium heat. Sauté onion for 5 to 7 minutes or until softened. Sprinkle with flour, mustard, salt and pepper and cook, stirring, for 1 minute. Gradually stir in milk and Worcestershire sauce; bring to a boil, stirring constantly. Cook, stirring, for 4 to 6 minutes or until thickened. Remove from heat and stir in pasteurized cheese until melted. Stir in cooked macaroni and half the Cheddar.

4. Spread half the macaroni mixture in prepared baking dish. Gently spread beef mixture on top. Top with the remaining macaroni mixture.

5. Cover and bake in preheated oven for 30 to 35 minutes or until bubbling. Sprinkle with the remaining Cheddar and bake, uncovered, for 5 minutes or until cheese is melted.

Layered Beef and Noodle Bake

I feel really good about serving this casserole to my little girl, because lean protein supplies energy and brain power. And getting her to eat this dish isn't hard — she loves it!

Tip

One bunch of green onions typically yields ½ cup (125 mL) chopped tops.

- Preheat oven to 350°F (180°C)
- 11- by 7-inch (28 by 18 cm) glass baking dish, greased
- Food processor

8 oz	extra-lean ground beef	250 g
2	cloves garlic, minced	2
1 cup	chopped green onion tops, divided	250 mL
2	cans (each 8 oz/227 mL) tomato sauce	2
	Salt and freshly ground black pepper	
6 oz	whole-wheat egg noodles	175 g
1 cup	low-fat cottage cheese	250 mL
1 cup	reduced-fat sour cream	250 mL
¼ cup	shredded reduced-fat Cheddar cheese	60 mL

1. In a large nonstick skillet, over medium-high heat, cook beef, garlic and half the green onions, breaking beef up with the back of a spoon, for 8 to 10 minutes or until beef is no longer pink. Drain off fat. Stir in tomato sauce, ½ cup (125 mL) water and a pinch each of salt and pepper; bring to a boil. Reduce heat to low, cover and simmer, stirring occasionally, for 10 minutes.

2. Meanwhile, in a large pot of boiling water, cook noodles according to package directions until just tender. Drain and set aside.

3. In a food processor, purée cottage cheese until smooth. Transfer to a medium bowl and stir in sour cream, the remaining green onions and a pinch each of salt and pepper.

4. Spread half the noodles in prepared baking dish. Top with half the cottage cheese mixture and half the meat sauce. Repeat layers with the remaining noodles, cottage cheese mixture and meat sauce. Sprinkle with Cheddar.

5. Bake in preheated oven for 30 to 40 minutes or until bubbling.

Side Dishes

Mom's Traditional Cornbread Dressing 262

John's Sausage Dressing 263

Oyster Dressing 264

Baked Potato Casserole 265

Delmonico Potatoes 266

Tif's Scalloped Potato Casserole 267

Kennedy's Two-Cheese Twice-Baked Potatoes 268

Potato and Cheese Casserole 269

Creamy Potato and Leek Casserole 270

Rice Casserole 271

Cheese Bread Pudding 272

Creamy Herbed Polenta 273

Green Chile Hominy 274

Creamy Broccoli Artichoke Bake 275

Savory Broccoli Casserole 276

Broccoli and Swiss Cheese Gratin 277

Broccoli Rice Casserole 278

Super-Easy Corn Casserole 279

Creamy Corn Casserole 280

Spicy Scalloped Corn 281

Corny Spoon Bread 282

Mexican Cornbread 283

Green Bean Casserole 284

Summer Squash Casserole 285

Butternut Squash, Leek and Tomato Casserole 286

Squash Corn Bake 287

Sweet Potato Custard with Pecans 288

Zucchini Casserole 289

Spicy Zucchini Cheese Bake 290

Zucchini with Cheese Casserole 291

Five-Bean Casserole 292

Barbecue and Honey Baked Beans 293

Scalloped Pineapple Casserole 294

Mom's Traditional Cornbread Dressing

Makes 10 to 12 servings

My mom made the best cornbread dressing on the face of the earth — so moist and perfect with the Thanksgiving meal.

Tips

Mom would crumble the cornbread and let it sit out overnight to dry. You can also bake it in a 350°F (180°C) oven for about 10 minutes for a similar effect.

If you do not have poultry drippings, substitute ¾ cup (175 mL) chicken broth mixed with ¼ cup (60 mL) melted butter.

- Preheat oven to 350°F (180°C)
- 13- by 9-inch (33 by 23 cm) glass baking dish, greased

2 tbsp	butter	30 mL
1 cup	chopped celery	250 mL
1 cup	chopped onion	250 mL
1	jar (2 oz/57 mL) chopped pimentos, drained	1
6 cups	crumbled cornbread	1.5 L
1 tsp	salt	5 mL
1 tsp	freshly ground black pepper	5 mL
1 tsp	dried rubbed sage	5 mL
½ tsp	poultry seasoning	2 mL
1	egg, beaten	1
1½ cups	chicken broth	375 mL
1 cup	turkey or chicken drippings (see tip, at left)	250 mL

1. In a large skillet, melt butter over medium heat. Sauté celery and onion for 5 to 7 minutes or until softened.

2. In a large bowl, combine celery mixture, pimentos, cornbread, salt, pepper, sage and poultry seasoning. Stir in egg, broth and drippings. Spread in prepared baking dish.

3. Bake in preheated oven for 45 minutes or until set but not dry.

John's Sausage Dressing

My friend John Sullivan
is a jack of all trades,
including cooking. His
sausage dressing recipe
has become one of my
favorites with Cornish
game hens, roast chicken
or turkey.

Tip
Sautéing vegetables in a
combination of olive oil
and butter adds flavor.

- Preheat oven to 350°F (180°C)
- 13- by 9-inch (33 by 23 cm) glass baking dish, greased

1 tbsp	olive oil	15 mL
1 tbsp	butter	15 mL
2	stalks celery, chopped	2
1	onion, finely chopped	1
1 lb	pork sausage (bulk or removed from casings)	500 g
1⅔ cups	chicken broth (approx.)	400 mL
1	package (14 oz/398 g) cubed herb-flavored stuffing mix	1

1. In a large skillet, heat oil and butter over medium heat. Sauté celery and onion for 5 to 7 minutes or until softened. Increase heat to medium-high; add sausage and cook, breaking it up with the back of a spoon, for 8 to 10 minutes or until no longer pink. Drain off fat.

2. Add enough broth to just cover ingredients in skillet; cook for 2 minutes. Add stuffing mix and toss thoroughly, adding more broth if it seems too dry. Spoon into prepared baking dish.

3. Bake in preheated oven for 45 minutes or until browned on top and hot in the center.

Oyster Dressing

When I was a child, extended family from the northeastern United States would bring this dish to Thanksgiving dinner as an alternative dressing option. Although it's very different from the cornbread dressing that is traditional in the South, I love its unique flavor.

- Preheat oven to 350°F (180°C)
- 13- by 9-inch (33 by 23 cm) glass baking dish, greased

2 tbsp	olive oil	30 mL
6 cups	raw oysters, drained, liquid reserved	1.5 L
1	loaf French bread, torn into chunks	1
¼ cup	butter	60 mL
3	cloves garlic, minced	3
1	bunch green onions (about 5), chopped	1
1	onion, chopped	1
2	eggs, beaten	2
2 tbsp	chopped fresh parsley	30 mL

1. In a large skillet, heat oil over medium-high heat. Add oysters, reduce heat to low and cook, stirring, for about 2 minutes or until edges begin to curl. Drain, adding liquid to the reserved oyster liquid, and transfer oysters to a cutting board.

2. Add bread to oyster liquid, tossing to help bread absorb the liquid. When bread is soft, transfer to the cutting board with the oysters. Chop bread and oysters into small pieces and transfer to a large bowl.

3. In the same skillet, melt butter over medium heat. Sauté garlic, green onions and onions for 5 to 7 minutes or until softened. Add oyster mixture and toss to coat. Stir in eggs and parsley. Spoon into prepared baking dish.

4. Cover and bake in preheated oven for 30 minutes or until internal temperature reaches 160°F (71°C).

Baked Potato Casserole

Makes 10 to 12 servings

My friend Pamela Weatherford confesses that this side dish is a splurge, but says it's well worth it. I am sure you will agree!

Tips

Butter is easiest to cube when it's cold and in stick form.

Instead of sprinkling the bacon and green onions on top as garnish, add them after the casserole has baked for 30 minutes and let them cook on top for the last 10 minutes.

- Preheat oven to 350°F (180°C)
- 13- by 9-inch (33 by 23 cm) glass baking dish, greased

7	cloves garlic	7
6	large red-skinned potatoes, each cut into 8 pieces	6
3 cups	shredded Cheddar cheese, divided	750 mL
2 cups	sour cream	500 mL
8 oz	cream cheese, cut into $1/2$-inch (1 cm) cubes	250 g
$3/4$ cup	butter, cut Into $1/2$-Inch (1 cm) cubes	175 mL
5	slices bacon, cooked crisp and crumbled	5
1	bunch green onions (about 5), sliced	1

1. Place garlic and potatoes in a large Dutch oven. Add enough cold water to cover and bring to a boil over high heat. Reduce heat and simmer for 20 to 25 minutes or until potatoes are tender. Drain and return to pot. Stir in 2 cups (500 mL) of the Cheddar and sour cream. Spread evenly in prepared baking dish.

2. Using the end of a wooden spoon, poke holes every 2 inches (5 cm) in potato mixture. Place a cream cheese cube in half the holes and a butter cube in the other half, alternating between cream cheese and butter. Cover cubes with potato mixture. Sprinkle with the remaining Cheddar.

3. Bake in preheated oven for 40 minutes or until cheese is melted and bubbling. Serve sprinkled with bacon and green onions.

Delmonico Potatoes

This is my adaptation of a classic recipe, using Yukon gold potatoes, cutting back a bit on the nutmeg and doubling the cheese — yum!

Tips

I love the buttery flavor of Yukon gold potatoes, but russets work just as well.

This is a different cooking technique for the potatoes (usually I start them in cold water) because you want them slightly softened but not cooked through, so they're firm enough to shred.

No white pepper on hand? You can use black pepper; just be aware that your cream sauce will have little black specks in it.

- Preheat oven to 425°F (220°C)
- 13- by 9-inch (33 by 23 cm) glass baking dish, greased

4	Yukon gold potatoes, peeled and cut into quarters lengthwise (about 2 lbs/1 kg)	4
	Ice water	
¾ cup	whole milk	175 mL
¼ cup	heavy or whipping (35%) cream	60 mL
½ tsp	salt	2 mL
¼ tsp	freshly ground white pepper	1 mL
⅛ tsp	ground nutmeg	0.5 mL
¼ cup	freshly grated Parmesan cheese, divided	60 mL

1. In a large saucepan, bring 8 cups (2 L) water to a boil over high heat. Add potatoes and boil for 10 minutes or until slightly tender. Drain and immerse in a bowl of ice water for 30 minutes or until well chilled. Drain and shred potatoes on the coarse side of a box cheese grater.

2. In a large bowl, combine milk, cream, salt, white pepper and nutmeg.

3. Heat a large skillet over medium heat. Add shredded potatoes and milk mixture; cook, stirring gently without mashing potatoes, for 10 to 12 minutes or until milk mixture is thickened. Remove from heat and stir in half the cheese.

4. Transfer potato mixture to prepared baking dish and sprinkle with the remaining cheese.

5. Bake in preheated oven for 30 minutes or until bubbling.

Tif's Scalloped Potato Casserole

My friends are always asking me for this recipe, but until now, I've never written it down. Here you go, folks!

Tip

For large parties, bake two or three dishes of this casserole, rotating them in the oven partway through to ensure even baking.

- Preheat oven to 350°F (180°C)
- 13- by 9-inch (33 by 23 cm) glass baking dish, greased

5 lbs	potatoes, peeled and thinly sliced	2.5 kg
6	cloves garlic	6
1	can (10 oz/284 mL) condensed cream of mushroom soup	1
1 cup	milk	250 mL
1/2 cup	sour cream	125 mL
1 tsp	salt	5 mL
1 tsp	freshly ground black pepper	5 mL
1/4 cup	butter, cut into pieces	60 mL
8	slices bacon, cooked crisp and crumbled	8
1/3 cup	chopped fresh chives	75 mL
2 1/2 cups	shredded Colby-Jack cheese	625 mL

1. Place potatoes and garlic in a large Dutch oven. Add enough cold salted water to cover and bring to a boil over high heat. Reduce heat and simmer for 10 minutes or until slightly tender. Drain and set aside.

2. In a large bowl, whisk together soup, milk, sour cream, salt and pepper.

3. Arrange half the potatoes in prepared baking dish. Layer with half each of the butter, bacon, chives, soup mixture and cheese. Repeat layers, ending with cheese.

4. Cover and bake in preheated oven for 50 to 55 minutes or until bubbling.

Kennedy's Two-Cheese Twice-Baked Potatoes

Makes 4 servings

My daughter, Kennedy, could live on mashed potatoes alone. She'd happily eat them at every meal, plus snacks. Although she adores them plain, this potato casserole with double the cheese is her favorite.

Tips

Russet potatoes also work well here, but I love the buttery taste of Yukon gold.

You can use other smoked cheeses, or even non-smoked varieties, in place of the Gouda.

For a cheesier potato and a beautiful presentation, add 1 tbsp (15 mL) shredded cheese to the top of each potato at the end of the baking time. Bake for an additional 5 minutes or until cheese is melted.

- Preheat oven to 425°F (220°C)
- 8-inch (20 cm) square glass baking dish, greased

4	Yukon gold potatoes (each about 1 1/4 lbs/625 g)	4
4 oz	smoked Gouda cheese, shredded	125 g
4 oz	cream cheese, softened	125 g
1/4 cup	milk	60 mL
1 tsp	salt	5 mL
1/2 tsp	freshly ground black pepper	2 mL
2 tbsp	chopped fresh chives	30 mL

1. Prick potatoes all over with a fork. Place directly on the rack in preheated oven and bake for 40 to 60 minutes or until tender. Remove from oven, leaving oven on.

2. Cut a lengthwise slice from the top of each potato. Discard skin from slice and place pulp in a large bowl. Gently scoop out flesh from each potato, leaving a thin shell, and add flesh to bowl.

3. Using a potato masher or an electric mixer on low speed, mash or beat potato flesh. Stir in Gouda, cream cheese, milk, salt and pepper. Stir in chives. Spoon into potato shells, dividing evenly. Place in prepared baking dish.

4. Bake for 20 to 25 minutes or until light brown.

Potato and Cheese Casserole

Makes 10 to 12 servings

This recipe was passed down to my friend Stacia Hernstrom from her grandmother, and she continues the family tradition by making it with her children. It's great for holiday gatherings!

Tip

If you like sharp cheese, use extra-sharp (extra-old) Cheddar or a combination of Cheddar and Swiss, Emmentaler or Gruyère.

- Preheat oven to 325°F (160°C)
- 13- by 9-inch (33 by 23 cm) glass baking dish, greased

2 tbsp	butter	30 mL
1	onion, finely chopped	1
2 lbs	frozen hash brown potatoes, thawed	1 kg
1	can (10 oz/294 mL) condensed cream of mushroom soup	1
2 cups	sour cream	500 mL
2 cups	shredded Cheddar cheese	500 mL
1 tsp	salt	5 mL
1/2 tsp	freshly ground black pepper	2 mL

1. In a large skillet, melt butter over medium heat. Sauté onion for 5 to 7 minutes or until softened.

2. In a large bowl, combine sautéed onion, hash browns, soup, sour cream, cheese, salt and pepper. Spread in prepared baking dish.

3. Bake in preheated oven for 55 minutes or until bubbling.

Creamy Potato and Leek Casserole

Potatoes and leeks are a classic combination, and this creamy casserole is one of my new favorites.

Tips

Yukon Gold potatoes truly make this recipe, but any other baking potato will work fine.

The cheeses in the Italian six-cheese blend are mozzarella, provolone, Parmesan, fontina, Romano and Asiago. You can use a combination of any of these if you don't have the packaged blend.

- Preheat oven to 375°F (190°C)
- 11- by 7-inch (28 by 18 cm) glass baking dish, greased

1 tbsp	extra virgin olive oil	15 mL
2	leeks (white part only), thinly sliced	2
3 lbs	Yukon gold potatoes, peeled and thinly sliced	1.5 kg
2	cloves garlic, minced	2
1⅔ cups	chicken broth	400 mL
½ tsp	freshly ground white pepper	2 mL
1	jar (15 oz/425 mL) Alfredo sauce	1
1 tsp	salt	5 mL
8 oz	shredded Italian six-cheese blend	250 g

1. In a large skillet, heat oil over medium heat. Sauté leeks for 5 to 7 minutes or until tender. Stir in potatoes, garlic, broth and white pepper; reduce heat and simmer, stirring occasionally, for 10 minutes or until liquid is absorbed. Gently stir in Alfredo sauce and salt just until coated. Spread in prepared baking dish and sprinkle with cheese.

2. Cover and bake in preheated oven for 20 minutes. Uncover and bake for 15 minutes or until cheese is lightly browned.

Rice Casserole

My friend and yoga student Becky Johnson kindly shared her mother-in-law's recipe. Nozik Smith makes this yummy side dish for family functions, with overwhelming approval.

Tip

If you like, you can sprinkle the top with more cheese 5 minutes before the end of the baking time.

- Preheat oven to 350°F (180°C)
- 11- by 7-inch (28 by 18 cm) glass baking dish, greased

1	can (4$\frac{1}{2}$ oz/127 mL) chopped mild green chiles	1
2 cups	cooked long-grain white rice	500 mL
2 cups	shredded Monterey Jack cheese	500 mL
1 cup	sour cream	250 mL
1 tsp	ground nutmeg	5 mL
$\frac{1}{4}$ tsp	salt	1 mL
$\frac{1}{4}$ tsp	freshly ground black pepper	1 mL

1. In a large bowl, combine chiles, rice, cheese, sour cream, nutmeg, salt and pepper. Spread in prepared baking dish.

2. Bake in preheated oven for 30 minutes or until bubbling.

Cheese Bread Pudding

This simple, economical, delicious side dish was my grandmother's invention.

Tip

Serve garnished with chopped green onion for added color and flavor.

- Preheat oven to 300°F (150°C)
- 6½-inch (16 cm) square glass baking dish, greased

5	slices bread, crusts removed	5
3	eggs, beaten	3
1½ cups	milk	375 mL
1 cup	shredded Cheddar cheese	250 mL
1 tsp	Worcestershire sauce	5 mL
1 tsp	salt	5 mL
1 tsp	freshly ground black pepper	5 mL

1. Using a serrated knife, cut bread into 1-inch (2.5 cm) squares. Layer in bottom of prepared baking dish.

2. In a medium bowl, whisk together eggs, milk, cheese, Worcestershire sauce, salt and pepper. Pour mixture over bread.

3. Bake in preheated oven for 45 to 50 minutes or until set.

Creamy Herbed Polenta

Makes 6 to 8 servings

I am a Southern girl through and through, and I adore this recipe! When I was growing up, grits were my thing, while Ellen, my gal pal from the northeastern U.S., enjoyed polenta. In my opinion, both have very much the same texture and, depending on the recipe, a similar taste, too.

Tips

For a creamier texture, do not bake the polenta; simply serve it after step 2.

Leftover polenta squares can be grilled over medium heat for 5 to 7 minutes per side.

Feel free to mix up the herbs, using the freshest options from your garden or the market.

- Preheat oven to 325°F (160°C)
- 13- by 9-inch (33 by 23 cm) glass baking dish, greased

1¾ cups	yellow cornmeal	425 mL
¾ cup	freshly grated Parmesan cheese	175 mL
¾ cup	whole milk	175 mL
6 tbsp	butter	90 mL
3 tbsp	chopped fresh parsley	45 mL
2 tsp	chopped fresh thyme	10 mL
1 tsp	chopped fresh oregano	5 mL
1 tsp	chopped fresh rosemary	5 mL
½ tsp	freshly ground black pepper	2 mL

1. In a large saucepan, bring 6 cups (1.5 L) salted water to a boil over high heat. Gradually whisk in cornmeal. Reduce heat to low and cook, stirring often, for about 15 minutes or until mixture thickens and cornmeal is tender.

2. Remove from heat and add Parmesan, milk, butter, parsley, thyme, oregano, rosemary and pepper, stir until butter and cheese melt.

3. Spread in prepared baking dish. Bake in preheated oven for 30 minutes or until firm. Cut into squares.

Green Chile Hominy

This recipe is a favorite
of my dear friends Tom
and Lisa Perini, owners of
Perini Ranch Steakhouse
in Buffalo Gap, Texas. It
is a great side dish that
looks terrific on a plate.
They often serve it in a
cast-iron skillet for a more
rustic effect. This recipe
is versatile — it's great for
breakfast, lunch or dinner
alongside almost any
entrée.

Tips

Once you open the can of
jalapeños to use the juice
for this recipe, transfer the
peppers and the remaining
juice to an airtight container
and refrigerate to use in
nachos, sandwiches or
salads.

This casserole can be
prepared through step 4,
then refrigerated for up
to 1 day or frozen for up
to 3 months (see freezing
instructions on page 13).
Increase the baking time
to 40 to 45 minutes.

- Preheat oven to 325°F (160°C)
- 13- by 9-inch (33 by 23 cm) glass baking dish, greased

10	slices bacon	10
1 cup	chopped white onion	250 mL
4	cans (each 15 oz/425 mL) white hominy, drained, reserving 1/2 cup (125 mL) liquid	4
1 tbsp	juice from pickled jalapeños	15 mL
2 cups	shredded Cheddar cheese, divided	500 mL
1 cup	chopped Anaheim pepper, divided	250 mL

1. In a large skillet, over medium-high heat, cook bacon until crisp. Using tongs, transfer to a plate lined with paper towels, reserving drippings in the pan. Let cool, then crumble.

2. Reduce heat to medium and add onion to drippings in skillet; sauté for 5 to 7 minutes or until softened. Remove from heat.

3. In a large saucepan, over medium heat, stir hominy until heated through. Add hominy liquid and jalapeño juice; increase heat to high and bring to a boil. Remove from heat and stir in 1 1/2 cups (375 mL) of the cheese until melted. Stir in sautéed onion, half the Anaheim pepper and half the bacon.

4. Pour into prepared baking dish and sprinkle with the remaining cheese, Anaheim pepper and bacon.

5. Bake in preheated oven for about 15 minutes or until cheese is melted.

Creamy Broccoli Artichoke Bake

Makes 6 to 8 servings

Broccoli and artichokes, two of my favorite vegetables, are sheer elegance in this rich side casserole.

Tip

Thawed frozen artichoke hearts also work well. Use 7 hearts.

- Preheat oven to 350°F (180°C)
- 8-inch (20 cm) square glass baking dish, greased

1	can (14 oz/398 mL) artichoke hearts, drained and quartered	1
2	eggs, lightly beaten	2
1	can (10 oz/284 mL) condensed cream of mushroom soup	1
1/2 cup	mayonnaise	125 mL
1 tsp	freshly squeezed lemon juice	5 mL
1 tsp	Worcestershire sauce	5 mL
1/4 tsp	garlic salt	1 mL
2	packages (each 10 oz/300 g) frozen chopped broccoli, thawed and drained	2
1 cup	shredded extra-sharp (extra-old) Cheddar cheese	250 mL
1/2 cup	dry bread crumbs	125 mL
1/4 cup	butter, melted	60 mL

1. Arrange artichokes evenly in bottom of prepared baking dish.

2. In a large bowl, whisk together eggs, soup, mayonnaise, lemon juice, Worcestershire sauce and garlic salt. Stir in broccoli. Pour over artichoke hearts and sprinkle with cheese and bread crumbs. Drizzle melted butter on top.

3. Bake in preheated oven for 30 minutes or until cheese is melted.

Savory Broccoli Casserole

Makes 8 servings

This savory favorite comes to you courtesy of our family friend Linda Sullivan.

Tip

Gently fold the blue cheese into this mixture — you don't want a blue sauce!

- Preheat oven to 350°F (180°C)
- 8-inch (20 cm) square glass baking dish, greased

¼ cup	butter	60 mL
¼ cup	all-purpose flour	60 mL
2 cups	milk	500 mL
6 oz	cream cheese, softened	175 g
½ cup	crumbled blue cheese	125 mL
4	packages (each 10 oz/300 g) frozen chopped broccoli, thawed and drained	4
20	buttery crackers, crumbled	20

1. In a medium saucepan, melt butter over medium heat. Whisk in flour and cook, whisking constantly, for 1 minute. Gradually whisk in milk and bring to a simmer, whisking constantly. Cook, whisking constantly, for about 5 minutes or until slightly thickened. Reduce heat to low and stir in cream cheese until melted. Stir in broccoli until coated with sauce.

2. Remove from heat and gently fold in blue cheese. Pour into prepared baking dish and sprinkle with crumbled crackers.

3. Bake in preheated oven for 30 minutes or until bubbling.

Broccoli and Swiss Cheese Gratin

Makes 8 servings

Fresh broccoli and creamy cheese melt in your mouth in this casserole — it's a true winner!

Tips

Frozen broccoli would also work well. There's no need to blanch it, just let it thaw, then drain it well.

Garnish with a pinch of hot pepper flakes for zing and color.

- Preheat oven to 375°F (190°C)
- Steamer basket
- 12-cup (3 L) casserole dish

2	heads broccoli, roughly chopped (about 12 cups/3 L)	2
	Ice water	
1/4 cup	butter	60 mL
1/4 cup	all-purpose flour	60 mL
2 cups	milk	500 mL
2 cups	shredded Swiss cheese, divided	500 mL
1/2 tsp	salt	2 mL
1/4 tsp	freshly ground black pepper	1 mL
1/4 tsp	garlic powder	1 mL

1. In a large saucepan fitted with a steamer basket, bring 1 inch (2.5 cm) of water to a simmer over medium heat. Place broccoli in basket, cover and steam for 3 to 4 minutes or until just tender. Drain and immerse in a bowl of ice water to stop the cooking process.

2. In a medium saucepan, melt butter over medium heat. Whisk in flour and cook, whisking constantly, for 1 minute. Gradually whisk in milk and bring to a simmer, whisking constantly. Reduce heat and simmer, whisking, for 3 to 4 minutes or until slightly thickened.

3. Remove from heat and stir in half the cheese, salt, pepper and garlic powder. Add broccoli and toss to coat with sauce. Pour into casserole dish and sprinkle with the remaining cheese.

4. Bake in preheated oven for 35 to 40 minutes or until bubbling and golden brown. Let cool for 10 minutes before serving.

Broccoli Rice Casserole

Longtime family friend Jeri Tribo discovered this dish many, many years ago when her husband was in the service and all the Air Force wives exchanged recipes.

Tip

If you don't care for pimentos, leave them out.

Variation

For extra crunch, add ½ cup (125 mL) drained sliced water chestnuts.

- Preheat oven to 325°F (160°C)
- 13- by 9-inch (33 by 23 cm) glass baking dish

2	packages (each 10 oz/300 g) frozen chopped broccoli, thawed and drained	2
1	can (10 oz/284 mL) condensed cream of celery soup	1
1	jar (8 oz/227 mL) pasteurized processed cheese spread	1
1	jar (2 oz/57 mL) chopped pimentos, drained	1
2 cups	cooked long-grain white rice	500 mL
½ cup	butter, melted	125 mL
1 cup	shredded Cheddar cheese	250 mL

1. In a large bowl, combine broccoli, soup, cheese spread, pimentos, rice and butter. Spoon into baking dish and sprinkle with Cheddar.

2. Bake in preheated oven for 45 minutes or until bubbling.

Super-Easy Corn Casserole

Of all the corn/cornbread combinations in the world, none is as easy or as tasty as this. It's perfect on cold winter days, with homemade chili, soup or stew.

Tip

If you have a different size package of cornbread mix, use 3½ cups (875 mL) dry mix. If you cannot find packaged mix, whisk together 2⅔ cups (650 mL) yellow cornmeal, ¾ cup (175 mL) all-purpose flour, 4 tsp (20 mL) baking powder, 2 tsp (10 mL) granulated sugar and 1 tsp (5 mL) salt; use in place of the mix.

- Preheat oven to 350°F (180°C)
- 13- by 9-inch (33 by 23 cm) glass baking dish, greased

4	eggs, beaten	4
2	boxes (each 8½ oz/241 g) cornbread mix	2
1	can (16 oz/454 mL) whole-kernel corn, with liquid	1
1	can (16 oz/454 mL) cream-style corn	1
1	can (4½ oz/127 mL) chopped mild green chiles	1
2 cups	sour cream	500 mL
½ cup	butter, melted	125 mL

1. In a large bowl, combine eggs, cornbread mix, whole-kernel corn, cream-style corn, chiles, sour cream and butter. Spread in prepared baking dish.

2. Bake in preheated oven for 45 to 60 minutes or until a tester inserted in the center comes out clean.

Creamy Corn Casserole

My dear friend David Oberg loves this side dish so much, he often eats it as an entrée.

Tips

During corn season, substitute fresh corn kernels for the frozen.

No seasoned salt on hand? Use salt and pepper.

- Preheat oven to 400°F (200°C)
- 12-cup (3 L) casserole dish, greased

3	eggs, beaten	3
1	can (14 oz/398 mL) cream-style corn	1
1 cup	frozen corn kernels	250 mL
1/3 cup	granulated sugar	75 mL
1/3 cup	whole milk	75 mL
1/3 cup	melted butter	75 mL
2 tbsp	cornstarch	30 mL
1 tsp	seasoned salt	5 mL
1/4 tsp	dry mustard	1 mL
1/4 tsp	onion powder	1 mL

1. In a large bowl, combine eggs, cream-style corn, frozen corn, sugar, milk, butter, cornstarch, salt, mustard and onion powder. Spread in prepared casserole dish.

2. Bake in preheated oven for 1 hour, stirring halfway through, until bubbling.

Spicy Scalloped Corn

This recipe mimics the creaminess of scalloped potatoes, but with the sweet flavor of fresh corn and a kick of heat from the cayenne pepper. It's delicious alongside grilled chicken or pork chops.

Tip

To add depth of flavor, substitute a mild or medium-heat green chile pepper for the bell pepper.

- Preheat oven to 400°F (200°C)
- 6-cup (1.5 L) casserole dish, greased

3 tbsp	all-purpose flour	45 mL
1 tsp	salt	5 mL
1/4 tsp	paprika	1 mL
1/4 tsp	dry mustard	1 mL
1/8 tsp	cayenne pepper	0.5 mL
3 tbsp	butter	45 mL
1	small green bell pepper, finely chopped	1
1/2	onion, finely chopped	1/2
1 cup	milk	250 mL
1	egg yolk, lightly beaten	1
2 cups	fresh or drained canned corn kernels	500 mL
2/3 cup	dry bread crumbs	150 mL

1. In a small bowl, combine flour, salt, paprika, mustard and cayenne; set aside.

2. In a skillet, melt butter over medium heat. Sauté green pepper and onion for 5 to 7 minutes or until softened. Stir in flour mixture and cook, stirring, for 1 minute. Gradually stir in milk and bring to a boil, stirring constantly.

3. Gradually whisk a little of the hot milk mixture into egg yolk. Stir egg mixture and corn into pan. Pour into prepared casserole dish and sprinkle with bread crumbs.

4. Bake in preheated oven for 25 to 30 minutes or until bubbling.

Corny Spoon Bread

I know you'll love this classic dish with a corny name!

Tip

When whisking the hot milk mixture into the eggs in step 3, make sure to pour the sauce in a thin, steady stream while whisking constantly. This will gradually warm the eggs (temper them) without causing them to scramble. To keep the sauce silky smooth, keep whisking while you add the egg mixture to the pan.

- Preheat oven to 350°F (180°C)
- 8-cup (2 L) casserole dish, greased

2⅓ cups	frozen corn kernels, thawed	575 mL
3 cups	whole milk, divided	750 mL
¾ cup	finely ground yellow cornmeal	175 mL
2	eggs, lightly beaten	2
2 tbsp	unsalted butter	30 mL
1½ tsp	dried thyme	7 mL
1½ tsp	salt	7 mL
1 tsp	granulated sugar	5 mL
¼ tsp	freshly ground black pepper	1 mL

1. In a large saucepan, combine corn and 2 cups (500 mL) of the milk; bring to a boil over medium heat.

2. In a small bowl, whisk together cornmeal and the remaining milk. Gradually add to the boiling milk, whisking constantly. Reduce heat and simmer gently, stirring often, for 3 minutes or until thickened. Remove from heat.

3. Gradually whisk a little of the hot milk mixture into eggs. Whisk egg mixture, butter, thyme, salt, sugar and pepper into pan. Spread in prepared casserole dish.

4. Bake in preheated oven for about 30 minutes or until golden and set. Serve hot or at room temperature.

Mexican Cornbread

I will always remember how our friend Jen O'Neil reacted when she first tasted this recipe at a party at our place. She couldn't get enough! Give it a try and see for yourself.

Tips

Removing the ribs and seeds from a jalapeño lessens its heat.

If your cornbread mix requires you to add oil, water and egg rather than just milk or water, use 3½ cups (875 mL) dry mix, increase the milk to 1½ cups (375 mL) and add 6 tbsp (90 mL) vegetable oil with the eggs when making the batter as directed in step 2. If you cannot find packaged mix, simply make 4 cups (500 mL) of your favorite cornbread batter and fold in the corn.

- Preheat oven to 400°F (200°C)
- 13- by 9-inch (33 by 23 cm) glass baking dish, greased

1 lb	lean ground beef	500 g
1	small onion, chopped	1
1	jalapeño pepper, seeded and chopped	1
1	envelope (1¼ oz/37 g) taco seasoning mix	1
1 tsp	Worcestershire sauce	5 mL
2	boxes (each 8½ oz/241 g) cornbread mix	2
2	eggs, beaten	2
⅔ cup	milk	150 mL
1	can (14 oz/398 mL) cream-style corn	1
2 cups	shredded Cheddar cheese	500 mL

1. In a large nonstick skillet, over medium-high heat, cook beef, onion and jalapeño, breaking beef up with the back of a spoon, for 8 to 10 minutes or until beef is no longer pink. Drain off fat. Stir in taco seasoning and Worcestershire sauce. Set aside.

2. In a large bowl, combine cornbread mix, eggs and milk. Batter will be slightly lumpy. Fold in corn.

3. Pour half the batter into prepared baking dish. Spread beef mixture on top. Sprinkle with cheese. Pour the remaining batter over top.

4. Bake in preheated oven for 20 to 25 minutes or until golden brown.

Green Bean Casserole

Makes 6 to 8 servings

Everyone I know has a version of this classic recipe. Most of us know it by heart. But I had to include it in this book, because it's a staple for my family.

Tip

You can use either French-cut green beans or whole green beans. And feel free to use blanched fresh or thawed frozen beans instead of canned.

- Preheat oven to 350°F (180°C)
- 8-inch (20 cm) square glass baking dish

1	can (10 oz/284 mL) condensed cream of mushroom soup	1
¾ cup	milk	175 mL
½ tsp	freshly ground black pepper	2 mL
½ tsp	garlic powder	2 mL
2	cans (each 14 oz/398 mL) green beans, drained	2
1	can (2¾ oz/79 g) french-fried onions, divided	1

1. In a medium bowl, combine soup, milk, pepper and garlic powder. Gently fold in green beans and half the onions. Pour into baking dish.

2. Bake in preheated oven for 25 minutes. Sprinkle with the remaining onions and bake for 5 minutes or until casserole is bubbling and onions are golden brown.

Summer Squash Casserole

Makes 8 to 10 servings

Back in her college days, my friend Ellen Harrison taught her roommates how to make this inexpensive casserole. Everyone loved it so much, they made it once a week for several weeks, bringing it to every potluck dinner they were invited to, always with rave reviews!

- Preheat oven to 350°F (180°C)
- 13- by 9-inch (33 by 23 cm) glass baking dish

1/4 cup	butter, divided	60 mL
1	large onion, chopped	1
3 cups	sliced yellow summer squash	750 mL
1	box (6 oz/175 g) herb-flavored stuffing mix	1
1	can (10 oz/284 mL) condensed cream of mushroom soup	1
1	can (10 oz/284 mL) condensed cream of chicken soup	1
1 cup	sour cream	250 mL
2	eggs, beaten	2
1/4 cup	freshly grated Parmesan cheese	60 mL

1. In a large skillet, melt half the butter over medium-high heat. Sauté onion and squash for 5 to 7 minutes or until softened. Transfer to a bowl and mash with a fork. Set aside.

2. In the same skillet, melt the remaining butter over medium heat. Stir in stuffing mix, mushroom soup, chicken soup, sour cream, eggs and onion mixture. Pour into baking dish and sprinkle with Parmesan cheese.

3. Bake in preheated oven for 30 minutes or until bubbling.

Butternut Squash, Leek and Tomato Casserole

This gorgeous combination of golden squash, green leeks and red tomatoes is perfect for a holiday buffet.

Tips

Soil hides deep inside leek leaves. Slice the leek lengthwise to the root but not through it. Soak and rinse leeks carefully to remove the soil.

If you need to substitute dried basil and thyme, use half the amount and add with the tomatoes.

- Steamer basket
- 13- by 9-inch (33 by 23 cm) glass baking dish, greased

3 lbs	butternut squash	1.5 kg
2 tbsp	olive oil	30 mL
3	leeks (white and light green parts only), thinly sliced	3
4 cups	canned diced tomatoes	1 L
1 tbsp	finely chopped fresh basil	15 mL
1 tsp	finely chopped fresh thyme	5 mL
1 tsp	salt	5 mL
1/2 tsp	freshly ground black pepper	2 mL
3 cups	shredded sharp (old) Cheddar cheese	750 mL

1. Using a sharp knife or a vegetable peeler, peel squash. Cut in half lengthwise and scoop out the seeds. Cut flesh crosswise into 1-inch (2.5 cm) slices.

2. In a large saucepan fitted with a steamer basket, bring 1 inch (2.5 cm) of water to a simmer over medium heat. Place squash in basket, cover and steam for 15 to 20 minutes or until fork-tender. Transfer to prepared baking dish.

3. Preheat oven to 425°F (220°C).

4. In a medium skillet, heat oil over medium heat. Sauté leeks for 5 to 7 minutes or until softened. Add tomatoes, increase heat to medium-high and boil gently, stirring frequently, for 5 minutes. Add basil and thyme; cook, stirring, for about 5 minutes or until thickened. Season with salt and pepper. Spoon over squash and sprinkle with cheese.

5. Bake for 15 to 20 minutes or until cheese is lightly browned and bubbling.

Squash Corn Bake

Even finicky eaters in the Collins family love this recipe, so it is a staple at any family gathering.

Tip

Mashed squash gives a smooth conslstency to the casserole. For a chunkier texture, omit step 1 and sauté the squash with the onion.

- Preheat oven to 350°F (180°C)
- 13- by 9-inch (33 by 23 cm) glass baking dish, greased

4	yellow summer squash, cut into 1-inch (2.5 cm) thick rounds	4
2 tbsp	butter, divided	30 mL
1	onion, chopped	1
2	eggs, beaten	2
2⅓ cups	frozen corn kernels	575 mL
1 cup	shredded Swiss cheese	250 mL
½ tsp	salt	2 mL
¼ cup	buttery cracker crumbs	60 mL
2 tbsp	freshly grated Parmesan cheese	30 mL

1. Place squash in a medium saucepan and cover with water; bring to a boil over high heat. Reduce heat to medium and cook for 5 to 7 minutes or until tender. Drain and mash with a fork; set aside.

2. In a large skillet, melt half the butter over medium heat. Sauté onion for 5 to 7 minutes or until softened.

3. In a large bowl, combine mashed squash, sautéed onion, eggs, corn, Swiss cheese and salt. Spread in prepared baking dish.

4. In a microwave-safe bowl, microwave the remaining butter on High for 15 seconds or until melted. Stir in cracker crumbs and Parmesan. Spread evenly over squash mixture.

5. Bake in preheated oven for 40 minutes or until golden brown.

Sweet Potato Custard with Pecans

The sweet potato fans in my family love this recipe, and especially the crunchy pecan topping.

Variations

Substitute ½ cup (125 mL) bourbon for the buttermilk.

Omit the pecan topping and sprinkle the casserole with 1 cup (250 mL) miniature marshmallows during the last 10 minutes of baking.

- Preheat oven to 350°F (180°C)
- 13- by 9-inch (33 by 23 cm) glass baking dish, greased

6	large sweet potatoes, cooked, peeled and sliced	6
2	eggs	2
¾ cup	granulated sugar	175 mL
¾ cup	buttermilk	175 mL
½ cup	butter	125 mL
1 tsp	baking powder	5 mL
1 tsp	ground cinnamon	5 mL
1 tsp	vanilla extract	5 mL

Pecan Topping

1 cup	packed brown sugar	250 mL
½ cup	all-purpose flour	125 mL
⅓ cup	butter, melted	75 mL
1 cup	chopped pecans	250 mL

1. In a large bowl, using an electric mixer on medium speed, beat sweet potatoes, eggs, sugar, buttermilk, butter, baking powder, cinnamon and vanilla until smooth. Spread in prepared casserole dish.

2. *Topping:* In a medium bowl, combine brown sugar, flour and butter. Stir in pecans until coated. Sprinkle evenly over sweet potato mixture.

3. Bake in preheated oven for 30 to 45 minutes or until bubbling.

Zucchini Casserole

Makes 6 to 8 servings

This rich casserole is a staple at my friend Lana Oberg's family functions.

Tips

In a hurry? Broccoli loves this combination of cheeses and doesn't need draining.

A food processor makes quick work of shredding the zucchini.

• 8-inch (20 cm) square glass baking dish

2 lbs	zucchini, coarsely shredded	1 kg
2 tsp	salt	10 mL
4	eggs, beaten	4
1 cup	shredded Cheddar cheese	250 mL
½ cup	cottage cheese	125 mL
¾ cup	dry bread crumbs	175 mL
3 tbsp	chopped fresh parsley	45 mL
½ tsp	freshly ground black pepper	2 mL
2 tbsp	butter	30 mL

1. In a medium bowl, toss zucchini and salt. Let stand for 30 minutes. Drain and squeeze liquid from zucchini.

2. Meanwhile, preheat oven to 350°F (180°C).

3. In a large bowl, whisk together eggs, Cheddar and cottage cheese. Add zucchini and toss to coat. Pour into baking dish.

4. In a small bowl, combine bread crumbs, parsley and pepper. Sprinkle over the zucchini mixture. Dot with butter.

5. Bake for 45 minutes or until bubbling.

Spicy Zucchini Cheese Bake

Makes 10 to 12 servings

This spicy, cheesy casserole is simply bursting with flavor!

Tip

To kick up the heat, try medium or hot green chiles and substitute pepper Jack cheese for the Monterey Jack.

- Preheat oven to 350°F (180°C)
- 13- by 9-inch (33 by 23 cm) glass baking dish, greased

2 tbsp	butter	30 mL
2	cloves garlic, minced	2
1	onion, chopped	1
3 lbs	zucchini, sliced	1.5 kg
2 tbsp	all-purpose flour	30 mL
1 tsp	salt	5 mL
1/2 tsp	freshly ground black pepper	2 mL
1/2 tsp	dried thyme	2 mL
1	egg, beaten	1
1	can (4 1/2 oz/127 mL) chopped mild green chiles	1
1 cup	ricotta cheese	250 mL
2 cups	shredded Monterey Jack cheese	500 mL
1 cup	freshly grated Parmesan cheese	250 mL
1/4 cup	chopped fresh parsley	60 mL

1. In a large skillet, melt butter over medium-high heat. Sauté garlic, onion and zucchini for 5 to 7 minutes or until softened. Sprinkle with flour, salt, pepper and thyme; cook, stirring, for 1 minute. Remove from heat and stir in egg, chiles, ricotta, Monterey Jack, Parmesan and parsley. Pour into prepared baking dish.

2. Bake in preheated oven for 25 to 30 minutes or until bubbling.

Zucchini with Cheese Casserole

Rich and creamy, hearty and delicious, this fresh zucchini casserole couldn't be easier!

Tip

Jarlsberg is a mild, creamy yellow semi-firm cheese. Good substitutes include Emmentaler, Gruyère and Swiss.

- Preheat oven to 350°F (180°C)
- Steamer basket
- 11- by 7-inch (28 by 18 cm) glass baking dish

3	zucchini, cut into ¼-inch (0.5 cm) slices	3
2 tbsp	butter or margarine	30 mL
2 tbsp	all-purpose flour	30 mL
¼ tsp	salt	1 mL
Pinch	freshly ground black pepper	Pinch
1 cup	mllk	250 mL
8 oz	Jarlsberg cheese, shredded	250 g

1. In a large saucepan fitted with a steamer basket, bring 1 inch (2.5 cm) of water to a simmer over medium heat. Place zucchini in basket, cover, leaving lid slightly ajar, and steam for 5 to 6 minutes or until tender. Transfer to baking dish.

2. In a small saucepan, melt butter over medium heat. Whisk in flour, salt and pepper; cook, whisking constantly, for 1 minute. Gradually whisk in milk; cook, whisking constantly, for about 5 minutes or until thick and bubbling. Pour over zucchini. Sprinkle with cheese.

3. Bake in preheated oven for 20 to 30 minutes or until top is golden brown.

Five-Bean Casserole

Makes 12 servings

My dear friend Lorinda, from Orange County, California, served this years ago at her July 4th celebration and I've loved it ever since. It's great with any style of barbecue, along with potato salad and coleslaw.

- Preheat oven to 350°F (180°C)
- 13- by 9-inch (33 by 23 cm) glass baking dish

8 oz	bacon, chopped	250 g
2	onions, chopped	2
½ cup	packed brown sugar	125 mL
⅓ cup	cider vinegar	75 mL
1 tsp	garlic salt	5 mL
1 tsp	dry mustard	5 mL
1	can (14 oz/398 mL) baked beans in tomato sauce	1
1	can (14 to 19 oz/398 to 540 mL) kidney beans, drained and rinsed	1
1	can (14 to 19 oz/398 to 540 mL) great Northern beans, drained and rinsed	1
1	can (14 to 19 oz/398 to 540 mL) chickpeas, drained and rinsed	1
1	can (14 to 19 oz/398 to 540 mL) butter beans, drained and rinsed	1
⅓ cup	blackstrap molasses	75 mL

1. In a large skillet, over medium heat, sauté bacon and onion for 5 to 7 minutes or until onion is softened. Stir in brown sugar, vinegar, garlic salt and dry mustard until sugar is dissolved. Reduce heat to low, cover and simmer, stirring occasionally, for 20 minutes.

2. In baking dish, combine baked beans, kidney beans, great Northern beans, chickpeas, butter beans and molasses. Spoon bacon mixture over top.

3. Bake in preheated oven for 1 hour or until bubbling.

Barbecue and Honey Baked Beans

Makes 8 to 10 servings

My friend Stephanie Collins always gets raves when she serves this dish at gatherings. Though she considers it a side, it's so hearty it could certainly be served as an entrée.

Tips

Bitters are typically used as a flavoring in cocktails, but can also be used to flavor food, as here.

Use your favorite sweet barbecue sauce to accent the savory ingredients in this recipe.

- Preheat oven to 350°F (180°C)
- 13- by 9-inch (33 by 23 cm) glass baking dish, greased

8 oz	lean ground beef	250 g
8 oz	hot Italian sausage (bulk or removed from casings)	250 g
1	onion, chopped	1
4	cans (each 16 oz/454 mL) baked beans with pork in tomato sauce	4
1⅔ cups	beef broth	400 mL
1 cup	barbecue sauce	250 mL
¾ cup	liquid honey	175 mL
1 tsp	cayenne pepper	5 mL
1 tsp	liquid smoke	5 mL
1 tsp	Worcestershire sauce	5 mL
½ tsp	salt	2 mL
½ tsp	bitters	2 mL
¼ tsp	hot pepper sauce	1 mL
8	slices bacon, cooked crisp and crumbled	8

1. In a large nonstick skillet, over medium-high heat, cook beef, sausage and onion, breaking beef and sausage up with the back of a spoon, for 8 to 10 minutes or until beef and sausage are no longer pink. Drain off fat.

2. Stir in beans, broth, barbecue sauce, honey, cayenne, liquid smoke, Worcestershire sauce, salt, bitters and hot pepper sauce. Pour into prepared baking dish and sprinkle with bacon.

3. Bake in preheated oven for 45 minutes or until bubbling.

Scalloped Pineapple Casserole

When my good friend David Oberg, aka "Dallas," heard I was writing this book, he reminded me how much I love his unusual pineapple recipe. Dessert or side? You decide.

Tips

Crushed pineapple is a great option too.

Look for canned pineapple packed in its own juices, which has a much fresher flavor and less sugar than pineapple packed in syrup.

- Preheat oven to 350°F (180°C)
- 13- by 9-inch (33 by 23 cm) glass baking dish, greased

1½ cups	granulated sugar	375 mL
1 cup	butter, softened	250 mL
2	eggs	2
1	can (20 oz/568 mL) pineapple chunks, with juice	1
6 cups	cubed bread, divided	1.5 L

1. In a large bowl, using an electric mixer on high speed, cream sugar and butter until pale yellow. Add eggs, one at a time, beating well after each addition. Reduce speed to low and mix in pineapple.

2. Arrange half the bread in prepared baking dish. Spoon pineapple mixture over top. Arrange remaining bread over pineapple.

3. Bake in preheated oven for 45 minutes or until golden brown.

Barbecue and Honey Baked Beans (page 293)

No-Pasta Lasagna (page 229)

Kid Stuff

Cherry Pecan Breakfast Casserole 296

Creamy Baked Apple Dip 297

Kids' Chicken and Apple Bake 298

Kids' Chicken and Rice. 299

Layered Meatballs. 300

Beef and Rice Bake 301

Quick Pizza Casserole 302

Kids' Pasta Casserole. 303

Taco Casserole. 304

Tater Nugget Taco Casserole 305

Tater Nugget Bake 306

Creamy Burger and Fries Bake 307

Corn Dog Casserole 308

Mashed Potato–Stuffed Hot Dogs. 309

Cheesy Beans and Hot Dogs 310

Mashed Potato Casserole. 311

Cheesy Potato Spinach 312

Cheesy Tex-Mex Squash 313

Brownies S'mores Style 314

Apple Dumplings 316

Cherry Pecan Breakfast Casserole

With sweet cherries and crunchy pecans, this breakfast casserole will be a hit with kids of all ages. If your child has a nut allergy, just leave the pecans out. Serve with whipped cream or flavored syrup.

Tip

Use day-old or stale bread when making this casserole. The bread will cut in cubes more easily and the casserole will be denser.

- 13- by 9-inch (33 by 23 cm) glass baking dish, greased

8 cups	cubed French bread (½-inch/1 cm cubes)	2 L
8 oz	cream cheese, softened	250 g
½ cup	granulated sugar, divided	125 mL
½ tsp	almond extract	2 mL
½ cup	dried cherries	125 mL
½ cup	chopped pecans	125 mL
4	eggs	4
1½ cups	half-and-half (10%) cream	375 mL
½ tsp	ground cinnamon	2 mL

1. Place half the bread in prepared baking dish.

2. In a large bowl, using an electric mixer on high speed, beat cream cheese, half the sugar and almond extract for about 3 minutes or until light and fluffy. On low speed, mix in cherries and pecans. Drop in spoonfuls over bread. Top with the remaining bread.

3. In the same bowl, using an electric mixer on medium speed, beat eggs until blended. Beat in cream, cinnamon and the remaining sugar; beat for about 1 minute or until frothy. Pour over bread. Cover and refrigerate for at least 6 hours or overnight.

4. Preheat oven to 350°F (180°C).

5. Uncover baking dish. Bake for 45 to 50 minutes or until browned. Let cool for 5 minutes before serving.

Creamy Baked Apple Dip

Makes 16 servings

I love to entertain, but I've noticed that kids often scorn the adult menu. So I developed this kid-friendly dip that adults eat with pleasure. Serve with pretzel rods or wheat crackers.

Tip

Baking apples give the best texture for this recipe.

- Preheat oven to 375°F (190°C)
- 8-inch (20 cm) square glass baking dish

8 oz	cream cheese, softened	250 g
2 tbsp	packed brown sugar	30 mL
1/2 tsp	pumpkin pie spice	2 mL
1/4 tsp	ground cinnamon	1 mL
1/4 tsp	ground nutmeg	1 mL
1	apple, finely chopped, divided	1
1/4 cup	shredded Cheddar cheese	60 mL
1 tbsp	finely chopped pecans	15 mL

1. In a medium bowl, beat cream cheese, brown sugar, pumpkin pie spice, cinnamon and nutmeg until well blended. Stir in half the apples. Spoon into baking dish and top with the remaining apples, Cheddar and pecans.

2. Bake in preheated oven for 12 to 15 minutes or until bubbling.

Kids' Chicken and Apple Bake

Makes 4 servings

The savory flavors of chicken and bacon meld beautifully with the tart tang of apples in this kid-approved recipe.

Tip

Fuji and McIntosh apples work well too.

- Preheat oven to 350°F (180°C)
- 13- by 9-inch (33 by 23 cm) glass baking dish, greased

2 tbsp	butter	30 mL
4	boneless skinless chicken breasts	4
2	slices bacon, chopped	2
1	onion, chopped	1
2	Granny Smith apples, peeled and cut into slices	2
½ cup	unsweetened apple cider	125 mL
½ tsp	salt	2 mL
½ tsp	freshly ground black pepper	2 mL

1. In a large skillet, melt butter over medium-high heat. Cook chicken, turning once, for about 8 minutes or until browned on both sides. Transfer chicken to a plate.

2. Add bacon and onion to skillet; sauté for 5 to 7 minutes or until bacon is crisp and onion is softened. Add apples and apple cider; cook, stirring occasionally, for 2 minutes.

3. Spoon apple mixture into prepared baking dish. Arrange chicken on top. Sprinkle with salt and pepper.

4. Cover and bake in preheated oven for 50 to 55 minutes or until chicken is no longer pink inside.

Creamy Baked Apple Dip (page 297)

Creamy Potato and Leek Casserole (page 270)

Kids' Chicken and Rice

This simple recipe has nothing "risky" in it, just flavors kids are sure to like. Their plates will be clean every time!

Tip

Serve garnished with sour cream, salsa and/or shredded cheese.

- Preheat oven to 350°F (180°C)
- 11- by 7-inch (28 by 18 cm) glass baking dish, greased

4	boneless skinless chicken breasts	4
½ tsp	salt	2 mL
½ tsp	freshly ground black pepper	2 mL
2 tbsp	butter	30 mL
1 cup	long-grain white rice	250 mL
1	package (5 oz/142 g) Spanish rice mix	1
1	can (28 oz/796 mL) diced tomatoes	1

1. Sprinkle chicken with salt and pepper. In a large skillet, melt butter over medium-high heat. Cook chicken, turning once, for about 8 minutes or until browned on both sides. Transfer chicken to prepared baking dish.

2. In a small bowl, combine white rice and Spanish rice mix. Stir in tomatoes and 1 cup (250 mL) water. Pour over chicken.

3. Cover and bake in preheated oven for 1 hour or until rice is tender and chicken is no longer pink inside.

Layered Meatballs

This wonderful one-dish meal is perfect for potlucks, and leftovers (if you have any) taste just as good, if not better!

Variation

If your kids will eat broccoli, add 2 cups (500 mL) chopped broccoli with the peas for extra nutrition.

- Preheat oven to 400°F (200°C)
- 13- by 9-inch (33 by 23 cm) glass baking dish

1	package (6 oz/170 g) stuffing mix for chicken	1
1	can (10 oz/284 mL) condensed cream of mushroom soup	1
1/4 cup	milk	60 mL
1	package (1 lb/454 g) frozen cooked meatballs, thawed	1
2 cups	frozen peas	500 mL
1 cup	shredded Cheddar cheese	250 mL

1. Prepare stuffing according to package directions.

2. In a medium bowl, combine soup and milk. Stir in meatballs and peas. Pour into baking dish and top with stuffing and cheese.

3. Bake in preheated oven for 20 to 25 minutes or until bubbling.

Beef and Rice Bake

Makes 4 to 6 servings

Here's another "safe" recipe that will satisfy even picky eaters.

Tips

I like to use a nonstick skillet when browning ground turkey, chicken or beef, as it eliminates the need for oil or butter.

Wrap leftovers in flour tortilla for an easy, delicious second meal.

- Preheat oven to 350°F (180°C)
- 11- by 7-inch (28 by 18 cm) glass baking dish, greased

1 lb	lean ground beef	500 g
1/2 cup	chopped onion	125 mL
1	large green bell pepper, chopped	1
1	can (14 oz/398 mL) diced tomatoes	1
1/2 cup	long-grain white rice	125 mL
2 tsp	Worcestershire sauce	10 mL
1/2 tsp	salt	2 mL
1/4 tsp	freshly ground black pepper	1 mL
1 cup	shredded Cheddar cheese	250 mL

1. In a large nonstick skillet, over medium-high heat, cook beef and onion, breaking beef up with the back of a spoon, for 8 to 10 minutes or until beef is no longer pink. Drain off fat.

2. Stir in green pepper, tomatoes, rice, 1/2 cup (125 mL) water, Worcestershire sauce, salt and pepper. Spoon into prepared baking dish.

3. Cover and bake in preheated oven for 1 hour or until rice is tender. Sprinkle with cheese and bake, uncovered, for 5 minutes or until cheese is melted.

Quick Pizza Casserole

What could be better than this recipe on a busy weeknight? It's quick and easy, and kids love it!

Tip

If your jar of pizza sauce is larger than 14 oz (398 mL), you'll need about 1⅔ cups (400 mL).

• Preheat oven to 400°F (200°C)
• 8-inch (20 cm) square glass baking dish, greased

1 lb	lean ground beef	500 g
1	jar (14 oz/398 mL) pizza sauce	1
2 cups	shredded mozzarella cheese	500 mL
2	eggs	2
1½ cups	milk	375 mL
¾ cup	biscuit mix	175 mL

1. In a large nonstick skillet, over medium-high heat, cook beef, breaking it up with the back of a spoon, for 8 to 10 minutes or until no longer pink. Drain off fat and transfer beef to prepared baking dish. Pour pizza sauce over top and sprinkle with cheese.

2. In a medium bowl, whisk together eggs, milk and biscuit mix until well blended. Pour over beef mixture.

3. Bake in preheated oven for 30 to 35 minutes or until top is golden. Let cool for 5 minutes before serving.

Kids' Pasta Casserole

**Makes 10 to
12 servings**

The fun pasta shapes in this casserole will delight your kids. They don't need to know you snuck some spinach in!

Tips

Use any type of fun pasta shapes, such as shells, wheels or characters.

It's important to let the meat sauce cool slightly at the end of step 3; otherwise, when you add the eggs in step 4, they will cook — which you don't want here. Adding the cool pasta and spinach to the beef mixture before the eggs reduces its temperature even further.

If your skillet isn't big enough to hold all of the ingredients, transfer the beef mixture to the pasta pot or to a large bowl before adding the pasta and spinach.

- Preheat oven to 350°F (180°C)
- 13- by 9-inch (33 by 23 cm) glass baking dish, greased

7 oz	small pasta shapes	210 g
1½ lbs	lean ground beef	750 g
1 cup	chopped onion	250 mL
1	clove garlic, minced	1
1	jar (14 oz/398 mL) spaghetti sauce	1
1	can (8 oz/227 mL) tomato sauce	1
1	can (6 oz/170 mL) tomato paste	1
1 tsp	dried Italian seasoning	5 mL
½ tsp	salt	2 mL
¼ tsp	freshly ground black pepper	1 mL
1	package (10 oz/300 g) frozen chopped spinach, thawed and squeezed dry	1
2	eggs, lightly beaten	2
1 cup	shredded sharp (old) Cheddar cheese	250 mL
½ cup	fresh bread crumbs	125 mL
¼ cup	freshly grated Parmesan cheese	60 mL

1. In a large pot of boiling water, cook pasta according to package directions until just tender. Drain and let cool.

2. Meanwhile, in a large nonstick skillet, over medium-high heat, cook beef, onion and garlic, breaking beef up with the back of a spoon, for 8 to 10 minutes or until beef is no longer pink. Drain off fat.

3. Stir in spaghetti sauce, tomato sauce, tomato paste, Italian seasoning, salt, pepper and ¾ cup (175 mL) water; bring to a boil. Reduce heat to low, cover and simmer, stirring occasionally, for 10 to 15 minutes or until slightly thickened. Remove from heat and let cool slightly.

4. Stir cooked pasta and spinach into beef mixture. Stir in eggs and Cheddar. Pour into prepared baking dish and sprinkle with bread crumbs and Parmesan.

5. Cover and bake in preheated oven for 40 to 45 minutes or until bubbling. Let cool for 5 minutes before serving.

Taco Casserole

The kids in my life love this Tex-Mex casserole served with ranch dressing and salsa.

Tip

I like to use a nonstick skillet when browning ground turkey, chicken or beef, as it eliminates the need for oil or butter.

- Preheat oven to 350°F (180°C)
- 13- by 9-inch (33 by 23 cm) glass baking dish, greased

2 lbs	lean ground beef	1 kg
1	envelope (1¼ oz/37 g) taco seasoning mix	1
1	can (8 oz/227 mL) tomato sauce	1
2 cups	crushed tortilla chips	500 mL
2 cups	shredded Cheddar cheese	500 mL
1 cup	chopped lettuce (optional)	250 mL
1 cup	chopped tomatoes (optional)	250 mL

1. In a large nonstick skillet, over medium-high heat, cook beef and taco seasoning, breaking beef up with the back of a spoon, for 8 to 10 minutes or until beef is no longer pink. Drain off fat. Stir in tomato sauce, reduce heat and simmer, stirring occasionally, for 10 minutes.

2. Arrange tortilla chips in bottom of prepared baking dish. Layer half the beef mixture and half the cheese on top. Repeat layers of beef mixture and cheese.

3. Bake in preheated oven for 25 to 30 minutes or until cheese is bubbling. Serve garnished with lettuce and tomatoes, if desired.

Tater Nugget Taco Casserole

This yummy casserole is full of flavors kids love: ground beef, corn, nacho cheese and crispy potato nuggets.

Tip
Choose lean ground beef whenever possible; you won't notice a loss of flavor in a dish like this one, where there are so many other flavors present.

- Preheat oven to 350°F (180°C)
- 13- by 9-inch (33 by 23 cm) glass baking dish, greased

2 lbs	lean ground beef	1 kg
1/2 cup	chopped onion	125 mL
1	envelope (1 1/4 oz/37 g) taco seasoning mix	1
1	can (11 oz/312 mL) whole-kernel corn, drained	1
1	can (10 oz/284 mL) condensed nacho cheese soup	1
2	packages (each 16 oz/454 g) frozen seasoned shredded potato nuggets, such as Tater Tots	2

1. In a large nonstick skillet, over medium-high heat, cook beef and onion, breaking beef up with the back of a spoon, for 8 to 10 minutes or until beef is no longer pink. Drain off fat.

2. Stir in taco seasoning and 2/3 cup (150 mL) water; reduce heat and simmer for 5 minutes. Stir in corn and soup. Spoon into prepared baking dish and arrange potato nuggets in a single layer on top.

3. Bake in preheated oven for 30 to 35 minutes or until potato nuggets are crispy and golden brown.

Tater Nugget Bake

Makes 8 servings

Kid-friendly ingredients are the stars in this creamy casserole — and it's super-easy to boot!

Variation

Add a 19-oz (540 mL) can of stewed tomatoes to the beef mixture for extra nutritional value.

- Preheat oven to 350°F (180°C)
- 13- by 9-inch (33 by 23 cm) glass baking dish, greased

2 lbs	lean ground beef	1 kg
1	small onion, chopped	1
½ tsp	freshly ground black pepper	2 mL
2	packages (each 16 oz/454 g) frozen seasoned shredded potato nuggets, such as Tater Tots	2
2	cans (each 10 oz/284 mL) condensed cream of mushroom soup	2
1⅓ cups	milk	325 mL
2 cups	shredded Cheddar cheese	500 mL

1. In a large nonstick skillet, over medium-high heat, cook beef and onion, breaking beef up with the back of a spoon, for 8 to 10 minutes or until beef is no longer pink. Drain off fat.

2. Spoon into prepared baking dish and stir in pepper. Arrange potato nuggets in a single layer on top.

3. In a medium bowl, combine soup and milk. Pour over potato nuggets. Sprinkle with cheese.

4. Bake in preheated oven for 35 to 40 minutes or until filling is bubbling.

Creamy Burger and Fries Bake

Makes 8 servings

An all-American favorite, burger and fries, combined in a casserole makes a dish that's perfect for kids!

Tip

I like using lean ground beef to reduce the fat, especially when a recipe contains a lot of flavor, as this one does.

- Preheat oven to 375°F (190°C)
- 13- by 9-inch (33 by 23 cm) glass baking dish

2 lbs	lean ground beef	1 kg
1 cup	onion, chopped	250 mL
1	can (10 oz/284 mL) condensed Cheddar cheese soup	1
1	can (10 oz/284 mL) condensed golden mushroom soup	1
1/4 tsp	freshly ground black pepper	1 mL
1	package (16 oz/454 g) frozen french fries	1
1 1/2 cups	shredded Cheddar cheese	375 mL

1. In a large nonstick skillet, over medium-high heat, cook beef and onion, breaking beef up with the back of a spoon, for 8 to 10 minutes or until beef is no longer pink. Drain off fat.

2. Stir in cheese soup, mushroom soup and pepper. Spoon into baking dish and arrange french fries on top.

3. Bake in preheated oven for 30 minutes or until fries are golden brown. Sprinkle with cheese and bake for 5 minutes or until cheese is melted. Let cool for 5 to 10 minutes before serving.

Corn Dog Casserole

Everyone in my family loves corn dogs and loves this yummy casserole! I make it when all of my nieces and nephews are visiting. Sweet coleslaw is a good side for this dish.

Tip

If your cornbread mix requires you to add oil, water and egg rather than just milk or water, use 3½ cups (875 mL) dry mix and add 6 tbsp (90 mL) vegetable oil with the eggs when making the batter as directed in step 3. If you cannot find packaged mix, whisk ½ cup (125 mL) vegetable oil or melted butter with the eggs and milk; in another bowl, whisk together 2⅓ cups (575 mL) yellow cornmeal, ¾ cup (175 mL) all-purpose flour, 4 tsp (20 mL) baking powder, 1 tbsp (15 mL) granulated sugar and ½ tsp (2 mL) salt; use in place of the mix, stirring it in with the corn, cheese and pepper.

- Preheat oven to 400°F (200°C)
- 13- by 9-inch (33 by 23 cm) glass baking dish, greased

2 tbsp	butter	30 mL
1 cup	sliced green onions	250 mL
1½ lbs	all-beef frankfurters	750 g
2	eggs	2
1½ cups	milk	375 mL
2	packages (each 8½ oz/241 g) cornbread mix	2
1	can (8½ oz/241 mL) cream-style corn	1
2 cups	shredded Cheddar cheese, divided	500 mL
¼ tsp	freshly ground black pepper	1 mL

1. In a skillet, melt butter over medium heat. Sauté green onions for 4 to 5 minutes or until tender. Transfer to a large bowl.

2. Cut frankfurters lengthwise into quarters, then cut each quarter crosswise into thirds. In the same skillet, over medium heat, sauté frankfurters for 5 minutes or until browned. Add to onion mixture and stir to combine. Remove 1 cup (250 mL) of the hot dog mixture and set aside.

3. In a medium bowl, whisk together eggs and milk. Stir in cornbread mix, corn, 1½ cups (375 mL) of the cheese and pepper. Add to the large bowl of hot dog mixture, stirring thoroughly.

4. Spread in prepared baking dish. Top with the reserved hot dog mixture and the remaining cheese.

5. Bake in preheated oven for 30 minutes or until golden brown.

Mashed Potato–Stuffed Hot Dogs

Kids love mashed potatoes, and they love hot dogs, so why not combine them?

Tip

Instant mashed potatoes work just fine in this recipe.

- Preheat oven to 350°F (180°C)
- 13- by 9-inch (33 by 23 cm) glass baking dish

5 cups	mashed potatoes	1.25 L
⅔ cup	finely chopped onion	150 mL
½ cup	chopped fresh parsley	125 mL
¼ cup	melted butter	60 mL
24	all-beef frankfurters (about 3 lbs/1.5 kg)	24
3 tbsp	prepared mustard	45 mL
1 cup	shredded Cheddar cheese	250 mL

1. In a large bowl, combine potatoes, onion, parsley and butter until well blended.

2. Slit frankfurters lengthwise, without cutting all the way through. Spread the cut surface with mustard. Place cut side up in baking dish. Fill each frankfurter with potato mixture. Sprinkle with cheese.

3. Bake in preheated oven for 20 minutes or until cheese is melted.

Cheesy Beans and Hot Dogs

Makes 4 to 6 servings

Beans, cheese and hot dogs — if you're a kid, you have to love this one!

Tip

When you're stirring the cheese into the sauce, if it looks like the cheese isn't incorporating smoothly, just remove the pan from the heat. The residual heat in the sauce will be enough to melt the cheese, and it's less likely to split.

- Preheat oven to 375°F (190°C)
- 8-inch (20 cm) square glass baking dish

1 tbsp	olive oil	15 mL
1	small onion, finely chopped	1
2½ tbsp	all-purpose flour	37 mL
1¾ cups	milk	425 mL
3 cups	shredded Cheddar cheese	750 mL
2	cans (each 14 to 19 oz/398 to 540 mL) pinto beans, drained and rinsed	2
8 oz	all-beef frankfurters, halved lengthwise and cut crosswise into ½-inch (1 cm) slices	250 g
½ tsp	salt	2 mL
¼ tsp	freshly ground black pepper	1 mL
½ cup	dry bread crumbs	125 mL

1. In a skillet, heat oil over medium heat. Sauté onion for 5 to 7 minutes or until softened. Sprinkle with flour and cook, stirring constantly, for 2 minutes. Gradually whisk in milk and cook, whisking constantly, for 2 to 3 minutes or until slightly thickened. Add cheese, 1 cup (250 mL) at a time, stirring until melted after each addition.

2. Remove from heat and stir in beans, frankfurters, salt and pepper. Spoon into baking dish and sprinkle with bread crumbs.

3. Bake in preheated oven for 15 to 20 minutes or until top is golden. Let cool slightly before serving.

Mashed Potato Casserole

This fantastic casserole, beloved by kids, works as either an entrée or a side dish.

Tip

My daughter, Kennedy, doesn't care for salami, so I leave it out when I'm making this casserole for her. Feel free to do the same for the picky eaters in your life.

- Preheat oven to 400°F (200°C)
- 11- by 7-inch (28 by 18 cm) glass baking dish, greased

2½ lbs	baking potatoes, peeled	1.25 kg
1 cup	freshly grated Parmesan cheese	250 mL
⅔ cup	milk	150 mL
4 tbsp	butter, softened, divided	60 mL
1	egg, beaten	1
½ tsp	salt	2 mL
½ tsp	freshly ground black pepper	2 mL
¼ tsp	ground nutmeg	1 mL
8 oz	mozzarella cheese, cut into ½-inch (1 cm) dice	250 g
4 oz	salami, diced	125 g
2 tbsp	dry bread crumbs	30 mL
2 tbsp	freshly grated Parmesan cheese	30 mL

1. Place potatoes in a large saucepan and add enough cold water to cover. Bring to a boil over high heat. Reduce heat and simmer for 20 to 25 minutes or until fork-tender. Drain.

2. Transfer potatoes to a large bowl and mash until smooth. Stir in 1 cup (250 mL) Parmesan, milk and 3 tbsp (45 mL) of the butter. Stir in egg, salt, pepper and nutmeg. Stir in mozzarella and salami.

3. Sprinkle bread crumbs in prepared baking dish, shaking to coat evenly. Spread potato mixture in dish, dot with the remaining butter and sprinkle with 2 tbsp (30 mL) Parmesan.

4. Bake in preheated oven for 40 to 45 minutes or until heated through and top is browned. Let cool for 10 minutes before serving.

Cheesy Potato Spinach

Makes 6 to 8 servings

Here's a great way to get vegetables into kids who are uncertain about green things.

Tip
Squeeze thawed and drained spinach several times to remove excess moisture.

- Preheat oven to 400°F (200°C)
- 11- by 7-inch (28 by 18 cm) glass baking dish, greased

8	Yukon gold potatoes, peeled and cubed	8
1	package (10 oz/300 g) frozen chopped spinach, thawed and squeezed dry	1
½ cup	sour cream	125 mL
¼ cup	butter, softened	60 mL
2 tbsp	chopped green onion	30 mL
1 tsp	salt	5 mL
¼ tsp	freshly ground black pepper	1 mL
1 cup	shredded Cheddar cheese	250 mL

1. Place potatoes in a large saucepan and add enough cold water to cover. Bring to a boil over high heat. Reduce heat and simmer for 20 to 25 minutes or until fork-tender. Drain.

2. Transfer potatoes to a large bowl and mash until smooth. Stir in spinach, sour cream, butter, green onions, salt and pepper. Spread in prepared baking dish.

3. Bake in preheated oven for 25 minutes. Sprinkle with cheese and bake for 5 minutes or until cheese is melted.

Cheesy Tex-Mex Squash

**Makes 10 to
12 servings**

Adding cheese is a mom-tested way to get kids to eat their vegetables.

Tip
Use mild or extra-mild green chiles and mild salsa unless your kids are more adventurous than most when it comes to heat.

Variation
For extra color and crunch, add 1 chopped red bell pepper to the squash mixture in step 1.

- Preheat oven to 400°F (200°C)
- 13- by 9-inch (33 by 23 cm) glass baking dish, greased

1	can (4½ oz/127 mL) diced mild green chiles	1
2¼ lbs	yellow summer squash, cut lengthwise into quarters, then thinly sliced crosswise	1.125 kg
2¼ cups	shredded extra-sharp (extra-old) Cheddar cheese, divided	550 mL
⅔ cup	finely chopped onion	150 mL
½ tsp	salt	2 mL
¼ cup	all-purpose flour	60 mL
¾ cup	salsa	175 mL

1. In a large bowl, combine chiles, squash, ¾ cup (175 mL) of the cheese, onion and salt. Sprinkle with flour and toss to coat. Spread in prepared baking dish.

2. Cover and bake in preheated oven for 40 to 45 minutes or until squash is tender. Spoon salsa on top and sprinkle with the remaining cheese. Bake, uncovered, for about 15 minutes or until cheese is melted and golden.

Brownies S'mores Style

Like all kids, my daughter, Kennedy, loves s'mores and the whole process of making those campfire delights. Although the campfire is missing from this casserole, the flavor is still there!

Tip

The wattage of your microwave will determine whether you should melt chocolate on Medium (50 %) or Medium-High (70%). You may have to experiment; if you burn the chocolate the first time, start over! If you prefer to use a saucepan over low heat, that works, too. Just use one large enough to add the rest of the ingredients, so you don't have to dirty an extra bowl.

- Preheat oven to 325°F (160°C), with rack positioned in the lower third
- 8-inch (20 cm) square metal baking pan, lined with foil, leaving a 1-inch (2.5 cm) overhang, foil lightly greased

Crust

1½ cups	crushed graham crackers	375 mL
2 tbsp	granulated sugar	30 mL
Pinch	salt	Pinch
6 tbsp	unsalted butter, melted	90 mL

Filling

4 oz	unsweetened chocolate, chopped	125 g
½ cup	unsalted butter	125 mL
1 cup	packed brown sugar	250 mL
¾ cup	granulated sugar	175 mL
1½ tsp	vanilla extract	7 mL
½ tsp	salt	2 mL
4	eggs	4
1 cup	all-purpose flour	250 mL
4 cups	mini marshmallows	1 L

1. *Crust:* In a medium bowl, combine graham crackers, sugar, salt and butter. Press evenly over bottom of prepared pan. Bake in preheated oven for about 20 minutes or until golden brown. Remove from oven, leaving oven on.

2. *Filling:* Place chocolate and butter in a large microwave-safe bowl. Microwave on Medium (50%) or Medium-High (70%) for 2 to 4 minutes, stirring every 30 seconds, until melted. Stir in brown sugar, granulated sugar, vanilla and salt. Beat in eggs to make a thick, glossy batter. Stir in flour until blended.

The marshmallows can burn quickly under the broiler, so keep an eye on them and remove the pan from the oven as soon as they're golden brown.

3. Pour batter over crust. Bake for 40 to 45 minutes or until a tester inserted in the center comes out clean. Remove from oven and carefully position a rack 6 inches (15 cm) from the broiler. Preheat broiler.

4. Layer marshmallows over brownies. Toast under the broiler for about 2 minutes or until golden brown. Let cool in pan on a wire rack for 5 minutes. Using foil overhang, gently lift brownies from pan. Remove foil and cut into bars.

Apple Dumplings

Kids and adults alike will love these apple dumplings, especially when you serve them with vanilla ice cream or frozen yogurt.

Tip

I love making these desserts look like little presents or packages by crimping the dough on top of the apples.

- Preheat oven to 375°F (190°C)
- 13- by 9-inch (33 by 23 cm) glass baking dish, greased

Dough

3 cups	all-purpose flour	750 mL
3 tbsp	granulated sugar	45 mL
1 tsp	baking powder	5 mL
1 tsp	salt	5 mL
½ cup	cold butter, cut into pieces	125 mL
1 cup	milk	250 mL

Filling

4	baking apples, peeled, cored and cut in half crosswise	4
½ cup	granulated sugar	125 mL
1 tsp	ground cinnamon	5 mL
⅛ tsp	ground nutmeg	0.5 mL

Glaze

¾ cup	packed brown sugar	175 mL
⅓ cup	butter, cut into cubes	75 mL
¼ tsp	salt	1 mL

1. *Dough:* In a large bowl, sift together flour, sugar, baking powder and salt. Using a pastry blender or two knives, cut in butter until mixture looks like coarse meal. Gradually stir in milk until a soft dough forms.

2. Transfer dough to a lightly floured work surface and knead for 30 seconds. Divide dough in half. Roll each half into a 10-inch (25 cm) square. Cut each into four 5-inch (12.5 cm) squares.

3. *Filling:* Place an apple half, cut side up, on each square. In a small bowl, combine sugar, cinnamon and nutmeg. Sprinkle each apple half with 1 tbsp (15 mL) sugar mixture. Moisten edges of dough and bring corners up over apples, pressing edges together. Place in prepared baking dish, with joined edges either on top or underneath dumplings.

4. *Glaze:* In a saucepan, bring 2 cups (500 mL) water to a boil. Stir in brown sugar, butter and salt; return to a boil, stirring until sugar is dissolved. Pour over dumplings.

5. Bake in preheated oven for 45 to 50 minutes or until apples are tender. Serve warm.

Desserts

Creamy Cheese Cherry Bake 318
Layered Rocky Road Bars 319
Southern Chocolate Pecan Pie Brownies 320
Tif's Favorite Blackberry Cobbler. 321
Mixed Berry Cobbler. 322
Simple Double-Cherry Cobbler 323
Mom's Summer Peach Cobbler 324
Fruit Crisp. 325
Zucchini Crisp. 326
Apple Cranberry Dessert Casserole 327
Layered Apple Gingerbread Bake 328
Blueberry and Nectarine Dessert Casserole 329
Hot Fruit Casserole. 330
Blintz Casserole 331
Better Than Sex Layered Dessert 332
Oven Crème Brûlée 333
Tart Apple Tapioca 334
Pilgrims' Spicy Cornmeal Pudding 335
Almond Rice Pudding. 336
Bread Pudding with Whiskey Sauce 337
Apple Cranberry Sauce. 338

Creamy Cheese Cherry Bake

Crescent dinner rolls make a surprising and pleasing crust for a cherry dessert.

Variation

Substitute apple pie filling for the cherry.

- Preheat oven to 350°F (180°C)
- 13- by 9-inch (33 by 23 cm) glass baking dish, greased

2	cans (each 8 oz/227 g) refrigerated crescent rolls, divided	2
1 lb	cream cheese, softened	500 g
1	egg white	1
1½ cups	confectioners' (icing) sugar, divided	375 mL
1 tsp	vanilla extract	5 mL
1	can (21 oz/596 mL) cherry pie filling	1
3 tbsp	milk	45 mL

1. Unroll one crescent roll sheet and press into prepared baking dish, pressing ¾ inch (2 cm) up the sides to form a crust.

2. In a large bowl, using an electric mixer on medium speed, beat cream cheese, egg white, half the confectioners' sugar and vanilla until well blended. Spread over crust and spread pie filling on top.

3. Unroll second crescent roll sheet, press into a 13- by 9-inch (33 by 23 cm) rectangle and place on top of dish, pressing to seal edges. Cut a few slits in the top to vent steam.

4. Bake in preheated oven for 25 to 30 minutes or until crust is golden brown. Let cool slightly.

5. Place the remaining confectioners' sugar in a small bowl. Gradually whisk in milk until well blended. Drizzle over warm dessert. Cut into 24 bars.

Layered Rocky Road Bars

Makes 25 bars

This recipe is so yummy-good, and individual bars are great reheated in the microwave!

Variation

It is very hard to improve on this, but I do love it with pecans in place of the peanuts!

- Preheat oven to 350°F (180°C)
- 8-inch (20 cm) square metal baking pan, greased and floured

1 cup	all-purpose flour	250 mL
¾ cup	quick-cooking rolled oats	175 mL
½ cup	granulated sugar	125 mL
½ cup	butter, softened	125 mL
½ tsp	baking soda	2 mL
¼ tsp	salt	1 mL
¼ cup	salted peanuts, chopped	1 mL
½ cup	caramel ice cream topping	125 mL
½ cup	whole salted peanuts	125 mL
1½ cups	mini marshmallows	375 mL
½ cup	semisweet chocolate chips	125 mL

1. In a medium bowl, using an electric mixer on low speed, beat flour, oats, sugar, butter, baking soda and salt for 1 to 2 minutes, stopping often to scrape down bowl, until mixture resembles coarse crumbs. Mix in chopped peanuts for 15 seconds. Reserve ¾ cup (175 mL) of the oat mixture. Press the remaining oat mixture into bottom of prepared baking pan.

2. Bake in preheated oven for 12 to 15 minutes or until lightly browned. Remove from oven, leaving oven on.

3. Spread caramel topping evenly over hot crust. Sprinkle with whole peanuts, marshmallows and chocolate chips. Sprinkle the reserved oat mixture on top.

4. Bake for 20 to 25 minutes or until lightly browned. Let cool completely, then refrigerate for 2 hours or until firm. Cut into bars.

Southern Chocolate Pecan Pie Brownies

Makes 40 brownies

Many years ago, at the start of my career in the food world, I stumbled upon an amazing brownie recipe while doing a live cooking show. I share with you my version — you won't believe how decadent this is!

Tip

Lining the pan with foil allows you to easily lift out the brownies.

- Preheat oven to 350°F (180°C)
- 13- by 9-inch (33 by 23 cm) metal baking pan, lined with foil, foil sprayed with nonstick cooking spray

1	9-inch (23 cm) frozen pecan pie	1
1¼ cups	semisweet chocolate chips	300 mL
½ cup	butter	125 mL
1 cup	granulated sugar	250 mL
2	eggs	2
1 cup	milk	250 mL
1½ cups	all-purpose flour	375 mL
1 tsp	baking powder	5 mL

1. Remove pie from wrapping and discard paper circle. Let thaw at room temperature for 2 hours.

2. Place chocolate chips and butter in a large microwave-safe glass bowl. Microwave on High for 1 minute. Stir and microwave on High in 30-second intervals, stirring after each interval, until smooth. Let cool slightly.

3. Using an electric mixer on low speed, beat sugar, eggs and milk into chocolate mixture until blended.

4. Cut pie in half and break one half into about 6 pieces. Add broken pieces to chocolate mixture. Add flour and baking powder. Beat on low until just blended.

5. Cut the remaining pie half into 1-inch (2.5 cm) chunks. Using a wooden spoon, stir into batter (batter will be thick). Spread in prepared baking pan.

6. Bake in preheated oven for 50 minutes. Let cool completely in pan on a wire rack. Cut into squares.

Tif's Favorite Blackberry Cobbler

When I was growing up, we had blackberry vines along our fence that produced huge, plump, delicious blackberries. Such fond childhood memories accompany this recipe, which my mom and I would make together. It is still my dessert of choice. It's fantastic served hot, with a scoop of vanilla ice cream, but I also love it cold, for breakfast.

Tip

I have made this recipe super-easy by using a refrigerated pie crust, but feel free to use 8 oz (250 g) of your favorite pastry (or half a recipe for a 9-inch/23 cm pie), rolled out to an 11-inch (28 cm) circle.

- Preheat oven to 425°F (220°C)
- 11- by 7-inch (28 by 18 cm) glass baking dish, greased

¾ cup	granulated sugar	175 mL
½ cup	all-purpose flour	125 mL
½ cup	butter, melted	125 mL
1 tsp	vanilla extract	5 mL
4 cups	blackberries	1 L
½	package (15 oz/426 g) refrigerated pie crust (see tip, at left)	½
1 tbsp	granulated sugar	15 mL

1. In a large bowl, combine ¾ cup (175 mL) sugar, flour, butter and vanilla. Gently stir in blackberries until coated. Transfer to prepared baking dish.

2. Cut pie crust into ½-inch (1 cm) wide strips. Arrange strips over blackberry mixture, overlapping in a decorative pattern. Sprinkle with 1 tbsp (15 mL) sugar.

3. Bake in preheated oven for 50 minutes or until crust is golden brown and center is bubbling.

Mixed Berry Cobbler

I adore berries, especially when they're baked into a cobbler, fresh from the oven. Here, I've mixed three of my favorites: blackberries, blueberries and raspberries. Serve warm with whipped cream or ice cream.

Tip

Mixed frozen berries are handy to have stashed in the freezer for last-minute desserts. You can use 7 cups (1.75 L) mixed berries (still frozen) in this recipe in place of the blackberries, blueberries and raspberries. If the strawberries in the mix are large, let them thaw slightly and cut them into halves or quarters.

- Preheat oven to 350°F (180°C)
- 6½-inch (16 cm) square glass baking dish, greased

3½ cups	blackberries	875 mL
2 cups	blueberries	500 mL
1½ cups	raspberries	375 mL
½ cup	granulated sugar	125 mL
½ cup	chopped pecans	125 mL
¼ cup	orange juice	60 mL
2 tbsp	quick-cooking tapioca	30 mL

Topping

1 cup	all-purpose flour	250 mL
⅓ cup	granulated sugar, divided	75 mL
¼ tsp	baking soda	1 mL
¼ tsp	salt	1 mL
6 tbsp	milk	90 mL
¼ cup	sour cream	60 mL
2 tbsp	butter, melted	30 mL

1. In a large bowl, gently combine blackberries, blueberries, raspberries, sugar, pecans, orange juice and tapioca. Transfer to prepared baking dish.

2. *Topping:* In the same bowl, whisk together flour, ¼ cup (60 mL) of the sugar, baking soda and salt.

3. In a small bowl, whisk together milk, sour cream and butter. Stir into flour mixture until well blended.

4. Drop batter by spoonfuls over fruit mixture. Sprinkle with the remaining sugar.

5. Bake in preheated oven for 35 to 40 minutes or until topping is golden brown.

Simple Double-Cherry Cobbler

This dessert is as easy as sliced bread — literally!

Tip

If you like the flavor of tart (sour) cherries, you can use 1½ cups (375 mL) drained tart cherries from a jar instead of the canned sweet cherries.

- Preheat oven to 350°F (180°C)
- 8-inch (20 cm) square glass baking dish, greased

2	cans (each 21 oz/596 mL) cherry pie filling	2
1	can (15 oz/426 mL) pitted dark sweet cherries in heavy syrup, drained	1
¼ cup	all-purpose flour, divided	60 mL
½ tsp	almond extract	2 mL
5	slices white bread, crusts removed	5
1¼ cups	granulated sugar	300 mL
1	egg, lightly beaten	1
½ cup	butter, melted	125 mL
1½ tsp	grated lemon zest	7 mL

1. In a large bowl, combine pie filling, cherries, half the flour and almond extract. Transfer to prepared baking dish.

2. Cut each bread slice into 5 strips. Arrange over fruit mixture.

3. In a small bowl, whisk together sugar, egg, butter and lemon zest. Stir in the remaining flour. Pour evenly over bread.

4. Bake in preheated oven for 40 to 45 minutes or until golden brown.

Mom's Summer Peach Cobbler

Makes 8 to 10 servings

I remember my mom greasing the dish for this cobbler by melting the butter in the oven. I thought that was kind of odd, but it worked every time. I give you this recipe in loving memory of my mother, Fay Tacker. It's amazing with vanilla ice cream.

- Preheat oven to 350°F (180°C)
- 13- by 9-inch (33 by 23 cm) glass baking dish

4 cups	sliced peeled peaches	1 L
2 cups	granulated sugar, divided	500 mL
1 tbsp	almond liqueur	15 mL
½ cup	butter	125 mL
1½ cup	self-rising flour	375 mL
1½ cup	milk	375 mL

1. In a large saucepan, combine peaches, half the sugar, liqueur and ¼ cup (60 mL) water; bring to a boil over medium heat. Reduce heat and simmer for 10 minutes or until slightly softened. Remove from heat.

2. Place butter in baking dish and place in preheated oven to melt.

3. In a medium bowl, combine flour and the remaining sugar. Gradually stir in milk until well combined.

4. Remove baking dish from oven and swirl to coat with melted butter. Pour in batter. Spread fruit mixture evenly on top.

5. Bake for 45 to 50 minutes or until golden brown and bubbling.

Fruit Crisp

Makes 4 servings

This delightful fruit crisp has an unusual topping of crushed corn flakes. Serve warm, with whipped cream.

Tip

For an easy, tidy and fun way to crush the corn flakes, place them in a sealable plastic bag, seal and place the bag on the counter. Use a rolling pin, a meat mallet or the bottom of a saucepan to gently crush them into crumbs. Kids are a terrific help with this task!

- Preheat oven to 375°F (190°C)
- 6½-inch (16 cm) square glass baking dish, greased

1	can (29 oz/824 mL) peaches, pitted sour red cherries or apricots, drained	1
2 tbsp	granulated sugar	30 mL
1 tbsp	butter, melted	15 mL
¼ tsp	salt	1 mL
½ tsp	ground cinnamon (optional)	2 mL

Topping

3 tbsp	butter	45 mL
⅓ cup	granulated sugar	75 mL
1 tbsp	all-purpose flour	15 mL
1 cup	crushed corn flakes cereal	250 mL

1. In a large bowl, combine peaches, sugar, butter, salt and cinnamon. Pour into prepared baking dish.

2. *Topping:* In a medium bowl, using an electric mixer on high speed, cream butter. On medium speed, mix in sugar and flour. Mix in cereal until crumbly. Sprinkle over peach mixture.

3. Bake in preheated oven for 25 minutes or until topping is crisp.

Zucchini Crisp

Although it may seem a bit unusual, this fragrant summer squash dessert is sure to be a hit! The sweet and sour flavors invite a sweet sherbet garnish, such as lemon pineapple.

Tip

You'll need about 3 medium zucchini to get 8 cups (2 L) sliced. If you have a very large zucchini with mature, firm seeds, it's best to cut it in half lengthwise and scrape out the seeds before slicing the flesh.

- Preheat oven to 375°F (190°C)
- 13- by 9-inch (33 by 23 cm) glass baking dish

8 cups	thinly sliced peeled zucchini	2 L
2/3 cup	freshly squeezed lemon juice	150 mL
1 cup	granulated sugar	250 mL
2 tsp	ground cinnamon, divided	10 mL
1/4 tsp	ground nutmeg	1 mL

Crust

4 cups	all-purpose flour	1 L
2 cups	granulated sugar	500 mL
1 1/2 cups	butter, cut into cubes	375 mL
Pinch	salt	Pinch

1. In a large saucepan, combine zucchini and lemon juice; bring to a simmer over medium heat. Stir in sugar, half the cinnamon and nutmeg; reduce heat to low and simmer for 10 to 15 minutes or until zucchini is tender. Remove from heat.

2. *Crust:* In a large bowl, using a blending fork or a pastry blender, combine flour, sugar, butter and salt until crumbly. Remove 1/2 cup (125 mL) and stir into zucchini mixture.

3. Pat half the remaining crust mixture into baking dish. Bake in preheated oven for 10 minutes. Remove from oven and reduce oven temperature to 350°F (180°C).

4. Spread zucchini filling evenly over hot crust. Sprinkle remaining crust mixture on top and pat down. Evenly sprinkle with the remaining cinnamon.

5. Bake for 30 minutes or until topping is crisp.

Apple Cranberry Dessert Casserole

This scrumptious tart-sweet dessert is great with vanilla ice cream or frozen yogurt.

Tip

I like to leave the skins on the apples for the added color and texture, but you can certainly peel them if you prefer.

- Preheat oven to 350°F (180°C)
- 13- by 9-inch (33 by 23 cm) glass baking dish, greased

1	bag (12 oz/375 g) fresh cranberries	1
5 cups	chopped baking apples	1.25 L
1½ cups	granulated sugar	375 mL
2 cups	quick-cooking rolled oats	500 mL
¾ cup	packed brown sugar	175 mL
½ cup	all-purpose flour	125 mL
½ cup	butter, softened	125 mL

1. In a large bowl, combine cranberries, apples and granulated sugar. Transfer to prepared baking dish.

2. In another large bowl, combine oats, brown sugar and flour. Using a pastry blender or two knives, cut in butter until crumbly. Sprinkle over cranberry mixture.

3. Bake in preheated oven for 1 hour or until topping is crisp and brown.

Layered Apple Gingerbread Bake

Makes 8 servings

This warm layered dessert is a wonderful treat in blustery cold winter weather.

Tip

For an extra-decadent touch, serve this warm dessert with whipped cream lightly sweetened with pure maple syrup or honey.

- Preheat oven to 375°F (190°C)
- 11- by 7-inch (28 by 18 cm) glass baking dish, greased

1	package (14½ oz/412 g) gingerbread mix, divided	1
¼ cup	packed brown sugar	60 mL
½ cup	butter, divided	125 mL
½ cup	chopped pecans	125 mL
2	cans (each 21 oz/596 mL) apple pie filling	2

1. In a medium bowl, stir together 2 cups (500 mL) of the gingerbread mix and ¾ cup (175 mL) water until smooth. Set aside.

2. In another medium bowl, combine the remaining gingerbread mix and brown sugar. Using a pastry blender or two knives, cut in half the butter until crumbly. Stir in pecans. Set aside.

3. In a large saucepan, over medium heat, combine apple pie filling and the remaining butter; cook, stirring, for 3 to 5 minutes or until heated through.

4. Spoon hot apple mixture into prepared baking dish. Spoon gingerbread-water mixture over hot apple mixture. Sprinkle with gingerbread-pecan mixture.

5. Bake in preheated oven for 30 to 35 minutes or until a tester inserted in the center of the cake layer comes out clean.

Blueberry and Nectarine Dessert Casserole

Makes 8 to 10 servings

I love the combination of fresh blueberries and nectarines. It works brilliantly in pie form, but when you don't feel like wrestling with pastry, try this easy casserole instead!

Variation

Substitute ripe peaches for the nectarines, if you wish.

- Preheat oven to 350°F (180°C)
- 8-inch (20 cm) square glass baking dish, greased

Topping

½ cup	granulated sugar	125 mL
⅓ cup	all-purpose flour	75 mL
½ tsp	ground cinnamon	2 mL
½ tsp	ground nutmeg	2 mL
¼ cup	cold butter, cut into pieces	60 mL

Batter

1⅓ cups	all-purpose flour	325 mL
½ tsp	salt	2 mL
¼ tsp	baking powder	1 mL
¾ cup	granulated sugar	175 mL
¾ cup	butter, softened	175 mL
1 tsp	vanilla extract	5 mL
3	eggs	3
2	nectarines, cut into 1-inch (2.5 cm) wedges	2
2 cups	blueberries	500 mL

1. *Topping:* In a small bowl, combine sugar, flour, cinnamon and nutmeg. Using a pastry blender or two knives, cut in butter until mixture resembles coarse crumbs. Refrigerate until ready to use.

2. *Batter:* In a small bowl, whisk together flour, salt and baking powder.

3. In a large bowl, using an electric mixer on high speed, cream sugar, butter and vanilla. On medium speed, beat in eggs, one at a time, until well blended. Beat in flour mixture. Using a wooden spoon, gently fold in nectarines and blueberries. Spread in prepared baking dish and sprinkle with topping.

4. Bake in preheated oven for 45 to 50 minutes or until a tester inserted in the center comes out clean.

Hot Fruit Casserole

Makes 12 to 14 servings

With a mix of peaches, pineapples, apples and apricots, this make-ahead dessert is a hit at any gathering. Serve warm, with whipped cream or vanilla ice cream.

Tip

Refrigerate or freeze any extra fruit juice drained from the canned fruit and use it in a smoothie or your favorite fruity cocktail.

- 13- by 9-inch (33 by 23 cm) glass baking dish

1	can (20 oz/568 mL) peach halves	1
2	cans (each 20 oz/568 mL) pineapple slices	2
1	can (20 oz/568 mL) apricot halves	1
2	McIntosh apples, peeled, cored and cut into rings	2
1 cup	butter	250 mL
1 cup	packed brown sugar	250 mL
¼ cup	all-purpose flour	60 mL
¼ cup	unsweetened apple cider	60 mL
¼ cup	dry sherry	60 mL

1. Drain peaches, pineapple and apricots, reserving all juices. Measure 1¾ cups (425 mL) juice (reserve any extra for another use).

2. Layer peaches, pineapples, apples and apricots in baking dish (in that order).

3. In a saucepan, melt butter over low heat. Stir in brown sugar, flour, apple cider, sherry and reserved fruit juice; cook, stirring, until smooth and thickened. Pour over fruit. Cover and refrigerate for at least 6 hours or overnight.

4. Preheat oven to 350°F (180°C).

5. Uncover baking dish. Bake in preheated oven for 45 to 50 minutes or until bubbling.

Hot Fruit Casserole (page 330)

Southern Chocolate Pecan Pie Brownies (page 320)

Blintz Casserole

This dessert casserole, which comes to you courtesy of my friend Chris Russo, uses prepared fruit blintzes, so it's incredibly easy. Serve sprinkled with confectioners' sugar or with dollops of sour cream, if desired.

Tip

If time permits and you have a favorite blintz recipe, by all means feel free to use homemade blintzes instead of frozen. You'll need about 12.

- Preheat oven to 350°F (180°C)
- 11- by 7-inch (28 by 18 cm) glass baking dish

½ cup	butter, melted	125 mL
2	packages (each 13 oz/369 g) frozen cherry, apple or blueberry blintzes	2
4	eggs, beaten	4
1½ cups	sour cream	375 mL
¼ cup	granulated sugar	60 mL
½ tsp	salt	2 mL
1 tsp	vanilla extract	5 mL

1. Pour butter into baking dish. Place frozen blintzes in a single layer on top.

2. In a large bowl, whisk together eggs, sour cream, sugar, salt and vanilla. Pour over blintzes.

3. Bake in preheated oven for 45 minutes or until top starts to brown.

Better Than Sex Layered Dessert

With a pecan crust, a rich cream cheese layer and a decadent chocolate pudding layer, this dish is more than worthy of its name.

Tip

I typically garnish this dessert with chopped nuts or chocolate shavings. I have also served it with fresh berries and a sprig of mint.

- Preheat oven to 350°F (180°C)
- 13- by 9-inch (33 by 23 cm) baking pan

1½ cups	chopped pecans, divided	375 mL
1 cup	all-purpose flour	250 mL
½ cup	butter, melted	125 mL
8 oz	cream cheese, softened	250 g
1 cup	confectioners' (icing) sugar	250 mL
2 cups	whipped topping, divided	500 mL
2	packages (each 3½ oz/105 g) chocolate instant pudding mix	2
3 cups	milk	750 mL

1. In a medium bowl, combine 1 cup (250 mL) of the pecans, flour and butter. Press into bottom of baking pan. Bake in preheated oven for 15 minutes or until golden and set. Remove from oven and let cool.

2. In a large bowl, using an electric mixer on medium speed, beat cream cheese and confectioners' sugar for 3 to 4 minutes or until smooth. Using a wooden spoon, gently fold in half the whipped topping. Spread evenly over crust.

3. In the same bowl, using an electric mixer on low speed, beat pudding mix and milk for about 3 minutes or until thick. Spread evenly over cream cheese mixture. Cover with plastic wrap and refrigerate for about 1 hour or until pudding is set.

4. Spread the remaining whipped topping evenly over pudding and sprinkle with the remaining pecans. Cover and refrigerate until ready to serve.

Oven Crème Brûlée

Makes 6 to 8 servings

Crème brûlée is one of my favorite desserts — so creamy inside, with the bite and crunch of caramelized sugar on top. Here's my casserole version.

Tip

Be careful: the water in the roasting pan will be very hot at the end of the baking time. Play it safe and let the water cool before removing it from the oven.

- Preheat oven to 300°F (150°C)
- 10- by 6-inch (25 by 15 cm) glass baking dish
- Roasting pan

2	egg yolks	2
2	eggs	2
¼ cup	granulated sugar	60 mL
Pinch	salt	Pinch
2 cups	heavy or whipping (35%) cream	500 mL
¾ cup	packed brown sugar	175 mL

1. In a medium bowl, using an electric mixer on medium speed, beat egg yolks and eggs until blended. Add granulated sugar and salt; beat for 2 to 3 minutes or until the sugar is dissolved. On low speed, gradually beat in cream. Pour into baking dish.

2. Place baking dish in roasting pan and pour enough hot water into roasting pan to come halfway up sides of dish. Bake in preheated oven for 25 to 30 minutes or until a tester inserted in the center comes out clean. Remove dish from roasting pan and let cool. Cover and refrigerate for at least 6 hours or overnight.

3. Preheat broiler. Using a paper towel, carefully blot moisture from top of custard. Press brown sugar through a fine-mesh sieve evenly over custard, making it no more than ¼ inch (0.5 cm) thick.

4. Broil, watching carefully and rotating dish as necessary, just until brown sugar melts and turns shiny. Serve immediately.

Tart Apple Tapioca

Makes 6 to 8 servings

So simple, so tart, so easy — I adore this dessert, especially on a cold winter day!

Tip

Granny Smiths are nice tart apples that hold their shape and flavor well when they're baked. Other apples good for baking include Crispin, Northern Spy and Jonathan.

- Preheat oven to 375°F (190°C)
- 11- by 7-inch (28 by 18 cm) glass baking dish, greased

3 cups	sliced Granny Smith apples	750 mL
2 tbsp	butter, cut into small pieces	30 mL
¼ tsp	ground cinnamon	1 mL
1 cup	packed brown sugar	250 mL
⅓ cup	quick-cooking tapioca	75 mL
2 tbsp	freshly squeezed lemon juice	30 mL
1 tsp	salt	5 mL

1. Arrange apples in prepared baking dish. Evenly dot with butter and sprinkle with cinnamon.

2. In a medium saucepan, whisk together brown sugar, tapioca, lemon juice, salt and $2\frac{1}{2}$ cups (625 mL) water. Bring to a boil over medium heat, stirring constantly. Pour over apples.

3. Cover and bake in preheated oven for 30 minutes or until apples are tender. Stir and serve warm.

Pilgrims' Spicy Cornmeal Pudding

Makes 8 to 10 servings

This recipe is similar to one made by the earliest settlers of the United States. I'd say that makes this fragrant, homey pudding a true American classic. Serve warm or cold, with whipped cream.

- Preheat oven to 275°F (140°C)
- 6½-inch (16 cm) square glass baking dish, greased
- Roasting pan

4 cups	whole milk, divided	1 L
½ cup	yellow cornmeal	125 mL
⅓ cup	packed brown sugar	75 mL
⅓ cup	granulated sugar	75 mL
⅓ cup	blackstrap molasses	75 mL
¼ cup	butter	60 mL
1 tsp	salt	5 mL
½ tsp	ground ginger	2 mL
½ tsp	ground cinnamon	2 mL
¼ tsp	ground nutmeg	1 mL

1. In a small saucepan, bring half the milk to a boil over medium-high heat, stirring constantly. Gradually stir in cornmeal, reduce heat to low and simmer, stirring constantly, for about 10 minutes or until creamy. Stir in brown sugar, granulated sugar, molasses, butter, salt, ginger, cinnamon and nutmeg.

2. Spread in prepared baking dish and pour the remaining milk on top. Place dish in roasting pan and pour enough hot water into roasting pan to come halfway up sides of dish.

3. Bake in preheated oven for 2½ to 3 hours or until a tester inserted in the center comes out clean. (As the pudding cools, it will become firmer.) Remove dish from roasting pan and let cool.

Almond Rice Pudding

This rice pudding is so simple and so yummy served warm or chilled. The flavor is even better the next day! Present each serving on a colorful plate, garnished with a mint leaf and perhaps a dollop of whipped cream.

Tip

Toast almonds in a dry skillet over medium heat, stirring and shaking pan constantly, for 3 to 4 minutes or until golden and fragrant. Immediately transfer to a bowl and let cool.

- Preheat oven to 350°F (180°C)
- 8-cup (2 L) casserole dish
- Roasting pan

4	eggs, lightly beaten	4
4 cups	milk	1 L
1⅓ cups	instant white rice	325 mL
⅔ cup	granulated sugar	150 mL
½ cup	slivered almonds, toasted	125 mL
½ tsp	ground nutmeg	2 mL
1 tsp	salt	5 mL
1 tsp	vanilla extract	5 mL
¼ tsp	almond extract	1 mL

1. In a large bowl, combine eggs, milk, rice, sugar, almonds, nutmeg, salt, vanilla and almond extract. Spoon into casserole dish. Place dish in roasting pan and pour enough hot water into roasting pan to come halfway up sides of dish.

2. Bake in preheated oven for 50 minutes or until top is set around the edges. Remove dish from roasting pan, stir pudding well and let cool for 30 minutes. Serve warm or let cool completely, cover and refrigerate for up to 2 days and serve chilled.

Bread Pudding
with Whiskey Sauce

This sinfully delicious, award-winning recipe was created by my friends Tom and Lisa Perini, owners of the Perini Ranch Steakhouse in Buffalo Gap, Texas. When I visit their restaurant, I am always tempted to order the bread pudding *first* and follow it with a meal.

- Preheat oven to 325°F (160°C)
- 9-inch (23 cm) round metal cake pan

Bread Pudding

2	eggs	2
2½ cups	milk	625 mL
2 tbsp	melted butter	30 mL
2 tbsp	vanilla extract, preferably Mexican	30 mL
2 cups	granulated sugar	500 mL
2 cups	cubed sourdough bread (1-inch/2.5 cm cubes)	500 mL
⅓ cup	chopped pecans	75 mL

Whiskey Sauce

½ cup	granulated sugar	125 mL
½ cup	butter, cut into cubes	125 mL
½ cup	heavy or whipping (35%) cream	125 mL
¼ cup	Tennessee whiskey (such as Jack Daniels)	60 mL

1. *Pudding:* In a large bowl, whisk eggs until blended. Whisk in milk, butter and vanilla. Gradually stir in sugar until dissolved.

2. Spread bread cubes in bottom of cake pan. Pour in egg mixture, making sure bread is evenly saturated. Sprinkle with pecans and push them down into the bread.

3. Bake in preheated oven for 50 to 60 minutes or until firm and golden.

4. *Sauce:* In a saucepan, combine sugar, butter, cream and whiskey. Bring to a low rolling boil over low heat, stirring constantly. Drizzle over individual servings of bread pudding.

Apple Cranberry Sauce

Makes about 6 cups (1.5 L)

This quick, easy recipe can be used in so many ways. It makes a wonderful dessert, with or without ice cream on top, but it's also a terrific filling for crêpes or can be stirred into your morning oatmeal for added flavor.

Tips

As the mixture cools, it will get thicker.

This sauce can be stored in an airtight container in the refrigerator for up to 1 week.

- Preheat oven to 350°F (180°C)
- 9-inch (23 cm) square glass baking dish

6	Gala apples, chopped	6
2 cups	dried cranberries	500 mL
1¼ cups	coarsely chopped walnuts	300 mL
1 cup	packed brown sugar	250 mL
2 tsp	ground cinnamon	10 mL

1. In a large bowl, combine apples, cranberries, walnuts, brown sugar, cinnamon and 1 cup (250 mL) water. Transfer to baking dish.

2. Bake in preheated oven for 25 to 30 minutes or until apples are tender. Let cool completely, then cover and refrigerate for at least 2 hours or until chilled.

Library and Archives Canada Cataloguing in Publication

Collins, Tiffany
    300 best casserole recipes / Tiffany Collins

Includes index.
ISBN 978-0-7788-0246-4

    1. Casserole cookery. I. Title. II. Title: Three hundred best casserole recipes.

TX693.C64 2010   641.8'21   C2010-903253-5

Index

À la King Chicken Casserole, 146
almonds
Almond Rice Pudding, 336
Crunchy Chow Mein Casserole, 232
Spiced Chicken Casserole, 137
Turkey and Green Onion Phyllo Layer, 163
Angel Hair Shrimp, 115
apples and applesauce
Apple Cranberry Dessert Casserole, 327
Apple Cranberry Sauce, 338
Apple Dumplings, 316
Apple French Toast Casserole, 17
Baked Kielbasa Appetizers, 64
Creamy Baked Apple Dip, 297
Creamy Cheese Cherry Bake (variation), 318
Hot Fruit Casserole, 330
Kids' Chicken and Apple Bake, 298
Layered Apple Gingerbread Bake, 328
Pork, Apple and Sweet Potato Casserole, 180
Tart Apple Tapioca, 334
apricots
Apricot Breakfast Bake, 20
Chicken Apricot Bake, 133
Fruit Crisp, 325
Hot Fruit Casserole, 330
Pork Chops and Savory Stuffing, 175
artichokes
Artichoke Cheddar Squares, 53
Artichoke Dip, The Best Ever, 54
Artichoke Quiche, 39
Artichokes Stuffed with Tuna, Potato and Cheddar, 108
Chicken and Artichoke Casserole, 148
Creamy Broccoli Artichoke Bake, 275
Creamy Crab and Artichoke Dip, 61
Layered Artichokes and Potatoes, 240
Layered Vegetable and Ziti Casserole, 90
Shrimp and Artichoke Divan, 119
Spicy Sausage, Artichoke and Sun-Dried Tomato Bake, 188
Spinach, Chicken Sausage and Artichoke Casserole, 255
Spinach and Artichoke Casserole, 55

asparagus
Asparagus, Bell Pepper and Cheese Frittata, 239
Deviled Egg Casserole, 24
Garden Vegetable Frittata, 37
Three-Cheese Ham Casserole, 168
bacon
Bacon, Ham and Cheese Casserole, 174
Bacon and Leeks in a Quiche, 41
Bacon Blue Cheese Dip, 51
Beef and Beans, 219
Brunch Casserole, 29
Cheesy Spinach Bacon Dip, 54
Chicken and Artichoke Casserole, 148
Eggs Benedict Bake, 25
Five-Bean Casserole, 292
Green Chile Hominy, 274
Leftover Pork and Baked Potato Casserole, 184
Low-Fat Hash Brown Casserole, 238
Noodle Quiche, 45
No-Pasta Lasagna, 229
Roasted Butternut Squash and Bacon Pasta Bake, 176
Scalloped Potato Casserole, Tif's, 267
Tex-Mex Green Chile Quiche, 45
beans. See also beans, green; beans, refried
Barbecue and Honey Baked Beans, 293
Beef and Beans, 219
Black Bean Enchilada Casserole, 99
Brunswick-Style Chicken Pot Pie, 160
Cheesy Beans and Hot Dogs, 310
Chicken, Sausage and Bean Cassoulet, 152
Chicken Enchilada Casserole with Teriyaki Sauce, 156
Corn Pone Pie, 200
Creamy Chipotle Black Bean Burrito Bake, 247
Five-Bean Casserole, 292
Kidney Bean and Rice Casserole, 101
Pasta Fazool Casserole, 224
Southwest Butternut Squash Tortilla Bake, 244
Southwestern Shepherd's Pie, 202
Vegetable Tamale Pie, 96

beans, green
Green Bean Casserole, 284
Italian Beef Pie (variation), 198
Potato, Green Bean and Ham Casserole, 172
Tater Nugget Casserole, 218
beans, refried
Baked Shrimp Enchiladas, 250
Burrito Pie, 201
Mexican Casserole, Kim's, 210
Tamale Pie, 134
Warm Mexican Layered Dip, 65
beef
Baked Spaghetti, 223
Baked Ziti, 230
Barbecue and Honey Baked Beans, 293
Beef, Brown Rice and Feta Cheese Casserole, 195
Beef and Beans, 219
Beef and Rice Bake, 301
Beef and Rice Keema, 216
Beef and Spinach Lasagna, 228
Beef Burgundy, 196
Beef Empanada Casserole, Spectacular, 212
Beef Pot Pie, 199
Beef Stroganoff Casserole, 203
Beef Ziti with Silky Béchamel, 220
Black Bean Enchilada Casserole (variation), 99
Burrito Pie, 201
Busy Day Hamburger Casserole, 207
Cabbage, Hamburger and Wild Rice Casserole, 208
Carnitas Casserole with Mole (variation), 186
Carry Along Casserole, 204
Cavatini Casserole, 225
Chai Chipotle Cheeseburger Casserole, 209
Corn Pone Pie, 200
Creamy Burger and Fries Bake, 307
Crunchy Chow Mein Casserole, 232
Easy Taco-Mac, 211
Enchilada Casserole, 214
Gammy's Delight, 205
Italian Beef Pie, 198
Italian Macaroni Casserole, 222
Johnny Mazetti, 231
Kids' Pasta Casserole, 303
King Ranch Casserole, 194
Lasagna, My Very Favorite, 226

Layered Beef and Noodle Bake, 260

Layered Beef and Zucchini Casserole, 206

Mexican Casserole, Kim's, 210

Mexican Cornbread, 283

No-Pasta Lasagna, 229

Pasta Fazool Casserole, 224

Quick Pizza Casserole, 302

The Reuben Casserole, 197

Santa Fe Stuffed Bell Peppers, 233

Sloppy Joe Mac and Cheese, 258

Southwestern Shepherd's Pie, 202

Stuffed Cabbage Rolls, 236

Taco Casserole, 304

Taco Quiche, 44

Tater Nugget Bake, 306

Tater Nugget Casserole, 218

Tater Nugget Taco Casserole, 305

Topsy-Turvy Pizza Casserole (variation), 191

Warm Mexican Layered Dip, 65

Zucchini, Tomato and Beef Casserole with Polenta Crust, 217

bell peppers. See peppers, bell

berries

Apple Cranberry Dessert Casserole, 327

Apple Cranberry Sauce, 338

Blackberry Cobbler, Tif's Favorite, 321

Blueberry and Nectarine Dessert Casserole, 329

Mixed Berry Cobbler, 322

The Best Artichoke Dip Ever, 54

Better Than Sex Layered Dessert, 332

biscuit mix

Chicken and Dumpling Casserole, 145

Quick Pizza Casserole, 302

Sausage and Cheddar Quiche, 42

Zucchini Squares, 59

Blintz Casserole, 331

bread (as ingredient). See also roll and bread dough

Apple French Toast Casserole, 17

Bread Pudding with Whiskey Sauce, 337

Breakfast Torta, Tiffany's, 33

Brunch Bake, Elegant, 30

Brunch Casserole, 29

Cheese Bread Pudding, 272

Cheese Strata, Cathy's, 34

Cherry Pecan Breakfast Casserole, 296

Crab Strata, 36

Crème Brûlée Bake, 21

Cremini Mushroom and Sausage Strata, 256

Eggs Benedict Bake, 25

French Toast Casserole, 16

Lavender French Toast Bake, Hummingbird Farms, 19

Orange French Toast Bake, 18

Oyster Dressing, 264

The Reuben Casserole, 197

Santa Fe Breakfast Casserole, 27

Scalloped Pineapple Casserole, 294

Simple Double-Cherry Cobbler, 323

Spinach, Chicken Sausage and Artichoke Casserole, 255

Tuna Crab Bake, 110

Wine-Soaked Bread Bake, 48

breakfast and brunch casseroles, 15–46, 296

broccoli

Baked White Fish with Broccoli Rice and Lemon Butter Sauce, 104

Broccoli and Swiss Cheese Gratin, 277

Broccoli Cheese Casserole, Jill's, 70

Broccoli Rice Casserole, 278

Cheese Strata, Cathy's, 34

Chicken Casserole, Tasty, 149

Creamy Broccoli Artichoke Bake, 275

Ham and Noodle Bake (variation), 170

Italian Beef Pie, 198

Layered Meatballs (variation), 300

Pork Chop and Potato Scallop (tip), 179

Savory Broccoli Casserole, 276

Shrimp Enchilada Casserole, 122

Three-Cheese Ham Casserole, 168

Turkey Divan, Classic, 162

Zucchini Casserole (tip), 289

Brownies S'mores Style, 314

Brown Rice and Chicken Bake, 146

Brunch Casserole, 29

Brunswick-Style Chicken Pot Pie, 160

Buffalo Chicken Dip, 62

Burrito Pie, 201

Busy Day Hamburger Casserole, 207

Butternut Squash, Leek and Tomato Casserole, 286

cabbage and sauerkraut

Cabbage, Hamburger and Wild Rice Casserole, 208

Mu Shu Pork Casserole, 182

Pork and Creamed Cabbage Casserole, 181

The Reuben Casserole, 197

Stuffed Cabbage Rolls, 236

Cajun Shrimp and Rice Casserole, 251

Cape Cod Casserole, 114

Caramelized Onion, Mushroom and Barley Casserole, 79

Carnitas Casserole with Mole, 186

carrots

Chicken and Artichoke Casserole, 148

Quinoa-Stuffed Bell Peppers, 242

Thanksgiving Leftover Casserole, 164

Carry Along Casserole, 204

casseroles

dishes and pans, 10–11

freezing, 13–14

ingredients, 12–13

Cathy's Cheese Strata, 34

Cavatini Casserole, 225

celery

Chicken Hot Dish, Mom's, 147

Johnny Mazetti, 231

Pork Rib Bake, 183

Chai Chipotle Cheeseburger Casserole, 209

Chai Chipotle Chicken Casserole, 135

cheese and cheese products. See also pasta; tortillas; specific cheeses (below)

Artichoke Dip, The Best Ever, 54

Asparagus, Bell Pepper and Cheese Frittata, 239

Bacon, Ham and Cheese Casserole, 174

Bacon Blue Cheese Dip, 51

Baked Feta with Marinara Sauce, 49

Baked Goat Cheese with Herbed Sun-Dried Tomatoes, 49

Beef, Brown Rice and Feta Cheese Casserole, 195

Breakfast Casserole, Country, 28

Broccoli Cheese Casserole, Jill's, 70

Broccoli Rice Casserole, 278

Brunch Bake, Elegant, 30

Buffalo Chicken Dip, 62

Cajun Shrimp and Rice Casserole, 251

Carry Along Casserole, 204

Chai Chipotle Cheeseburger Casserole, 209

Cheese Strata, Cathy's, 34

Cheesy Baked Vegetables, 87

Cheesy Grits Casserole with Mushrooms and Prosciutto, 31

Cheesy Phyllo Appetizers, 52

Cheesy Spinach Bacon Dip, 54

Chicken Casserole, King Ranch, 142

Chicken Croquette Casserole, 138

Christmas Omelet Casserole, 23

Corn Dip, 60

cheese (continued)
Couscous Bake, 102
Crab Strata, 36
Creamed Jalapeño Spinach Dip, 56
Creamy Crab and Artichoke Dip, 61
Creamy Potato and Leek Casserole, 270
Cremini Mushroom and Sausage Strata, 256
Cremini Mushroom Potato Dish, 78
Eggplant Parmesan Bake, 77
Greek Spinach Pie, 243
Ham and Eggplant Parmigiana, 169
Herb-Stuffed Eggplant with Roma Tomato, 75
Italian Baked Polenta, 248
Latin Pork Chop Casserole, 177
Layered Beef and Noodle Bake, 260
Layered Beef and Zucchini Casserole, 206
Layered Italian Antipasto Squares, 66
Layered Sweet Onions, Potatoes and Tomatoes with Romano Cheese, 80
Layered Vegetable and Ziti Casserole, 90
Mashed Potato Casserole, 311
Mushroom, Spinach and Sausage Breakfast Casserole, Ellen's, 22
No-Crust Green Chile Pie, 71
Noodle Quiche, 45
No-Pasta Lasagna, 229
Potato and Leek Swiss Bake, 81
Sara's Dip, 64
Savory Broccoli Casserole, 276
Scalloped Potato Casserole, Tif's, 267
Spicy Shrimp and Grits, 121
Spicy Zucchini Cheese Bake, 290
Spinach and Cheese Pie, 38
Spinach Quiche Nibbles, 57
Three-Cheese Ham Casserole, 168
Tuna Crab Bake, 110
Two-Cheese Twice-Baked Potatoes, Kennedy's, 268
Warm Mexican Layered Dip, 65
Zucchini, Tomato and Beef Casserole with Polenta Crust, 217
Zucchini Casserole, 289
Zucchini with Cheese Casserole, 291
cheese, Cheddar
Artichoke Cheddar Squares, 53
Artichoke Quiche, 39

Artichokes Stuffed with Tuna, Potato and Cheddar, 108
Baked Pimento Cheese, Tif's, 50
Baked Potato Casserole, 265
Baked Tuna Mac, 106
Baked White Fish with Broccoli Rice and Lemon Butter Sauce, 104
Beef and Rice Bake, 301
Breakfast Torta, Tiffany's, 33
Brunch Casserole, 29
Butternut Squash, Leek and Tomato Casserole, 286
Cabbage, Hamburger and Wild Rice Casserole, 208
Cape Cod Casserole, 114
Cheddar Cheese Bake, 48
Cheese Bread Pudding, 272
Cheesy Beans and Hot Dogs, 310
Cheesy Hash Brown Casserole, 32
Cheesy Potato Spinach, 312
Cheesy Tex-Mex Squash, 313
Chicken and Cheddar Dip with Four Chiles, 63
Chicken Casserole, Tasty, 149
Chicken Florentine with Wild Rice, 140
Chicken Noodle and Green Pea Casserole, 161
Corn Dog Casserole, 308
Creamy Broccoli Artichoke Bake, 275
Creamy Burger and Fries Bake, 307
Deviled Egg Casserole, 24
Easy Tamale Casserole, 215
Gammy's Delight, 205
Green Chile Hominy, 274
Ham and Noodle Bake, 170
Layered Chicken with Poblano Peppers and Cheese, 151
Layered Meatballs, 300
Leftover Pork and Baked Potato Casserole, 184
Low-Fat Hash Brown Casserole, 238
Mashed Potato–Stuffed Hot Dogs, 309
Mexican Cornbread, 283
Potato and Cheese Casserole, 269
Santa Fe Stuffed Bell Peppers, 233
Sausage, Tomato and Rice Casserole, 190
Sausage and Cheddar Quiche, 42
Sausage Egg Casserole, 26
Shrimp and Rice Casserole, 116
Southwestern Shepherd's Pie, 202
Taco Casserole, 304
Tater Nugget Bake, 306
Tater Nugget Casserole, 218
Tater Nugget Taco Casserole, 305
Tuna Casserole, Fay's, 107

cheese, cream
Apple French Toast Casserole, 17
Better Than Sex Layered Dessert, 332
Cherry Pecan Breakfast Casserole, 296
Crab Bake, 61
Creamy Baked Apple Dip, 297
Creamy Cheese Cherry Bake, 318
Creamy Smoked Salmon Dip, 60
cheese, Jack
Chai Chipotle Chicken Casserole, 135
Chile Cheese Casserole, 72
Layered Mexican Vegetable Bake with Red and Green Chile Sauce, 246
Rice Casserole, 271
Santa Fe Breakfast Casserole, 27
South of the Border Pork Chop Casserole, 178
Tamale Pie, 134
Tex-Mex Green Chile Quiche, 45
Turkey and Green Onion Phyllo Layer, 163
cheese, mozzarella
Chicken à la Candace, 136
Chicken and Artichoke Casserole, 148
Crustless Pizza Quiche, 43
Eggplant, Pepper, Onion and Tomato Bake, 76
Eggplant Gratin, 73
Italian Beef Pie, 198
Kidney Bean and Rice Casserole, 101
Quick Pizza Casserole, 302
Sausage, Sweet Pepper and Rice Casserole, 185
Spinach, Chicken Sausage and Artichoke Casserole, 255
Topsy-Turvy Pizza Casserole, 191
cheese, Parmesan
Creamy Herbed Polenta, 273
Layered Artichokes and Potatoes, 240
Lighten Up Tuna Casserole, 249
Tuna Noodle Casserole, 105
Turkey Divan, Classic, 162
cheese, Swiss
Broccoli and Swiss Cheese Gratin, 277
Creamy Vegetable Bake with Swiss Cheese, 85
Crescent Chicken Casserole, 144
Eggs Benedict Bake, 25
Potato, Green Bean and Ham Casserole, 172
The Reuben Casserole, 197
Spinach-Mushroom Quiche, 40
Squash Corn Bake, 287
Wine-Soaked Bread Bake, 48

cherries
    Cherry Pecan Breakfast Casserole, 296
    Creamy Cheese Cherry Bake, 318
    Fruit Crisp, 325
    Simple Double-Cherry Cobbler, 323
chicken. *See also* chicken breasts; turkey
    Chicken and Artichoke Casserole, 148
    Chicken and Cheddar Dip with Four Chiles, 63
    Chicken and Dumpling Casserole, 145
    Chicken Bell Pepper Bake, 150
    Chicken Casserole, Tasty, 149
    Chicken Casserole D'Iberville, 130
    Chicken Hot Dish, Mom's, 147
    Chicken Noodle and Green Pea Casserole, 161
    Chicken Pie, 143
    Crescent Chicken Casserole, 144
    Jambalaya Casserole, 158
    King Ranch Chicken Casserole, 142
    Mexican Chicken Lasagna, 153
    Seafood Spaghetti (variation), 128
    Spiced Chicken Casserole, 137
    Spinach, Chicken Sausage and Artichoke Casserole, 255
    Tamale Pie, 134
chicken breasts
    À la King Chicken Casserole, 146
    Baked Chicken Tetrazzini, 253
    Black Bean Enchilada Casserole (variation), 99
    Brown Rice and Chicken Bake, 146
    Brunswick-Style Chicken Pot Pie, 160
    Buffalo Chicken Dip, 62
    Chai Chipotle Chicken Casserole, 135
    Chicken, Sausage and Bean Cassoulet, 152
    Chicken à la Candace, 136
    Chicken Apricot Bake, 133
    Chicken Croquette Casserole, 138
    Chicken Enchilada Casserole with Teriyaki Sauce, 156
    Chicken Florentine with Wild Rice, 140
    Creamy Chicken Casserole, 159
    Easy Chicken Penne Pasta Bake, 252
    Kids' Chicken and Apple Bake, 298
    Kids' Chicken and Rice, 299
    Layered Chicken with Poblano Peppers and Cheese, 151

No Peeking Chicken, Mari's, 132
    Sour Cream Chicken Enchiladas, My Very Favorite, 254
    Southwestern Chicken Lasagna, 154
    Verde Chicken Casserole, 157
Chile Cheese Casserole, 72
chile peppers. *See* peppers, hot chile; peppers, mild chile
Chiles Rellenos Casserole, 241
chocolate
    Brownies S'mores Style, 314
    Carnitas Casserole with Mole, 186
    Layered Rocky Road Bars, 319
    Southern Chocolate Pecan Pie Brownies, 320
Christmas Omelet Casserole, 23
Classic Turkey Divan, 162
cobblers, 321–24
corn. *See also* cornmeal and grits
    Baked Shrimp Enchiladas, 250
    Brunswick-Style Chicken Pot Pie, 160
    Corn Dip, 60
    Corn Dog Casserole, 308
    Corny Spoon Bread, 282
    Creamy Chipotle Black Bean Burrito Bake, 247
    Creamy Corn Casserole, 280
    Easy Tamale Casserole, 215
    Green Chile Hominy, 274
    Layered Chicken with Poblano Peppers and Cheese, 151
    Layered Mexican Vegetable Bake with Red and Green Chile Sauce, 246
    Mexican Cornbread, 283
    Santa Fe Stuffed Bell Peppers, 233
    Sausage, Tomato and Rice Casserole, 190
    Shrimp and Rice Casserole, 116
    Southwest Butternut Squash Tortilla Bake, 244
    Southwestern Shepherd's Pie, 202
    Spicy Scalloped Corn, 281
    Squash Corn Bake, 287
    Summer Harvest Corn Casserole, 72
    Super-Easy Corn Casserole, 279
    Tater Nugget Taco Casserole, 305
    Vegetable Tamale Pie, 96
Cornbread Dressing, Mom's Traditional, 262
cornbread mix. *See also* cornmeal and grits
    Chicken, Sausage and Bean Cassoulet, 152
    Corn Dog Casserole, 308
    Corn Pone Pie, 200
    Easy Taco-Mac, 211
    Mexican Cornbread, 283
    Super-Easy Corn Casserole, 279

cornmeal and grits. *See also* corn; cornbread mix
    Bacon, Ham and Cheese Casserole, 174
    Cheesy Grits Casserole with Mushrooms and Prosciutto, 31
    Corny Spoon Bread, 282
    Creamy Herbed Polenta, 273
    Italian Baked Polenta, 248
    Pilgrims' Spicy Cornmeal Pudding, 335
    Southern Ham and Greens with Cornbread Crust, 173
    Spicy Shrimp and Grits, 121
    Tamale Pie, 134
    Vegetable Tamale Pie, 96
    Zucchini, Tomato and Beef Casserole with Polenta Crust, 217
Country Breakfast Casserole, 28
Couscous Bake, 102
crabmeat. *See* seafood
cranberries
    Apple Cranberry Dessert Casserole, 327
    Apple Cranberry Sauce, 338
    Thanksgiving Leftover Casserole, 164
cream cheese. *See* cheese, cream
Creamed Jalapeño Spinach Dip, 56
Creamy Baked Apple Dip, 297
Creamy Broccoli Artichoke Bake, 275
Creamy Burger and Fries Bake, 307
Creamy Cheese Cherry Bake, 318
Creamy Chicken Casserole, 159
Creamy Chipotle Black Bean Burrito Bake, 247
Creamy Corn Casserole, 280
Creamy Crab and Artichoke Dip, 61
Creamy Herbed Polenta, 273
Creamy Potato and Leek Casserole, 270
Creamy Seafood Bake, 111
Creamy Smoked Salmon Dip, 60
Creamy Vegetable Bake with Swiss Cheese, 85
Crème Brûlée Bake, 21
Cremini Mushroom and Sausage Strata, 256
Cremini Mushroom Potato Dish, 78
Crescent Chicken Casserole, 144
crisps, 325–26
Crunchy Chow Mein Casserole, 232
Crunchy Shrimp Casserole, 120
Crustless Pizza Quiche, 43

Delmonico Potatoes, 266
desserts, 314–38
Deviled Egg Casserole, 24
dips, 51, 54, 56, 60–65, 297
dressings (stuffing), 262–64

Easy Chicken Penne Pasta Bake, 252
Easy Taco-Mac, 211
Easy Tamale Casserole, 215
Easy Vegan Enchiladas, 100
eggplant
    Eggplant, Pepper, Onion and
        Tomato Bake, 76
    Eggplant Gratin, 73
    Eggplant Parmesan Bake, 77
    Eggplant Walnut Bake, 74
    Ham and Eggplant Parmigiana,
        169
    Herb-Stuffed Eggplant with Roma
        Tomato, 75
    Ratatouille Casserole, 98
eggs
    Apple French Toast Casserole, 17
    Apricot Breakfast Bake, 20
    Asparagus, Bell Pepper and
        Cheese Frittata, 239
    Breakfast Casserole, Country, 28
    Breakfast Torta, Tiffany's, 33
    Brunch Bake, Elegant, 30
    Brunch Casserole, 29
    Cheese Strata, Cathy's, 34
    Chile Cheese Casserole, 72
    Christmas Omelet Casserole, 23
    Crab Strata, 36
    Crème Brûlée Bake, 21
    Deviled Egg Casserole, 24
    Eggs Benedict Bake, 25
    French Toast Casserole, 16
    Garden Vegetable Frittata, 37
    Lavender French Toast Bake,
        Hummingbird Farms, 19
    Onion Frittata with Crème
        Fraîche Drizzle, 58
    Orange French Toast Bake, 18
    Oven Crème Brûlée, 333
    Santa Fe Breakfast Casserole, 27
    Southwest Strata, 35
    Spinach, Chicken Sausage and
        Artichoke Casserole, 255
Elegant Brunch Bake, 30
Ellen's Mushroom, Spinach and
    Sausage Breakfast Casserole, 22
Enchilada Casserole, 214

Fay's Tuna Casserole, 107
fish. See also seafood; tuna
    Baked White Fish with Broccoli
        Rice and Lemon Butter Sauce,
        104
    Creamy Seafood Bake, 111
    Creamy Smoked Salmon Dip, 60
    Oven Paella, 112
Five-Bean Casserole, 292
Fragrant Lamb and Ziti Casserole,
    234
frankfurters
    Cheesy Beans and Hot Dogs, 310
    Corn Dog Casserole, 308

Mashed Potato–Stuffed Hot Dogs,
        309
French Toast Casserole, 16
fruit. See also berries; specific fruits
    Fruit Crisp, 325
    Hot Fruit Casserole, 330
    Pork Chops and Savory Stuffing,
        175
    Scalloped Pineapple Casserole,
        294

Gammy's Delight, 205
Garden Vegetable Frittata, 37
grains. See also oats; rice
    Caramelized Onion, Mushroom
        and Barley Casserole, 79
    Quinoa and Mixed Veggie Bake,
        245
    Quinoa-Stuffed Bell Peppers, 242
Greek Spinach Pie, 243
Green Bean Casserole, 284
Green Chile Hominy, 274
greens. See also spinach
    Cheesy Baked Vegetables, 87
    Southern Ham and Greens with
        Cornbread Crust, 173
    Taco Quiche, 44
grits. See cornmeal and grits

ham and prosciutto
    Bacon, Ham and Cheese
        Casserole, 174
    Baked Turkey and Ham Casserole,
        166
    Cheese Strata, Cathy's, 34
    Cheesy Grits Casserole with
        Mushrooms and Prosciutto, 31
    Chicken à la Candace, 136
    Chicken Croquette Casserole, 138
    Deviled Egg Casserole, 24
    Ham and Eggplant Parmigiana,
        169
    Ham and Noodle Bake, 170
    Ham and Potato Bake, 171
    Layered Italian Antipasto Squares,
        66
    Potato, Green Bean and Ham
        Casserole, 172
    Southern Ham and Greens with
        Cornbread Crust, 173
    Three-Cheese Ham Casserole, 168
    Wine-Soaked Bread Bake, 48
Harvest Gratin, 86
Harvest Lasagna with Infused Sage
    White Sauce, 88
hash browns. See potatoes, hash
    brown
Herb-Stuffed Eggplant with Roma
    Tomato, 75
hominy. See corn
hot dogs. See frankfurters
Hot Fruit Casserole, 330

Hummingbird Farms Lavender
    French Toast Bake, 19

Italian Baked Polenta, 248
Italian Beef Pie, 198
Italian Macaroni Casserole, 222

Jambalaya Casserole, 158
Jill's Broccoli Cheese Casserole, 70
Johnny Mazetti, 231
John's Sausage Dressing, 263

Kennedy's Two-Cheese Twice-Baked
    Potatoes, 268
Kidney Bean and Rice Casserole, 101
Kids' Chicken and Apple Bake, 298
Kids' Chicken and Rice, 299
Kids' Pasta Casserole, 303
Kim's Mexican Casserole, 210
King Ranch Casserole, 194
King Ranch Chicken Casserole, 142

Lamb and Ziti Casserole, Fragrant,
    234
lasagna, 88, 153–55, 226–29
Latin Pork Chop Casserole, 177
Lavender French Toast Bake,
    Hummingbird Farms, 19
leeks
    Bacon and Leeks in a Quiche, 41
    Butternut Squash, Leek and
        Tomato Casserole, 286
    Cheesy Baked Vegetables, 87
    Creamy Potato and Leek
        Casserole, 270
    Potato and Leek Swiss Bake, 81
Leftover Pork and Baked Potato
    Casserole, 184
Lighten Up Tuna Casserole, 249
Low-Fat Hash Brown Casserole, 238

macaroni
    Baked Macaroni with Fresh
        Shrimp and Mushrooms, 118
    Baked Tuna Mac, 106
    Cheesy Macaroni and Cheese, 68
    Easy Taco-Mac, 211
    Italian Macaroni Casserole, 222
    Sloppy Joe Mac and Cheese, 258
    Smoked Gouda Mac and Cheese,
        69
Mari's No Peeking Chicken, 132
marshmallows
    Brownies S'mores Style, 314
    Layered Rocky Road Bars, 319
    Sweet Potato Custard with Pecans
        (variation), 288
Mashed Potato Casserole, 311
Mashed Potato–Stuffed Hot Dogs,
    309
Mexican Chicken Lasagna, 153
Mexican Cornbread, 283

Mixed Berry Cobbler, 322
Mom's Chicken Hot Dish, 147
Mom's Summer Peach Cobbler, 324
Mom's Traditional Cornbread
    Dressing, 262
mushrooms. *See also* mushroom
    soup
    Baked Chicken Tetrazzini, 253
    Baked Macaroni with Fresh
        Shrimp and Mushrooms, 118
    Baked Spaghetti, 223
    Beef, Brown Rice and Feta Cheese
        Casserole, 195
    Beef Burgundy, 196
    Beef Stroganoff Casserole, 203
    Cape Cod Casserole, 114
    Caramelized Onion, Mushroom
        and Barley Casserole, 79
    Cheesy Grits Casserole with
        Mushrooms and Prosciutto, 31
    Chicken Casserole D'Iberville,
        130
    Chicken Croquette Casserole, 138
    Cremini Mushroom and Sausage
        Strata, 256
    Cremini Mushroom Potato Dish,
        78
    Crescent Chicken Casserole, 144
    Crunchy Shrimp Casserole, 120
    Eggplant Gratin, 73
    Garden Vegetable Frittata, 37
    Harvest Lasagna with Infused
        Sage White Sauce, 88
    Italian Baked Polenta, 248
    Jambalaya Casserole, 158
    Johnny Mazetti, 231
    Lighten Up Tuna Casserole, 249
    Mexican Seafood Casserole, Sara's,
        124
    Mushroom, Spinach and Sausage
        Breakfast Casserole, Ellen's, 22
    Mu Shu Pork Casserole, 182
    No-Pasta Lasagna, 229
    Quinoa and Mixed Veggie Bake,
        245
    Quinoa-Stuffed Bell Peppers, 242
    Sausage Egg Casserole, 26
    Shrimp, Mushroom and Rice
        Casserole, 117
    Shrimp and Artichoke Divan, 119
    Spinach-Mushroom Quiche, 40
    Topsy-Turvy Pizza Casserole, 191
    Tuna Noodle Casserole, 105
mushroom soup (condensed)
    Broccoli Cheese Casserole, Jill's,
        70
    Cajun Shrimp and Rice Casserole,
        251
    Chicken Casserole, À la King,
        146
    Chicken Casserole, King Ranch,
        142

Creamy Broccoli Artichoke Bake,
    275
Creamy Burger and Fries Bake,
    307
Creamy Vegetable Bake with Swiss
    Cheese, 85
Green Bean Casserole, 284
Ham and Noodle Bake, 170
Italian Beef Pie, 198
Layered Meatballs, 300
Low-Fat Hash Brown Casserole,
    238
No Peeking Chicken, Mari's, 132
Pork Chop and Potato Scallop, 179
Potato and Cheese Casserole, 269
Scalloped Potato Casserole, Tif's,
    267
Seafood Spaghetti, 128
Summer Squash Casserole, 285
Tater Nugget Bake, 306
Tater Nugget Casserole, 218
Three-Cheese Ham Casserole, 168
Tuna Casserole, Fay's, 107
Mu Shu Pork Casserole, 182
My Very Favorite Lasagna, 226
My Very Favorite Sour Cream
    Chicken Enchiladas, 254

No-Crust Green Chile Pie, 71
noodles. *See also* pasta
    Baked Turkey and Ham Casserole,
        166
    Beef Stroganoff Casserole, 203
    Busy Day Hamburger Casserole,
        207
    Cape Cod Casserole, 114
    Carry Along Casserole, 204
    Chicken Hot Dish, Mom's, 147
    Chicken Noodle and Green Pea
        Casserole, 161
    Crunchy Chow Mein Casserole,
        232
    Ham and Noodle Bake, 170
    Johnny Mazetti, 231
    Layered Beef and Noodle Bake,
        260
    Lighten Up Tuna Casserole, 249
    Noodle Quiche, 45
    Three-Cheese Ham Casserole, 168
    Tuna Casserole, Fay's, 107
    Tuna Noodle Casserole, 105
No-Pasta Lasagna, 229
nuts. *See also* almonds; pecans
    Apple Cranberry Sauce, 338
    Couscous Bake, 102
    Eggplant Walnut Bake, 74
    Layered Rocky Road Bars, 319

oats (rolled)
    Apple Cranberry Dessert
        Casserole, 327
    Layered Rocky Road Bars, 319

olives
    Baked Spaghetti, 223
    Burrito Pie, 201
    Easy Chicken Penne Pasta Bake,
        252
    Layered Italian Antipasto Squares,
        66
    Sara's Dip, 64
    Tuna Casserole, Fay's, 107
    Turkey and Green Onion Phyllo
        Layer, 163
onions
    Bacon and Leeks in a Quiche
        (variation), 41
    Caramelized Onion, Mushroom
        and Barley Casserole, 79
    Creamy Vegetable Bake with Swiss
        Cheese, 85
    Eggplant, Pepper, Onion and
        Tomato Bake, 76
    Eggplant Gratin, 73
    Green Bean Casserole, 284
    Layered Sweet Onions, Potatoes
        and Tomatoes with Romano
        Cheese, 80
    Onion Frittata with Crème
        Fraîche Drizzle, 58
    Spinach, Zucchini and Sweet
        Onion Casserole, 83
    Turkey and Green Onion Phyllo
        Layer, 163
Orange French Toast Bake, 18
Oven Crème Brûlée, 333
Oven Paella, 112
Oyster Dressing, 264

pasta, 13, 14. *See also* noodles
    Angel Hair Shrimp, 115
    Baked Chicken Tetrazzini, 253
    Baked Macaroni with Fresh
        Shrimp and Mushrooms, 118
    Baked Rigatoni, 92
    Baked Spaghetti, 223
    Baked Tuna Mac, 106
    Baked Ziti, 230
    Beef and Spinach Lasagna, 228
    Beef Ziti with Silky Béchamel, 220
    Busy Day Hamburger Casserole,
        207
    Cavatini Casserole, 225
    Cheesy Macaroni and Cheese, 68
    Cheesy Spaghetti Casserole, 192
    Creamy Chicken Casserole, 159
    Easy Chicken Penne Pasta Bake,
        252
    Easy Taco-Mac, 211
    Harvest Lasagna with Infused
        Sage White Sauce, 88
    Italian Macaroni Casserole, 222
    Kids' Pasta Casserole, 303
    Lamb and Ziti Casserole, Fragrant,
        234

pasta (continued)
Lasagna, My Very Favorite, 226
Layered Vegetable and Ziti
Casserole, 90
Pasta Fazool Casserole, 224
Ravioli Casserole, 93
Roasted Butternut Squash and
Bacon Pasta Bake, 176
Seafood Spaghetti, 128
Sloppy Joe Mac and Cheese,
258
Smoked Gouda Mac and Cheese,
69
Southwestern Chicken Lasagna,
154
Spicy Sausage, Artichoke and
Sun-Dried Tomato Bake, 188
Spinach- and Ricotta-Stuffed
Shells, 82
peaches and nectarines
Blueberry and Nectarine Dessert
Casserole, 329
Fruit Crisp, 325
Hot Fruit Casserole, 330
Summer Peach Cobbler, Mom's,
324
peas
Baked Chicken Tetrazzini, 253
Beef and Rice Keema, 216
Brown Rice and Chicken Bake,
146
Chicken and Dumpling Casserole,
145
Chicken Casserole, À la King,
146
Chicken Noodle and Green Pea
Casserole, 161
Crab and Shrimp Casserole, 123
Layered Meatballs, 300
Lighten Up Tuna Casserole, 249
Southern Ham and Greens with
Cornbread Crust, 173
Tuna Noodle Casserole, 105
Vegetarian Casserole with Indian
Spices, 94
Pecan Pie Brownies, Southern
Chocolate, 320
pecans
Better Than Sex Layered Dessert,
332
Bread Pudding with Whiskey
Sauce, 337
Cherry Pecan Breakfast Casserole,
296
Chicken Apricot Bake, 133
Layered Apple Gingerbread Bake,
328
Layered Rocky Road Bars
(variation), 319
Mixed Berry Cobbler, 322
Sweet Potato Custard with Pecans,
288

pepperoni and salami. See also
sausage
Cavatini Casserole, 225
Crustless Pizza Quiche, 43
Layered Italian Antipasto Squares,
66
Mashed Potato Casserole, 311
peppers, bell. See also pimentos
Asparagus, Bell Pepper and
Cheese Frittata, 239
Baked Turkey and Ham Casserole,
166
Chicken Bell Pepper Bake, 150
Eggplant, Pepper, Onion and
Tomato Bake, 76
Harvest Gratin, 86
King Ranch Casserole, 194
Layered Italian Antipasto Squares,
66
Layered Vegetable and Ziti
Casserole, 90
Quinoa-Stuffed Bell Peppers, 242
Ratatouille Casserole, 98
Santa Fe Stuffed Bell Peppers, 233
Sausage, Sweet Pepper and Rice
Casserole, 185
Shrimp Enchilada Casserole, 122
peppers, hot chile. See also peppers,
mild chile
Carnitas Casserole with Mole, 186
Cheddar Cheese Bake (variation),
48
Chicken and Cheddar Dip with
Four Chiles, 63
Corn Dip, 60
Corn Pone Pie, 200
Creamed Jalapeño Spinach Dip,
56
Creamy Chipotle Black Bean
Burrito Bake, 247
Enchilada Casserole, 214
Green Chile Hominy, 274
Layered Chicken with Poblano
Peppers and Cheese, 151
Layered Mexican Vegetable Bake
with Red and Green Chile
Sauce, 246
Mexican Cornbread, 283
Mexican Seafood Casserole, Sara's,
124
Shrimp Enchilada Casserole, 122
Southwest Butternut Squash
Tortilla Bake, 244
peppers, mild chile (green). See also
peppers, hot chile
Baked Shrimp Enchiladas, 250
Black Bean Enchilada Casserole,
99
Burrito Pie, 201
Cheesy Tex-Mex Squash, 313
Chicken Casserole, King Ranch,
142

Chile Cheese Casserole, 72
Chiles Rellenos Casserole, 241
Easy Tamale Casserole, 215
Eggplant, Pepper, Onion and
Tomato Bake (variation), 76
Leftover Pork and Baked Potato
Casserole, 184
No-Crust Green Chile Pie, 71
Rice Casserole, 271
Santa Fe Breakfast Casserole, 27
Sour Cream Chicken Enchiladas,
My Very Favorite, 254
Southwestern Chicken Lasagna,
154
Spicy Shrimp and Grits, 121
Spicy Zucchini Cheese Bake, 290
Super-Easy Corn Casserole, 279
Tex-Mex Green Chile Quiche, 45
Turkey and Green Onion Phyllo
Layer, 163
Verde Chicken Casserole, 157
phyllo pastry
Cheesy Phyllo Appetizers, 52
Greek Spinach Pie, 243
Turkey and Green Onion Phyllo
Layer, 163
Pilgrims' Spicy Cornmeal Pudding,
335
pimentos
Artichoke Dip, The Best Ever, 54
Baked Pimento Cheese, Tif's, 50
Broccoli Rice Casserole, 278
Chicken Casserole, À la King, 146
Cornbread Dressing, Mom's
Traditional, 262
Crunchy Shrimp Casserole, 120
pork. See also specific pork products
Carnitas Casserole with Mole,
186
Johnny Mazetti, 231
Lasagna, My Very Favorite
(variation), 226
Latin Pork Chop Casserole, 177
Leftover Pork and Baked Potato
Casserole, 184
Mu Shu Pork Casserole, 182
Pork, Apple and Sweet Potato
Casserole, 180
Pork and Creamed Cabbage
Casserole, 181
Pork Chop and Potato Scallop,
179
Pork Chops and Savory Stuffing,
175
Pork Rib Bake, 183
South of the Border Pork Chop
Casserole, 178
Stuffed Cabbage Rolls, 236
potatoes, 13. See also potatoes, hash
brown; sweet potatoes
Artichokes Stuffed with Tuna,
Potato and Cheddar, 108

Baked Potato Casserole, 265
Beef and Rice Keema, 216
Beef Empanada Casserole, Spectacular, 212
Cheesy Potato Spinach, 312
Creamy Burger and Fries Bake, 307
Creamy Potato and Leek Casserole, 270
Cremini Mushroom Potato Dish, 78
Delmonico Potatoes, 266
Ham and Potato Bake, 171
Latin Pork Chop Casserole, 177
Layered Artichokes and Potatoes, 240
Layered Sweet Onions, Potatoes and Tomatoes with Romano Cheese, 80
Leftover Pork and Baked Potato Casserole, 184
Mashed Potato Casserole, 311
Mashed Potato–Stuffed Hot Dogs, 309
Pork Chop and Potato Scallop, 179
Potato, Green Bean and Ham Casserole, 172
Potato and Leek Swiss Bake, 81
Scalloped Potato Casserole, Tif's, 267
Southwestern Shepherd's Pie, 202
Tater Nugget Bake, 306
Tater Nugget Casserole, 218
Tater Nugget Taco Casserole, 305
Thanksgiving Leftover Casserole, 164
Two-Cheese Twice-Baked Potatoes, Kennedy's, 268
Vegetarian Casserole with Indian Spices, 94
potatoes, hash brown
Breakfast Torta, Tiffany's, 33
Chai Chipotle Chicken Casserole, 135
Cheesy Hash Brown Casserole, 32
Country Breakfast Casserole, 28
Low-Fat Hash Brown Casserole, 238
Potato and Cheese Casserole, 269
prosciutto. See ham and prosciutto

quiches, 39–46, 57
Quick Pizza Casserole, 302
Quinoa and Mixed Veggie Bake, 245
Quinoa-Stuffed Bell Peppers, 242

raisins
Spiced Chicken Casserole, 137
Turkey and Green Onion Phyllo Layer, 163

Ratatouille Casserole, 98
Ravioli Casserole, 93
The Reuben Casserole, 197
rice, brown
Beef, Brown Rice and Feta Cheese Casserole, 195
Beef and Rice Keema, 216
Brown Rice and Chicken Bake, 146
Crunchy Chow Mein Casserole, 232
Santa Fe Stuffed Bell Peppers, 233
rice, white, 14
Almond Rice Pudding, 336
Baked White Fish with Broccoli Rice and Lemon Butter Sauce, 104
Beef and Rice Bake, 301
Broccoli Cheese Casserole, Jill's, 70
Broccoli Rice Casserole, 278
Chicken Bell Pepper Bake, 150
Chicken Casserole, Tasty, 149
Crab and Shrimp Casserole, 123
Crunchy Shrimp Casserole, 120
Jambalaya Casserole, 158
Kidney Bean and Rice Casserole, 101
Kids' Chicken and Rice, 299
No Peeking Chicken, Mari's, 132
Oven Paella, 112
Ratatouille Casserole, 98
Rice Casserole, 271
Sausage, Sweet Pepper and Rice Casserole, 185
Sausage, Tomato and Rice Casserole, 190
Shrimp, Mushroom and Rice Casserole, 117
Shrimp and Rice Casserole, 116
South of the Border Pork Chop Casserole, 178
Spiced Chicken Casserole, 137
Stuffed Cabbage Rolls, 236
Turkey and Rice Enchiladas, 165
rice, wild
Cabbage, Hamburger and Wild Rice Casserole, 208
Cajun Shrimp and Rice Casserole, 251
Chicken and Artichoke Casserole, 148
Chicken Casserole D'Iberville, 130
Chicken Florentine with Wild Rice, 140
Gammy's Delight, 205
Shrimp, Mushroom and Rice Casserole, 117
Roasted Butternut Squash and Bacon Pasta Bake, 176

roll and bread dough (as ingredient)
Apricot Breakfast Bake, 20
Beef Empanada Casserole, Spectacular, 212
Brunswick-Style Chicken Pot Pie, 160
Chai Chipotle Cheeseburger Casserole, 209
Creamy Cheese Cherry Bake, 318
Crescent Chicken Casserole, 144
Layered Italian Antipasto Squares, 66
Potato and Leek Swiss Bake, 81
Spinach Quiche Nibbles, 57
Topsy-Turvy Pizza Casserole, 191

salami. See pepperoni and salami
salsa. See also tomato sauces
Chicken Enchilada Casserole with Teriyaki Sauce, 156
Creamy Chipotle Black Bean Burrito Bake, 247
Easy Vegan Enchiladas, 100
Santa Fe Stuffed Bell Peppers, 233
Sara's Dip, 64
Tamale Pie, 134
Turkey and Rice Enchiladas, 165
Warm Mexican Layered Dip, 65
Santa Fe Breakfast Casserole, 27
Santa Fe Stuffed Bell Peppers, 233
Sara's Dip, 64
Sara's Mexican Seafood Casserole, 124
sauerkraut. See cabbage and sauerkraut
sausage. See also frankfurters; pepperoni and salami
Baked Kielbasa Appetizers, 64
Baked Ziti, 230
Barbecue and Honey Baked Beans, 293
Breakfast Casserole, Country, 28
Breakfast Torta, Tiffany's, 33
Brunch Bake, Elegant, 30
Cheesy Spaghetti Casserole, 192
Chicken, Sausage and Bean Cassoulet, 152
Cremini Mushroom and Sausage Strata, 256
Jambalaya Casserole, 158
Mushroom, Spinach and Sausage Breakfast Casserole, Ellen's, 22
No-Pasta Lasagna, 229
Oven Paella, 112
Pasta Fazool Casserole, 224
Pork Chops and Savory Stuffing, 175
Santa Fe Breakfast Casserole, 27
Sausage, Sweet Pepper and Rice Casserole, 185
Sausage, Tomato and Rice Casserole, 190

sausage *(continued)*
    Sausage and Cheddar Quiche, 42
    Sausage Dressing, John's, 263
    Sausage Egg Casserole, 26
    Southwest Strata, 35
    Spicy Sausage, Artichoke and
      Sun-Dried Tomato Bake, 188
    Spinach, Chicken Sausage and
      Artichoke Casserole, 255
    Topsy-Turvy Pizza Casserole, 191
Scalloped Pineapple Casserole, 294
seafood. *See also* fish
    Angel Hair Shrimp, 115
    Bacon, Ham and Cheese Casserole
      (variation), 174
    Baked Crab with Sherry White
      Sauce, 126
    Baked Macaroni with Fresh
      Shrimp and Mushrooms, 118
    Baked Sea Scallops, 113
    Baked Shrimp Enchiladas, 250
    Cajun Shrimp and Rice Casserole,
      251
    Cape Cod Casserole, 114
    Crab and Shrimp Casserole, 123
    Crab Bake, 61
    Crab Strata, 36
    Creamy Crab and Artichoke Dip,
      61
    Creamy Seafood Bake, 111
    Crunchy Shrimp Casserole, 120
    Mexican Seafood Casserole, Sara's,
      124
    Oven Paella, 112
    Seafood Spaghetti, 128
    Shrimp, Mushroom and Rice
      Casserole, 117
    Shrimp and Artichoke Divan, 119
    Shrimp and Rice Casserole, 116
    Shrimp Enchilada Casserole, 122
    Spicy Shrimp and Grits, 121
    Tuna Crab Bake, 110
Sloppy Joe Mac and Cheese, 258
Smoked Gouda Mac and Cheese, 69
sour cream
    Baked Potato Casserole, 265
    Beef Stroganoff Casserole, 203
    Blintz Casserole, 331
    Potato and Cheese Casserole, 269
    Sour Cream Chicken Enchiladas,
      My Very Favorite, 254
Southern Chocolate Pecan Pie
    Brownies, 320
Southern Ham and Greens with
    Cornbread Crust, 173
South of the Border Pork Chop
    Casserole, 178
Southwest Butternut Squash Tortilla
    Bake, 244
Southwestern Chicken Lasagna, 154
Southwestern Shepherd's Pie, 202
Southwest Strata, 35

Spiced Chicken Casserole, 137
Spicy Sausage, Artichoke and Sun-
    Dried Tomato Bake, 188
Spicy Scalloped Corn, 281
Spicy Shrimp and Grits, 121
Spicy Zucchini Cheese Bake, 290
spinach
    Artichoke Dip, The Best Ever, 54
    Artichoke Quiche, 39
    Baked Ziti, 230
    Beef and Spinach Lasagna, 228
    Cheesy Baked Vegetables, 87
    Cheesy Potato Spinach, 312
    Cheesy Spinach Bacon Dip, 54
    Chicken Florentine with Wild
      Rice, 140
    Couscous Bake, 102
    Creamed Jalapeño Spinach Dip,
      56
    Easy Chicken Penne Pasta Bake,
      252
    Eggs Benedict Bake, 25
    Greek Spinach Pie, 243
    Ham and Noodle Bake (variation),
      170
    Harvest Lasagna with Infused
      Sage White Sauce, 88
    Kids' Pasta Casserole, 303
    Mexican Seafood Casserole, Sara's,
      124
    Mushroom, Spinach and Sausage
      Breakfast Casserole, Ellen's, 22
    Quinoa-Stuffed Bell Peppers, 242
    Spinach, Chicken Sausage and
      Artichoke Casserole, 255
    Spinach, Zucchini and Sweet
      Onion Casserole, 83
    Spinach and Artichoke Casserole,
      55
    Spinach and Cheese Pie, 38
    Spinach- and Ricotta-Stuffed
      Shells, 82
    Spinach-Mushroom Quiche, 40
    Spinach Quiche Nibbles, 57
squash. *See also* zucchini
    Butternut Squash, Leek and
      Tomato Casserole, 286
    Cheesy Tex-Mex Squash, 313
    Harvest Gratin, 86
    Layered Vegetable and Ziti
      Casserole, 90
    Roasted Butternut Squash and
      Bacon Pasta Bake, 176
    Southwest Butternut Squash
      Tortilla Bake, 244
    Squash Corn Bake, 287
    Summer Squash Casserole, 285
    Two-Squash Skillet Bake, 84
stratas, 34–36, 256
Stuffed Cabbage Rolls, 236
Summer Harvest Corn Casserole, 72
Summer Squash Casserole, 285

Super-Easy Corn Casserole, 279
Sweet Onions, Potatoes and
    Tomatoes with Romano
    Cheese, Layered, 80
sweet potatoes
    Harvest Lasagna with Infused
      Sage White Sauce, 88
    Pork, Apple and Sweet Potato
      Casserole, 180
    Sweet Potato Custard with Pecans,
      288

Taco Casserole, 304
Taco Quiche, 44
Tamale Pie, 134
Tart Apple Tapioca, 334
Tater Nugget Bake, 306
Tater Nugget Casserole, 218
Tater Nugget Taco Casserole, 305
Tex-Mex Green Chile Quiche, 45
Thanksgiving Leftover Casserole,
    164
Three-Cheese Ham Casserole, 168
Tiffany's Breakfast Torta, 33
Tif's Baked Pimento Cheese, 50
Tif's Favorite Blackberry Cobbler, 321
Tif's Scalloped Potato Casserole, 267
tomatoes. *See also* tomatoes,
    sun-dried; tomato sauces
    Baked Rigatoni, 92
    Baked Spaghetti, 223
    Beef, Brown Rice and Feta Cheese
      Casserole, 195
    Beef and Rice Bake, 301
    Beef and Rice Keema, 216
    Beef Empanada Casserole,
      Spectacular, 212
    Beef Ziti with Silky Béchamel, 220
    Brunswick-Style Chicken Pot Pie,
      160
    Butternut Squash, Leek and
      Tomato Casserole, 286
    Cabbage, Hamburger and Wild
      Rice Casserole, 208
    Cavatini Casserole, 225
    Chicken, Sausage and Bean
      Cassoulet, 152
    Christmas Omelet Casserole, 23
    Corn Pone Pie, 200
    Couscous Bake, 102
    Easy Chicken Penne Pasta Bake,
      252
    Easy Taco-Mac, 211
    Eggplant, Pepper, Onion and
      Tomato Bake, 76
    Eggplant Gratin, 73
    Eggplant Parmesan Bake, 77
    Ham and Eggplant Parmigiana,
      169
    Herb-Stuffed Eggplant with Roma
      Tomato, 75
    Italian Baked Polenta, 248

Johnny Mazetti, 231
Kidney Bean and Rice Casserole, 101
Kids' Chicken and Rice, 299
King Ranch Casserole, 194
King Ranch Chicken Casserole, 142
Lamb and Ziti Casserole, Fragrant, 234
Lasagna, My Very Favorite, 226
Latin Pork Chop Casserole, 177
Layered Sweet Onions, Potatoes and Tomatoes with Romano Cheese, 80
Pasta Fazool Casserole, 224
Quinoa and Mixed Veggie Bake, 245
Ratatouille Casserole, 98
Sausage, Sweet Pepper and Rice Casserole, 185
Sausage, Tomato and Rice Casserole, 190
Shrimp Enchilada Casserole, 122
Sloppy Joe Mac and Cheese, 258
Sour Cream Chicken Enchiladas, My Very Favorite, 254
Southwest Butternut Squash Tortilla Bake, 244
Southwestern Shepherd's Pie, 202
Southwest Strata, 35
Spicy Shrimp and Grits, 121
Stuffed Cabbage Rolls, 236
Tater Nugget Bake (variation), 306
Vegetable Tamale Pie, 96
Zucchini, Tomato and Beef Casserole with Polenta Crust, 217
tomatoes, sun-dried
Baked Goat Cheese with Herbed Sun-Dried Tomatoes, 49
Baked Rigatoni, 92
Cheddar Cheese Bake (variation), 48
Chicken à la Candace, 136
Spicy Sausage, Artichoke and Sun-Dried Tomato Bake, 188
tomato sauces. See also salsa; tomatoes
Baked Feta with Marinara Sauce, 49
Baked Shrimp Enchiladas, 250
Baked Ziti, 230
Beef and Beans, 219
Beef and Spinach Lasagna, 228
Black Bean Enchilada Casserole, 99
Busy Day Hamburger Casserole, 207
Carry Along Casserole, 204
Chai Chipotle Cheeseburger Casserole, 209
Cheesy Spaghetti Casserole, 192
Chicken Bell Pepper Bake, 150

Creamy Chicken Casserole, 159
Enchilada Casserole, 214
Italian Macaroni Casserole, 222
Kids' Pasta Casserole, 303
Layered Beef and Noodle Bake, 260
Layered Beef and Zucchini Casserole, 206
Layered Mexican Vegetable Bake with Red and Green Chile Sauce, 246
Mexican Chicken Lasagna, 153
No-Pasta Lasagna, 229
Quick Pizza Casserole, 302
Ravioli Casserole, 93
South of the Border Pork Chop Casserole, 178
Southwestern Chicken Lasagna, 154
Spinach- and Ricotta-Stuffed Shells, 82
Taco Casserole, 304
Topsy-Turvy Pizza Casserole, 191
Topsy-Turvy Pizza Casserole, 191
tortillas
Baked Shrimp Enchiladas, 250
Black Bean Enchilada Casserole, 99
Burrito Pie, 201
Carnitas Casserole with Mole, 186
Chicken Enchilada Casserole with Teriyaki Sauce, 156
Chiles Rellenos Casserole, 241
Creamy Chipotle Black Bean Burrito Bake, 247
Easy Vegan Enchiladas, 100
Enchilada Casserole, 214
King Ranch Casserole, 194
King Ranch Chicken Casserole, 142
Mexican Casserole, Kim's, 210
Mexican Chicken Lasagna, 153
Mexican Seafood Casserole, Sara's, 124
Shrimp Enchilada Casserole, 122
Sour Cream Chicken Enchiladas, My Very Favorite, 254
Southwest Butternut Squash Tortilla Bake, 244
Southwest Strata, 35
Taco Quiche, 44
Turkey and Rice Enchiladas, 165
Verde Chicken Casserole, 157
tuna
Artichokes Stuffed with Tuna, Potato and Cheddar, 108
Baked Tuna Mac, 106
Lighten Up Tuna Casserole, 249
Tuna Casserole, Fay's, 107
Tuna Crab Bake, 110
Tuna Noodle Casserole, 105

turkey. See also chicken
Baked Turkey and Ham Casserole, 166
Classic Turkey Divan, 162
Lasagna, My Very Favorite (variation), 226
Low-Fat Hash Brown Casserole, 238
Thanksgiving Leftover Casserole, 164
Turkey and Green Onion Phyllo Layer, 163
Turkey and Rice Enchiladas, 165
Warm Mexican Layered Dip, 65
Two-Squash Skillet Bake, 84

vegan recipes, 96, 100
vegetables. See greens; specific vegetables
Vegetable Tamale Pie, 96
Vegetarian Casserole with Indian Spices, 94
Verde Chicken Casserole, 157

Warm Mexican Layered Dip, 65
water chestnuts
Broccoli Rice Casserole (variation), 278
Crescent Chicken Casserole, 144
Crunchy Shrimp Casserole, 120
Mu Shu Pork Casserole, 182
wild rice. See rice, wild
wine
Beef Burgundy, 196
Eggplant Gratin, 73
Wine-Soaked Bread Bake, 48

zucchini. See also squash
Garden Vegetable Frittata, 37
Harvest Gratin, 86
Layered Beef and Zucchini Casserole, 206
Layered Mexican Vegetable Bake with Red and Green Chile Sauce, 246
Layered Vegetable and Ziti Casserole, 90
No-Pasta Lasagna, 229
Quinoa and Mixed Veggie Bake, 245
Ratatouille Casserole, 98
Spicy Zucchini Cheese Bake, 290
Spinach, Zucchini and Sweet Onion Casserole, 83
Two-Squash Skillet Bake, 84
Vegetable Tamale Pie, 96
Zucchini, Tomato and Beef Casserole with Polenta Crust, 217
Zucchini Casserole, 289
Zucchini Crisp, 326
Zucchini Squares, 59
Zucchini with Cheese Casserole, 291

More Great Books
from Robert Rose

Appliance Cooking

- The Mixer Bible (Second Edition) *by Meredith Deeds and Carla Snyder*
- The Dehydrator Bible *by Jennifer MacKenzie, Jay Nutt & Don Mercer*
- 650 Best Food Processor Recipes *by George Geary and Judith Finlayson*
- Slow Cooker Winners *by Donna-Marie Pie*
- Canada's Slow Cooker Winners *by Donna-Marie Pie*
- 200 Best Pressure Cooker Recipes *by Cinda Chavich*
- The 150 Best Slow Cooker Recipes *by Judith Finlayson*
- Delicious & Dependable Slow Cooker Recipes *by Judith Finlayson*
- 125 Best Vegetarian Slow Cooker Recipes *by Judith Finlayson*
- The Healthy Slow Cooker *by Judith Finlayson*
- The Best Convection Oven Cookbook *by Linda Stephen*
- 300 Best Bread Machine Recipes *by Donna Washburn and Heather Butt*
- 300 Best Canadian Bread Machine Recipes *by Donna Washburn and Heather Butt*

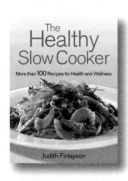

- Slow Cooker Winners *by Donna-Marie Pie*

Baking

- The Cheesecake Bible *by George Geary*
- The Complete Book of Baking *by George Geary*
- 1500 Best Bars, Cookies, Muffins, Cakes & More *by Esther Brody*
- The Complete Book of Bars & Squares *by Jill Snider*
- Complete Cake Mix Magic *by Jill Snider*
- 750 Best Muffin Recipes *by Camilla V. Saulsbury*
- The Complete Book of Pies *by Julie Hasson*
- 125 Best Cupcake Recipes *by Julie Hasson*

Healthy Cooking

- The Vegetarian Cook's Bible *by Pat Crocker*
- The Vegan Cook's Bible *by Pat Crocker*
- The Smoothies Bible (Second Edition) *by Pat Crocker*
- The Juicing Bible (Second Edition) *by Pat Crocker*
- 125 Best Vegan Recipes *by Maxine Effenson Chuck and Beth Gurney*
- 200 Best Lactose-Free Recipes *by Jan Main*

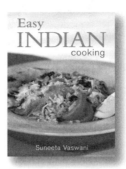

- Complete Gluten-Free Diet & Nutrition Guide
  by Alexandra Anca, MHSc, RD, and Theresa Santandrea-Cull
- 250 Gluten-Free Favorites
  by Donna Washburn and Heather Butt
- Complete Gluten-Free Cookbook
  by Donna Washburn and Heather Butt
- The Best Gluten-Free Family Cookbook
  by Donna Washburn and Heather Butt
- Diabetes Meals for Good Health
  by Karen Graham, RD
- Canada's Diabetes Meals for Good Health
  by Karen Graham, RD
- America's Complete Diabetes Cookbook
  Edited by Katherine E. Younker, MBA, RD
- Canada's Complete Diabetes Cookbook
  Edited by Katherine E. Younker, MBA, RD

Recent Bestsellers

- The Complete Book of Pickling
  by Jennifer MacKenzie
- Baby Blender Food
  by Nicole Young
- 200 Fast & Easy Artisan Breads
  by Judith Fertig

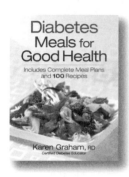

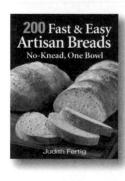

- 12,167 Kitchen and Cooking Secrets
  by Susan Sampson
- Easy Indian Cooking
  by Suneeta Vaswani
- Simply Thai Cooking
  by Wandee Young and Byron Ayanoglu

Health

- 55 Most Common Medicinal Herbs (Second Edition)
  by Dr. Heather Boon, B.Sc.Phm., Ph.D., and Michael Smith, B.Pharm, M.R.Pharm.S., ND
- Canada's Baby Care Book
  by Dr. Jeremy Friedman, MBChB, FRCP(C), FAAP, and Dr. Norman Saunders, MD, FRCP(C)
- The Baby Care Book
  by Dr. Jeremy Friedman, MBChB, FRCP(C), FAAP, and Dr. Norman Saunders, MD, FRCP(C)
- Better Baby Food (Second Edition)
  by Daina Kalnins, MSc, RD, and Joanne Saab, RD
- Better Food for Kids (Second Edition)
  by Daina Kalnins, MSc, RD, and Joanne Saab, RD
- Crohn's & Colitis
  by Dr. A. Hillary Steinhart, MD, MSc, FRCP(C)
- Crohn's & Colitis Diet Guide
  by Dr. A. Hillary Steinhart, MD, MSc, FRCP(C), and Julie Cepo, BSc, BASc, RD